DARK LADY

Winston Churchill's Mother
and Her World

Charles Higham

To Richard V Palafox
and Dorris Halsey

This edition published in Great Britain in 2007 by
Virgin Books Ltd
Thames Wharf Studios
Rainville Road
London
W6 9HA

First published in hardback in Great Britain in 2006 by
Virgin Books Ltd

A catalogue record for this book is available
from the British Library.

ISBN 978 0 7535 1200 5

The paper used in this book is a natural, recyclable product
made from wood grown in sustainable forests.
The manufacturing process conforms to the regulations
of the country of origin.

Typeset by TW Typesetting, Plymouth, Devon
Printed and bound in Great Britain by Clays Ltd, St Ives PLC

Praise for *Dark Lady* by Charles Higham

'*Dark Lady*, like all of Charles Higham's biographies, is vivacious, sensational and revelatory. Jennie Churchill emerges as an intensely individual and passionate figure, and the book is indispensable reading for a full and proper understanding of her great son, Winston.'
Simon Callow

'A fascinating biography, told with panache.'
YOU Magazine, *Mail on Sunday*

'A vibrant look at the life of society beauty Jennie Jerome covering murder, espionage, love affairs and political machinations.'
Daily Express

'Charles Higham's biography of Mr Churchill's irrepressible mama should come with a health warning – this may induce repetitive bouts of jaw-dropping . . . Unmissable stuff – so long as you take sensible precautions for your chin.'
Scottish Daily Record

'Higham's colourful tale is the stuff of fiction, featuring espionage and political manoeuvres of breathtaking audacity.'
Good Book Guide

'A fascinating story about a neglected historical figure.'
Glasgow Evening Times

'Charles Higham's book offers a portrait of a remarkable woman and of the society and its dramas, in which the young Winston Churchill grew up.'
Leicester Mercury

'This book talks about the remarkable, tempestuous life of controversial American society girl and mother of Winston Churchill, Jennie Jerome – feminist, advocate of Irish independence, and, above all, notoriously promiscuous. It charts her luxurious New York upbringing, eyebrow-raising entry into the British aristocracy through marriage to Lord Randolph Churchill, her endless line of liaisons with much younger men and a very different sort of affair in the highest of places – with the Prince of Wales, the future King Edward VII (one of many kings and princes to win her affection). Finally, Higham reveals the woman for whom advancing age was never an obstacle to pursuing her wildest passions while retaining the favour of the Establishment. Her death in a household accident came at the dawn of the Swinging Twenties – a period that could have been written for her.'
Scottish Parliament/Politico's Bookstore

Enough, if something from our hands have power
To live, and act, and serve the future hour;
And if, as toward the silent tomb we go,
Through love, through hope, and faith's transcendent dower
We feel that we are greater than we know.

WORDSWORTH

CONTENTS

CHAPTER ONE

In severe winter weather, on 9 January 1854, Jeanette Jerome was born in a modest, three-storey red-brick Greek Revival house at 8 Amity Street, Brooklyn, in the Cobble Hill section of Brooklyn Heights, NY.

The America of that time still had aspects of the frontier. Children were taught at a mother's knee or in schools where they used slates for writing; they were required to follow the religious and patriotic precepts of the ubiquitous McGuffey's Readers that taught literature in even the most remote communities, as well as the virtues of simple living, thrift, chastity before marriage and, above all, Americanism. Geography was taught in song, as each child memorised lyrics set to music, referring to every capital city and state in the nation. At graduation, children were expected to deliver speeches extolling the school, parents, the town, and God.

The horse-drawn plough was paramount, and wheat was still scythed; it was an age without any of the physical comforts taken for granted in the twenty-first century. There were no refrigerators, no electric light or heat, no antibiotics, and countless infant deaths. There was not much proper surgery, and amputations were often carried out without chloroform. Cities were dirty and overcrowded, with great, teeming tenements for the poor. Clothing was heavy and encumbering, in order to conceal the human body and prevent feelings of desire; in summer, the woollen suits and dresses proved painful, and no man, even at home, and no matter how poor, would think of coming to meals without jacket and tie. Even swimming costumes concealed their owners' physiques.

It would not be until three years after Jennie's death in 1921 that radio would be a reality; television lay much further in the future. In the mid-1850s, more than ninety years ahead of that medium's wide popular use, and forty years before the cinema was even thought of, a telephone was something that could not be imagined. The theatre was largely restricted to the rich, and opera an extreme luxury; for the vast majority of Americans, evening entertainment consisted of families gathered around pianos and singing, or, if the religious rules were not too tight, innocent games of cards. Prayers were said every morning, attendance at church was at least twice a week, and no meal could begin without grace being said. When young men left home there was the neighbourhood saloon after a hard day's work, and for women of means, sewing bees or charity work.

Working hours were long and crushing; in factories now mushrooming across the country, young women toiled on assembly lines or stitched clothes, where a pierced finger could result in instant dismissal. Many with no home slept on cotton waste in obscure corners of industrial plants until removed by business police.

For Jennie, these harsh realities were little known. Brooklyn was an airy, comparatively clean oasis in industrial New York State, swept by salty Atlantic winds that brought relief in summer and gusts of snow in winter, creating a paradise for children as they made snowmen or pelted each other with snowballs.

Street vendors made a cheerful racket, selling chestnuts, wrapped sweets, bunches of flowers, toys and ribbons. Several mail deliveries a day brought greetings, invitations to parties or birth announcements. Children believed that

Santa Claus had a reindeer sleigh and came down chimneys from the sky, and that babies were brought by a stork.

Against the rural innocence of a great nation still in the making, though, could be set the unbridled corruption of the financial centres and at the seat of government in Washington. There was no limit to the election fixing, manipulation of the stock market, buying of Congressmen and senators, or dark injustice in the courts for those who were not rich. Insurance, shipping, railroads, road development and big-city buildings were all riddled with deception and double-cross. And Leonard W Jerome, Jennie's father, his name whitewashed ever since, was among the most corrupt of all.

He was a genially ruthless manipulator of Wall Street, who used the press to raise or lower the value of stocks, and whose almost daily shifts of fortune kept his household in a constant state of uproar.

Of British origin, he could trace his family back to sixteenth-century Cornwall; Cornishmen and women were traditionally famous for their dark skin and romantic temperaments. Early Jerome immigrants had settled in New England: Rhode Island at first, then in New Hampshire, Massachusetts, and Connecticut. The story that Jennie's mother, Clarissa Hall Jerome, was part-Iroquois native American has added lustre to the family legend, fostered not least by Winston Churchill, but Anna Baker, the ancestor stated to have Indian blood, was in fact born and raised in Nova Scotia, where no Iroquois lived.

For generations, the Jeromes retained the flinty courage and steadfastness of Cornishmen, fond of horses and cattle, and of the harsh life of the sea. After much wandering, Jennie's paternal grandparents settled in the small, brick-and-clapboard town of Pompey Hill, in New York State, where they raised eleven children in a house made of planks, with a small outbuilding for raising livestock, most of which wound up on the family dinner table at meals.

As soon as they were old enough, each boy and girl would have to shovel snow, clear mud with their bare hands, chop logs, clean the house, wash dishes and chase off marauding animals. When they were only ten, the boys were armed with buckshot rifles; there were often wolves about.

The patriarch Isaac was a Bible-bashing tyrant, a stony, implacable despot whose word was law; his whip ruled every child. Every morning there was private worship, and each meal was preceded not only by grace but by a confession of sins.

Music other than religious was, Isaac held, the devil's own work and once when Leonard dared to play his second-hand fiddle on the Sabbath, Isaac seized it and smashed it to pieces. From then on, thrashings or no thrashings, Leonard and his brother Lawrence refused to worship God, and announced that they no longer believed in such a thing as Divine Providence.

When Leonard was admitted to the College of New Jersey (later Princeton) as a tall and strapping sophomore of nineteen, he behaved like so many young men who had been raised in morose and straitened circumstances: rebelling against authority, he became a card and a character. He once dragged a reluctant mule up three flights of stairs at Nassau Hall, and he stole street signs, gateposts and henhouses from the nearby villages and made a bonfire of them on the back campus. He ruined his chemistry professor's experiments by switching solutions in the laboratory bottles and test tubes and, to show his everlasting contempt for religion, he smeared the Prayer Hall with tar.

While Leonard was at the college, he was involved in an incident that became legendary on the night before 4 July 1835. To celebrate Independence Day, he and his patriotic friends stole a cannon, moved by the attacking British to New Brunswick during the Revolutionary War, and dragged it by horse-cart until it fell into a field. The youths left it there until they could bring up a sturdier cart, then returned it to its original position at the college, where it remains today.

Vividly emerging in debates at the famous Whig Hall, Leonard, himself a Whig, had to leave when his father's funds failed to meet a rise in fees; instead, he went to Union College, Schenectady. He was soon dubbed a 'potboiler', a constant nuisance, inattentive and feigning illness to avoid classes. He would never have obtained his BA degree if his influential uncle, Judge Hiram K Jerome, had not pulled the necessary strings.

Once they graduated, Leonard and Lawrence joined the staff of Judge Jerome's Palmyra, NY offices, but they were far too restive to take up legal careers. The young men met attractive sisters, Catherine and Clarissa Hall, and married them, though several years apart. The rules of courtship called for attending church services together, joining in family events such as singing songs at the piano, or seeing who could peel apples the fastest.

Tall, rangy and athletic, with square shoulders, long, lean physiques and flourishing moustaches, the genial brothers were immensely popular. By contrast with Jerome's laughing, charming extroversion and good cheer, his wife Clarissa was static, chill and snobbish. Her beauty – black, shiny hair parted in the middle, finely chiselled features and a perfect figure – was not accompanied by sensuality. There was no hint of the alleged Iroquois background in this puritanical descendant of God-fearing colonials: in fact, one of her ancestors had wiped out an entire tribe of Pequot Indians.

Unlike the Jeromes, the Halls were gentlefolk and Clarissa never let anyone forget it. Her parents had died within three months of each other when she was two, and this painful knowledge propelled her into self-sufficiency as an orphan.

Another anguish that drove her deep into herself was that her older sister Jane Anne Hall was insane, and lived and died in the Hartford, Connecticut Lunatic Asylum. In those times insanity in a family was a disgrace, a cause not of compassion but of calumny. Almost equally painful was the fact that the children were not adopted by one couple but were split up among several, all of whom denuded the children's land inheritances to pay for their upbringing.

Thriving in various enterprises in Rochester, Leonard and Lawrence started up a printing press and, keener Whigs than ever, published a polemical newspaper, the *Daily American*, which offered glowing support to Millard Fillmore, the vice president at the time, who had much in common with them.

He also was born in New York State, and was sprung from a long line of itinerant farming folk; he also had toiled as a legal clerk, but had gone on to become a successful attorney; as a young Congressman he had supported the growing science of telegraphy, in which, then and later, the brothers invested. When, on 9 July 1850, he succeeded to the presidency on the death in office of Zachary Taylor, he at once took care of the Jeromes.

Knowing that Lawrence was a tough businessman, he made him deputy collector of debts and taxes of the city of Rochester; knowing of Clarissa's longing to go abroad and Leonard's love of fine arts and music, he sent him as Consul to the Adriàtic independent state of Trieste, a great centre of culture. The Jeromes took with them their daughter Clarita and her friend from Rochester, seven-year-old Lillie Greenough, daughter and granddaughter of men prominent in the history of Vassar Women's College; later, she would be taught by the poet Longfellow and would be one of Jennie Jerome's closest companions.

When Franklin Pierce replaced Millard Fillmore as president in March, 1853, the Jeromes' days in Trieste were numbered. Pierce, under the malign influence of the Kentucky anarchist George Nicholas Sanders, was busy placing controversial figures in European embassies and consulates; he was bent on disrupting the old royalist regimes. There could be no place in such a conspiracy for an unsophisticated Rochester newspaperman, and Leonard was withdrawn.

It was a blow, but there were larger shocks ahead. The oldest Jerome boy, Isaac Jr, was butchered in a rebel uprising in Nicaragua, and the family purchases of paintings and sculptures were lost when a ship foundered off the coast of Spain.

Leonard and his family moved bag and baggage into his brother Addison's house at 292 Henry Street, Brooklyn Heights. Lawrence was also there briefly, with Catherine and his boys Roswell and Lovell, before he moved to Manhattan, where he had started up as a stockbroker.

When Clarissa became pregnant with her second child, she and Leonard, who had decided to join Lawrence in business, moved to the row house at 8 (today 197) Amity Street, where Jeanette was born.

She was not born, as has been stated repeatedly, at 292 Henry Street; that, as stated, was the home of her Uncle Addison (and of his wife Julia whose nickname was Jennie, hence Jeanette's use of it for the rest of her life).

There is no record of her baptism. Normally, the eminent clergyman Reverend Henry Ward Beecher, brother of Harriet Beecher Stowe, writer of *Uncle Tom's Cabin*, whose church was just a short walk away, christened the children of the rich; it was the ultimate social requirement in any family. But his records show no mention of a Jerome and there are no other entries in any church. Some records were destroyed and others removed by a renegade minister in a local quarrel in the Presbyterian community, but the absence of a mention in any newspaper makes it clear that Leonard Jerome, as a happy heathen, overruled Clarissa in the matter, and – according to the then-current orthodoxy – risked the child going to limbo with dogs and cats, by not having her baptised.

Among the errors often repeated in books on Jennie is that Jeanette was nicknamed for the famous soprano Jenny Lind, known as the Swedish Nightingale. Ralph G Martin wrote in his 1969 biography, 'Jerome had renewed his earlier [romantic] relationship with [Lind] and only months after Jennie's birth did Clara [sic] realise why [her husband] had insisted on the name.' This is incorrect; there is no evidence to support his even meeting Lind.

For years, the star had been deeply and exclusively involved with her handsome, brilliant and devoted young piano accompanist Otto Goldschmidt, who converted from

Judaism for her sake. By 1852, when the Jeromes left for Trieste, they were already married. They also went that year to Europe, where they remained happy and faithful for years. Certainly they were not in Trieste, or on board ships on which the Jeromes were passengers.

The day Jennie was born, a blizzard had just blown out, leaving piles of snow several feet deep. The night before, two Manhattan landmarks had burned down: the Metropolitan Hall and the Lafarge Hotel. The conflagrations sent clouds of smoke, mingled with chimney soot and burning ashes, over the city, as far as Brooklyn Heights across the river, blackening the sky as Jennie uttered her first cries.

When she took her first ferry ride to the metropolis, it was an adventure into another world. From the quiet Brooklyn backwater the visitor was plunged into an inferno of noise, dirt and overcrowding. A ride in a hansom cab was perilous; the driver had to thrash his horse through a bedlam of shouting mid-street vendors, beggars and tradesmen's carts. Crowds, talking at the tops of their voices, charged from sidewalk to sidewalk, and there was a jumble of vermin-ridden horse-drawn omnibuses, open to all weathers, dangerous swaying coaches, frustrated and angry mounted police, and frequent outbursts of violence.

During Jennie's teenage years, learning French, sewing, needlework, singing, pony-riding and ice-skating, she soon emerged as a 'character'. She was no infant Florence Nightingale, mending dolls that other children had torn apart. She was strong-willed, sharp, single-minded and passionately in love with life. She adored her laughing Blackbeard the Pirate of a father far more than she cared for her still, chaste and humourless mother, and she and her sister Clarita were very close.

Insecurity was the very air she breathed. In two short years, Leonard became a lion of Wall Street, a brutal stockjobber and manipulator; one day he would come home to announce he had made a killing, the next that he had almost been ruined. Even as a child, Jennie learned that playing the stock market was like playing poker for the highest of stakes and that her father was the ultimate in gamblers.

Leonard used a typical ploy of his time: he would have his friend James Gordon Bennett Jr, son of the owner of the *New York Herald*, announce in his newspaper that a company was in trouble; shareholders would sell the stock, then Jerome would buy it at the bottom of its price. Then he would have his other friend, Henry Jarvis Raymond, owner of the *New York Times*, publish a statement that the same company was doing well and that all previous reports were false; as a result, the stock rose and he made a killing.

These newspaper geniuses ruled Jennie's childhood: Bennett, unfashionably clean-shaven, strapping, with a great yoke of shoulders, battering any man who stood in his way with a pair of powerful fists; Raymond, tall and burly, running a little to fat, with a *farouche* countenance almost hidden behind a formidable shrubbery of black moustache and beard, and a shock of hair that resisted all efforts with brush and comb.

At offices off Wall Street and a shared house at 33 West 19th, Leonard and Lawrence flourished, despite the collapse of the New York and New Haven Railroad, in which they had an interest, and of several banks; it was only when their favourite Union Trust Company folded that Leonard decided it might be prudent to move to Europe for a time.

With their three daughters – Jennie had another sister now, Camille – the Jeromes spent two years in Paris. They were, as American nouveaux riches, received far more warmly than in New York, where they were emphatically not included in Mrs Astor's top Four Hundred – the curdled cream of corrupt East Coast society. They returned in 1858; a new daughter, Leonie was born in 1859. In his colourful (and indispensable) *Lights and Shadows of New York Life*, the social historian James D McCabe described the life of a child of a wealthy family of the time. At six, Jennie would have been taught deportment, the correct order of knives, forks and spoons at the family table, the proper way to drink tea with little finger extended, and the way to greet visitors, standing when they entered a room until given permission to sit.

Learning how to stitch an embroidered alphabet was an essential accomplishment for a child; French was already, after the Jeromes' trip to Paris, a second language. The classics were required early reading: *Uncle Tom's Cabin*, *The Scarlet Letter*, and *Walden: or Life in the Woods* were texts along with the McGuffey Readers for children between six and nine. Piano and voice lessons were mandatory; from the beginning, Jennie was an accomplished pianist and singer.

In addition, a child was required to learn the correct order of a household: the butler came first, followed by the housekeeper and the maids, from ladies' maid to kitchen hand, down to the humblest drudge. Every inch of the house had to be cleansed of New York dust and every floor polished every day; sheets must be changed daily, and washed in the basement-area copper, thence to be folded away in the linen closets in strictest rotation.

The parlour was the protecting womb, a shelter from the noise and dirt of a barbaric metropolis. This centre of activities was traditionally crammed with antiques in the British Victorian manner, the tables groaning with gewgaws, the heavily wallpapered walls covered in a display of the best art money could buy. Thick velvet curtains shut out the wicked street; they were often pulled close all day.

Christmas and New Year were visiting days: first, the children would accompany their parents to visit the poor, bringing gifts of food in wicker baskets and small amounts of cash; then they would attend well-to-do households with salutations; back at home, they would receive the rich until very late at night. Everyone knew everybody else and the slightest hint of scandal was a subject for whispers across potted palms or behind fans at society soirées and balls. It would never do for the rich to let their promiscuities be known to the bourgeoisie; an illusion of propriety, however fragile, was spun like a delicate spiderweb over the sordid truth.

Jennie's first major social event was on 12 October 1860, when she was six: a welcome for the Prince of Wales, who was on a private visit to promote Anglo-American relations; Jennie and her sisters were allowed to watch from a balcony. Three thousand people had been invited, but two thousand more crashed the party. As Jennie watched aghast, the weight of the huge throng causing the hastily improvised dance floor to collapse, leaving New York society in a heap of flying skirts, spilled jewels, rumpled cutaways and ruined uniforms.

In 1861, Leonard Jerome became entangled in a business adventure that would one day almost cost him his career. Fear of imminent Civil War led him to plunge a substantial amount of cash into the corrupt Pacific Mail Steamship Company, which ran cargo ships around Cape Horn to California, avoiding any trade between the states of North and South and picking up and delivering produce to Latin American countries. James Gordon Bennett Jr again proved indispensable: he published a statement in the *New York Herald* that the Pacific's crack mail packet, the *John L Stephens*, wasn't seaworthy; the stock fell and Leonard and Bennett bought it at bottom; days later, the *Herald* printed an apology and a correction. The stock soared, and both men made a killing. By 1863, Pacific Mail had risen from $64 to $329 a share.

At the outbreak of Civil War in 1861, Jennie was seven; and seven-year-old rich children were in those days allowed certain privileges. They could carry pocket money in purses or pockets; they could have a front-door latch key; they could take trips with children of their own age; they could dabble in painting and sculpture; they could express opinions at mealtime. A twirl of a parasol, or a coquettish glance at boys while walking out with governesses, were not considered improper. A child of Jennie's age and background invariably had a pigskin or Russian leather purse, a solid silver and satin-lined needlework box, and matching African ivory hairbrushes; her mirrors would be made of the finest antique silver. And when she travelled, even a short distance out of town, she would be accompanied by a red morocco-lined, brass-studded and fitted travelling trunk.

Jennie was a beautiful girl: she had her mother's dark hair, her father's pink, glowing skin, and sparkling amber eyes whose colour seemed to change with every shift of light. She was challenging and strong; already a tiny adult.

When the Civil War prevented shipments from Paris of fashionable gowns, supplied by the houses of Paquin and Worth, the New York dressmakers and milliners came into their own. The vast marble palace of AT Stewart's Emporium on the muddy, crowded corner of Broadway and Chambers Street was a wonderland for a child. The toy and doll departments were enormous and glowing, crammed with delectable items. The clothing departments, shamelessly copying Worth originals, offered a young lady hours of pleasure, with staff like a sultan's slaves and gas-lit mirrors that flattered both face and figure. No female (woman or child) of society wore the same dress twice; changes had to be made at a rate of at least three times a day, with maids at the ready to deal in bustles, hooped skirts and corsets. Flounces of Brussels lace, lace overskirts, velour and piqué, Swiss muslin, Indian muslin, Lyons silk . . . A dressmaker's bill could run into figures approaching the equivalent today of half a million dollars a year.

Leonard's attitude to Abraham Lincoln was ambiguous. His lawyers, Samuel Barlow, Jeremiah Larocque and partners, were outright Copperheads, opponents of the Washington administration and enemies of the President because of his high-handedness in disposing of the right of habeas corpus – the right of an accused person to be brought before a court – and his prevention of trade arrangements with Europe through tariff and blockade. Jerome's friend, August Belmont, as agent for the Rothschild banking empire in Europe, was similarly unhappy. Millard Fillmore hated Lincoln with all his heart. Jerome was also, like his brothers, still a Whig.

But much as he may have belonged to a powerful anti-Lincoln faction, Leonard would, at all costs, be loyal to the Union. He supplied money for warships, he raised funds at a mass meeting at Utica and he entered, albeit ill-advisedly, into a Lincolnian scheme to give an example to the South in the proper way to treat blacks.

On Lincoln's orders dated 31 December 1862, he shipped African-Americans to a Liberia-like colony on the Isle of Vache off the coast of Haiti, where they would enjoy self-rule in democratic conditions. However, the resettlement agent absconded with the money, leaving the settlers stranded. At the same time, he engaged an African-American nursemaid for his daughters, the colourfully dressed and beloved Dobbie, who accompanied the family for years, on travels out of New York, and eventually in Europe.

Leonard saw no reason not to profit from the war: he arranged, through his own private telegraphic company, to receive inside information from the battlefronts before either government or press: THE BOY IS BACK meant a reversal; THE BOY IS BETTER a victory. This schoolboy code enabled him to buy and sell stock accordingly and added considerably to his riches. Since he was helping to finance the Union, there were no complaints from Washington.

By 1862, at the age of eight, it was time for Jennie to go to boarding school. Soon after the family moved to their own house at 30 West 21st Street, she was enrolled at Miss Lucy Green's exclusive establishment for girls, at 1 Fifth Avenue, on the northeastern corner of fashionable Washington Square.

The red-brick building stood on the site of a former execution ground, where convicts had been hanged in public. Its atmosphere was appropriately grim: the hatchet-faced Miss Green, dressed in the severe grey costume of a Quaker woman, ran the school with all the freezing severity of Miss Scatcherd at Lowood in Charlotte Brontë's *Jane Eyre*.

The days began with a harsh bell that summoned the pupils to clean up their rooms and make their beds. They had to carry heavy chairs, placed as far away as possible, to the dining room, then fetch china and cutlery from the kitchen and lay them neatly on the table. At eight o'clock they would return this tableware to the kitchen, wash and dry it, and take the chairs back to their original location.

Mornings were taken up first with attendance at the Church of the Ascension, reached through sunshine, snow or rainstorm, where the bleak old theologian Dr George B Cheever would give fire-and-brimstone sermons, seeking to strike terror in the girls, warning of the fearful consequences if they should stray from the narrow path of virtue.

Back at school, the young ladies had to repeat the morning sermon, which they were supposed to have memorised by heart, and recite from sacred texts. After a meagre lunch they had to study French, German, Latin, Greek and Italian, while all conversation had to be in French. Jennie and the other pupils had to spend long hours in the evenings at lectures given by Lucy Green's influential older brother Andrew on Latin literature or such abstruse subjects as fourteenth-century jurisprudence; on Saturday afternoons, at the New York Society and Astor Libraries, she had to memorise ancient Greek manuscripts.

Severe though the training was, it gave Jennie a matchless grounding in politics, languages and history that is unthinkable in the modern world, and would stand her in good stead in her future career in England. And she also learned about newspapers from Henry J Raymond, who lectured at the school on the press in wartime, and from Elihu Root, the young future statesman, who taught political science. His looks were such that to subdue fluttering hearts, he had to be accompanied to his talks by a repressive and glaring chaperone.

Both at school and at home, Jennie continued her devotion to musical studies. She was encouraged by her father, who shared her addiction, a fact that has led successive chroniclers to state that at the time he was both the lover and sponsor of the great Italian-American diva Adelina Patti, then on the brink of her spectacular international career, and whom he and August Belmont presented at the Academy of Music at her debut in November

1859. But he had no romantic interest in the sour, plain, contentious future star; she was locked in battles with her father and manager, whom she later sued for misusing her, and by the time she was supposed to be in love with Leonard Jerome, she had already left for Europe, where she remained for many years.

Yet another musical error is that Jennie's closest friend of the Civil War period, the gifted mezzo-soprano Minnie Hauk, who would one day rival Lind and Patti in fame, was Jerome's illegitimate daughter. This was impossible: conceived in Europe to a German carpenter and his laundress wife, Amalia Hauck was born during their very brief stopover in New York on 16 November 1852; they moved at once to the newly growing town of Sumner, in the Kansas heartland, a hamlet so fragile that years later it blew away in a tornado, leaving no trace.

The parents, who had run a lodging house, made their way by riverboat to New Orleans, where Minnie won approval in concerts for the Civil War relief fund. Sent by adoring citizens to New York, she was adopted jointly by Jerome and August Belmont as sponsors; she was trained by Jennie's own teacher, the great Achille Ernani.

In July 1863, in record-breaking heat, the Draft Riots tore New York City apart; as the mob pillaged, raped and murdered, Leonard rushed to the defence of Henry J Raymond's *Times*, of which he was now a director. With laughing enthusiasm and deadly aim, he manned a Gatling gun and shot at the mob through the windows; to his and Raymond's surpassing delight, he drove the rioters into ransacking their competitor, Horace Greeley's *New York Tribune*. It was necessary for Leonard to get his family out of town and away from danger, so he bundled them onto a train for Newport, Rhode Island, where so many of his ancestors had settled, finding them a temporary home on breezy Narragansett Avenue.

In those days, Newport was a quiet, unassuming backwater that offered airy clapboard houses, tree-lined streets and a bright waterfront where a few small yachts tossed prettily at anchor. August Belmont had built a house there, and so had Peter Lorillard Ronalds, eccentric heir of a tobacco dynasty, whose enchantingly spirited wife Fanny adored Jennie and her sisters and took them on donkey-cart rides by the sea; Jennie and she would be lifelong friends.

Sadly the successful escape from New York was quickly overshadowed. Despite its fresh look, Newport was plagued by bad plumbing, supplied by Lorillard himself, and soon dysentery ravaged the city, followed by typhus. Camille, Jennie's younger sister, succumbed at the age of seven years and eight months; it was a devastating blow to the family. And Jerome clearly remained unsettled by it; after buying a $20,000 lot and beach rights, he sold them in less than two years on 2 June 1865. He was never able to make Newport his home, and his future visits were few.

The family found compensations. As a major fundraiser for the Union cause, a group headed by the Belmonts, with Clarissa Jerome and Fanny Ronalds on the ladies' committee, raised over a million dollars for the United States Sanitary Commission's New York City Metropolitan Fair. From January 1864, the backers kept hammering away at Mayor Charles G Gunther to arrange for city buildings to house the fair stalls. At last, he handed over an empty structure near Tammany Hall on the north side of Union Square, and another on West 14th Street. At the same time, Leonard was in the process of completing a grand faux-French chateau on 26th Street and Madison Square, designed by Tammany Hall's architect Thomas R Jackson at a cut price of $55,000 (about $7,000,000 today). The five-storey extravagance had a slanted roof in the style of Louis XIV's François Mansart, a marble portico, a marble-floored entrance hall and a grand ballroom that rivalled August Belmont's on Fifth Avenue. The stables where Jerome kept his horses were carpeted wall-to-wall, and he had walnut and African mahogany fixtures. Upstairs, Leonard built an elegantly appointed theatre that he lent to the Sanitary Commission for theatrical and operatic performances.

The grand opening of the fair on 4 April 1864 was a tremendous occasion. A public holiday had been declared and all of New York not opposed to the war turned out to greet a procession of 11,600 soldiers marching to a brass band and a chorus singing 'The Star-Spangled Banner'. Flags flew from every building and the harbours were alive with horns tooting and sailors cheering as they poured ashore. The Jerome family manned a booth on Union Square; everything was sold from captured Confederate flags all the way up to family jewels; Jennie and Clarita were there to sell to other children.

They were also present to see Fanny Ronalds, the exemplar of beauty and style, appear in a tableau vivant with Mrs Caroline Belmont at the 14th Street Floral Temple; later, Ronalds sang at the Theatre San Jeronimo over the stables, in the quartet from *Rigoletto*. It was a long festivity of excitement for Jennie, and even Miss Lucy Green could not deny her days of leave to attend it.

CHAPTER TWO

Like so many men of his generation, Leonard Jerome saw his future in railroads. It was his dream, shared with his wife and children, to bring trains into the heart of Manhattan, and preferably close to his own residence at West 26th Street. His first move was to join the New York City Board of Aldermen known as the forty thieves, and owned outright by 'Boss' William Marcy Tweed; that Democrat operator's 6-foot, 300-pound figure and flaring temper dominated all meetings. The Board sold franchises in streetcars, markets, department and dry-goods stores, and now railroads – and smashed all attempted legislation that threatened their plans.

Armed by backing from Tweed and up to his eyes in cheerful corruption, Jerome, who also had presidential support because of his paying for Union battleships, army equipment and uniforms, set out to double-cross the formidable Commodore Cornelius Vanderbilt, supreme tycoon of the age, whose approach to business dealings was well known. For example, when flagged down by one of the skippers of his yachting fleet that he must at once return to make another killing on Wall Street, he would order full steam ahead, and any small craft that got in his vessel's way was cut through and sunk, leaving the crew floundering.

Jerome had invested heavily in the New York and New Haven Railroad, which had started to penetrate the metropolis in partnership with Vanderbilt's Harlem line. NY & NH supplied the rolling stock, while the commodore provided the tracks. Jerome could see that if he built a track of his own, he would no longer have to share the profits with the Vanderbilts. Acting in secret, he personally snapped up, for $300 an acre, a stretch of land that could be used to provide such a line: Saw Mill River Valley, in Lower Westchester County, including the derelict Bathgate Farm, and he began laying tracks under cover of darkness.

Vanderbilt had an army of spies and he soon found out about this. He strode into the offices of the New York and New Haven when Jerome was out and bought up the board of directors as well as all of the common and preferred stock. This left Jerome facing ruin with hundreds of useless acres, as Vanderbilt had the rails pulled up and the plan abandoned. But then, with his horse-loving daughters clearly in mind, Jerome found a solution.

New York City needed a new racetrack for the fashionable set, and Jerome had only to watch Jennie and Clarita happily cantering about his Bathgate Farm property to know how much they would love the idea. But how could he get society to come from the heart of Manhattan to the track? The elite, with their cavalcade of carriages, must be able to get across the Harlem river and it had no bridge, only the old, jerry-built, collapsing one at Macombs' Dam. A brand-new road and bridge would have to be provided, but the cost would be crushing – even for a Jerome. He found a characteristic solution. He went to see the mayors of two nearby towns, Morisanea and West Farms, and talked them into floating city bonds, at two per cent, maturing in two hundred years, to pay for the bridge and road which, he persuaded them, would bring them riches and prestige. Through advertising in his *New York Times* and in Bennett's *Herald* the issue was sold out in a week. And so the road known as Central Avenue was laid down, and the bridge was rapidly built.

* * *

With increasing investments in railroads, Leonard began a regular column in the *Times*, running almost every day from 21 December 1864, recommending the public to buy railroad stock. To eliminate a competitor, he denounced the Erie Railroad Company on 15 January 1865, accusing its owners of illegal stock trading, market manipulation and issuing false prospectuses (a clear case of the pot calling the kettle black). Anxious to keep in with the government when a Congressional investigation into his activities was threatened, he soothed the troubled waters by urging his readers to snap up government bonds.

There can be no doubt that Jennie was, even at ten, an avid reader of his column; indeed, it is certain that reading it at home was mandatory. She remained even more passionately fond of her father than ever and he somehow talked Lucy Green into breaking the school rules of Sunday worship so he could take his daughter on the famous weekend society parades through Central Park. In gaudy calèches and four-in-hands, watched by cheering crowds, the peers of New York would ride in all weathers led by Jerome, Peter Lorillard Ronalds, and August Belmont, the spanking horses scrubbed and polished to a fault, the carriage doors painted with the owners' colours, and the entire gaudy procession guarded by Chief of Detective John M Young's hand-picked, mounted police.

Jennie rode proudly with her father on the box seat, adoring him as he cracked his whip, his top hat barely staying on his head in the high winds, his flourish of mustachios the bushiest in New York. His carriage was black-bodied with bright-red wheels, the blue-and-white Jerome colours vividly displayed on the doors.

Then came the grand opening of the Jerome Park Racetrack, dedicated to Clarissa, Clarita and an ecstatic Jennie, on 22 September 1866. Despite threats of rain, the sun shone brilliantly as Jennie and her family left West 26th Street that afternoon in their four-in-hand, cutting through street crowds along Fifth Avenue to Central Park, then up Eighth Avenue across the newly completed Harlem River

Macombs' Dam Bridge by way of Central Avenue in the Bronx, to the magnificent new concourse and members stand.

With great ingenuity, Jerome had devised a new form of track: a double loop in S formation, which, in hilly country, precluded the judges from seeing certain turns, so a sharply applied kick or whip on a rival horse's flanks could result in a shady victory. Society turned a blind eye, and there was high praise for the revolutionary track design as Jennie and her family walked up the hill to the clubhouse situated under a handsome, tree-covered bluff.

General Ulysses S Grant was on hand to greet the Jeromes, accompanied by August and Caroline Belmont; as Dodsworth's Brass Band played 'Hail, the Conquering Hero Comes', the general nodded in acceptance, but actually, as a waspish *New York Times* made clear, the music was intended for Leonard Jerome. Liveried servants by the dozen unpacked hampers of vintage champagne, Scotch and rye whiskey, claret, burgundy, and lemonade for the children. The food was the best that money could buy: terrapin, pâté de foie gras, partridge, tongue, Virginia ham and rare cheeses. Coffee flowed from a dozen silver urns, and the air was filled with expensive perfume and the best Havana cigars.

Jennie would have had time to explore the clubhouse with its Louis XIV furniture imported from France, its ballroom copied from the Tuileries Palace, its fine paintings and sculptures. And then, even though their horses didn't win, there was the excitement of seeing the family entries romp around the course, jockeys resplendent in blue-and-white satin suits and caps.

Back in New York, Jennie had more excitement ahead. Minnie Hauk, trained to perfection under Jerome's and Belmont's financial support, gave a brilliant debut performance at the Brooklyn Academy of Music on 13 October. Jennie joined society in cheering the fifteen-year-old's singing in Vincenzo Bellini's popular opera *La Sonnambula*, in which she played a sleepwalking girl who is mistaken by villagers for a ghost.

With the Jerome family's enthusiastic support, and to Jennie's lasting delight, Minnie was signed by the impresario Max Maretzek to a contract that eventually led her to astonish the world as the first great Carmen. A singer herself, Jennie was devoid of envy; she rejoiced in her friend's musical success as if it were her own. It was only laziness, lack of resolution and ambition, and the inability to develop latent talent in oneself that maddened her. In this respect and others, she was – and would remain – an arrogant New Yorker.

There were still more thrills in store for Jennie as her father told her he would be making a pioneer voyage across the Atlantic in James Gordon Bennett's yacht *Henrietta* for a $60,000 prize against competitors Pierre Lorillard (cousin of the aforementioned Peter Lorillard Ronalds) in the *Vesta* and the wealthy Osgood brothers in the *Fleetwing*. Such a sailing in winter storms at that time seems incredible; but there was no stopping these mid-nineteenth-century tycoons.[1]

On 11 December 1866, Jennie, her mother and sisters arrived at Sandy Hook on the coast near New York to see Leonard off. Thousands were gathered in snow flurries on the shore as Manhattan was closed for business, and some 3,000 Stars and Stripes fluttered from harbour-front rooftops. Hundreds of ships and small craft sounded horns and whistles, and a brass band played 'Hail, Columbia', 'Rally Round the Flag, Boys' and 'The Star-Spangled Banner'. As the three white yachts scudded round the headland, the roars of goodwill were deafening. One cannot doubt that Jennie's were among the loudest.

In those pre-cable days, it would be weeks before she would learn the facts of her father's voyage: the *New York Herald*'s reporter Stephen Fisk smuggled aboard the *Henrietta* in a champagne crate; divine service in the teeth of the Roaring Forties, when the worshippers crashed to the floor; Jerome and Bennett spilled from their bunks with laughter as the yacht took a sixteen-degree list; wind-driven snow

---

[1] As it turned out, only Bennett, Jerome, and his brother Lawrence in a rival boat made the trip.

beating through the rigging and ropes turned into spider webs of ice; and at last the triumphant sailing, ahead of the competition, past the Needles on England's coast to a wild reception from a waiting crowd.

Queen Victoria and several political and financial leaders sent their congratulations, and the Royal Yacht Squadron at Cowes on the Isle of Wight gave an elaborate reception. It was then that Leonard Jerome managed a typical stunt. Knowing that 9 January was Jennie's birthday – and he had never missed one yet – he was determined to make his way back to New York in time. It was now 30 December, so how could he possibly make it?

His brother Lawrence had come on a rival yacht. He agreed to 'become' Leonard; nobody would know the difference except the other contestants, and they wouldn't talk. Lawrence as Leonard gave a brilliant acceptance speech; alive with his customary humour, it brought the house down. Meanwhile, Leonard was on a fast train to Liverpool to catch the *City of Baltimore*, which just made it across the Atlantic by 9 January.

Jennie was at Jerome Park for her birthday celebrations and the opening of a brand-new ice-skating rink. There was no calculating her astonishment when she saw her father arrive by donkey cart; recorded in the *New York Times*, it was his loveliest gesture as a parent.

Within weeks, however, Leonard had a less happy experience. On 6 February he was at his office when a courier arrived with $100,000 in negotiable bonds and placed them on a desk for lodging in the safe. A tall man with red hair and a goatee beard picked up the package and walked out with it tucked under his coat. The man was Daniel Noble, burglar and forger, who had not served a term in jail despite a series of similar robberies. When he was finally caught and sent to prison in 1871, he had long since disposed of the bonds.

Clarissa had had enough. She insisted the family go to Paris. If Jerome did hesitate, that hesitation would have been ended by a snub that he would have felt keenly: when he offered $5,000 to his alma mater of the College of New

Jersey, the interest to be paid in annual prizes for senior classmen, he was turned down. His career at the college and his subsequent shady business dealings had resulted in this slap in the face. But so far as Jennie was concerned, there could be no doubt of her feelings: Paris was gloriously ahead!

The family settled happily in the City of Lights. While Jerome travelled to and from America after the first few months, Jennie's mother and older sister relished, in regular sallies from their apartment on the Rue Malesherbes, visits to the Imperial Circle, which ranged from Biarritz in the summer to Compiègne in the autumn to the Tuileries in the winter. Jennie, who had graduated from Miss Green's, was enlisted at the age of thirteen in the equally severe Lycée Coulon, with governesses in holiday periods. She enjoyed the continuing friendship of Lillie Greenough, who had married the American expatriate banker Charles Moulton, and lived at the magnificent Château de la Petit Val, some thirty miles from Paris, with a moat, a drawbridge, and ornamental gardens. Another good friend of the time was (again) the enchanting Fanny Ronalds; despite oft-repeated tales that she was Jerome's (and August Belmont's) mistress, she was still faithful to, and living with, her husband in Paris until late 1871, and had three children who took up most of her time. Her parents, the well-known Carters of Boston, also lived in her Paris house.

The big event of 1867 was the Paris Universal Exposition, with the Prince of Wales (remembered by Jennie from the 1860 New York City party fiasco) in attendance along with, at various times, Napoleon III, popinjay Emperor of France, and Eugénie, his pretty but superficial consort, and also the Czar of Russia and the Emperor of Austria-Hungary. For Jennie, we cannot doubt that the Egyptian House, with its gilded Pharaonic relics, the Ottoman Palace, a dazzle of minarets, domes and jewels, and the American Pavilion, a triumph of machinery, were surpassed by the musical events: Offenbach conducting his own orchestra, the great

French operetta star Hortense Schneider appearing in *The Grand Duchess of Gerolstein*, and Minnie Hauk giving a recital.

Three women captivated Paris at that time. Princess Metternich, wife of the Austro-Hungarian ambassador was as ugly as an organ grinder's monkey ('But what an interesting monkey!' she said of herself), matchlessly stylish in her Worth wardrobe and brilliant displays of diamonds and emeralds. Cora Pearl, mistress of kings, stunned all Paris in the stage show *The Commentaries of Caesar*, summoning up the Spirit of the Future in the handsome eleven-year-old form of the Prince Imperial, heir to the French throne. And finally there was Princess Mathilde, the richest woman in France after shedding the fabled monster Count Anatole Damidoff, heir to an incalculable coal-mining fortune of the Ural Mountains in Russia, who had whipped and beaten her when she refused him his marital privileges. Not even the death by firing squad of Napoleon's puppet, Mexican Emperor Maximilian, the attempted assassination in the Paris streets of Czar Alexander II, or the riot stimulated by the Italian revolutionary Giuseppe Garibaldi to greet the arrival of Emperor Francis Joseph of Austria-Hungary could put a damper on the exposition.

Ships' passenger manifests show Leonard Jerome in constant transit across the Atlantic from France to New York and back again, up to 1870 and beyond. Despite his cheerful, resolute outward appearance – all flushed cheeks, heroic moustache and loud, confident laughter – it is safe to say he was in a constant state of panic, trying to appease his cold wife and oldest daughter by spending time with them in the court circles of the Emperor, while at the same time shoring up a series of collapsing business ventures in Manhattan.

He had hung on against all odds to his investment in Pacific Mail, his vessels plying the Cape Horn route to California and Washington State. Greedy for spoils, and aware that the company was in a shaky condition, he had joined the Brown Brothers banking pool in Pacific, expanding the line by floating twenty million dollars in shares to start a new trade route to China; the vessels would also ship missionaries, leaving now for the Orient by the score. He was hoist by his own petard when one of his fellow directors used Leonard's well-tested device of declaring in the right places that Pacific Mail was in trouble, depressing the shares and buying at bottom.

Pacific Mail shares dropped 30 per cent; Leonard had bought the bulk of the stock 'on margin' and had guaranteed he would buy five million of new stock on the basis of the China route. He could have been ruined but, though he was badly affected, he survived, making money through other swindles.

There can be no doubt that Jennie and her sisters were informed of the matter; it was a policy in the Jerome family to hide nothing from even the youngest. Jennie continued to enjoy Paris, although she would have to be sixteen before she could go to the balls at the Tuileries or the October events at Compiègne. She was compensated by the friendships of Fanny Ronalds and Lillie Greenough Moulton, and now by the self-styled Comte de Persigny, the unprincipled former journalist whose title was in fact extinct, but who was very close to the Emperor and had secured his position by placing his wife firmly in the royal bed.

Persigny's loyalty had earned him a term in prison following an earlier revolution; it had also earned him millions in concessions in roads and railways, and such useful sinecures as the ambassadorship to Great Britain. He was no more a suitable exemplar than Jerome's corrupt friends in New York, but Jennie had an eye for pirates, and may well have had a crush on this handsome but heartless adventurer.

At fifteen in 1869, Jennie was already a full-blown beauty, with dark-brown hair, eyes full of life and laughter, perfect nose and chin, and a blossoming figure that would soon be large-breasted, with athletic lines obtained from daily rides on the Bois de Boulogne, figure-skating all winter long, and many brisk walks the length and breadth of Paris. She was spirited, full of wonder, unspoiled due to severe training at school and home, outspoken and strong; her love of her father and sisters was unchecked by adversity. Which is just as well, because on 4 April 1869, the family experienced what could have been its most shattering blow to date.

Their friend James Gordon Bennett led a chorus of anger, betraying Jerome completely, when a notorious incident became headline news. A squad of sheriffs, some sixteen in all, broke into the strongroom of the Union Pacific Railroad/Crédit Mobilier offices in New York and carried out a mass of documents that revealed, in the words of a Bennett editorial in the *Herald* dated 5 April, 'The most gigantic swindle ever perpetrated under the shadow of the law', the writer going on to say that 'the company [must] disgorge the millions they have plundered from the American people by their system of management in the trust confided in them'. Worn out and broken locomotives, defective tracks, vanished bonds, looted cash – the picture was appalling and one of the first names to come out of the vault as director and stockholder was Leonard Walter Jerome.

The famous crook Jim Fisk, annoyed he had not been given his share of the spoils, and another criminal, Boss Tweed's son William, were behind the raid; but they achieved nothing, because it soon became clear to the Congressional committee investigating the matter that dozens of politicians on Capitol Hill had been bought and paid for, and the investigation predictably collapsed.

CHAPTER THREE

J ennie was, in those Paris years, taught the piano to concert standard by the famous and irascible composer Stephen Heller, whose bristle of white hair and beard, cheeks flushed with anger, and demanding emphasis on aspects of keyboard technique became difficult daily experiences. Another burden of her existence was that, before she was sixteen, she was not of an age to be admitted, as her older sister was, to court occasions; and by the end of 1869, with a rapidly deteriorating political situation in Paris, it was clear that she would never become part of the royal circle; one ball and banquet after another was cancelled without warning. The extravagance of court events and the poverty of millions of Frenchmen had brought about a threat of revolution that stirred memories of the Terror, the murderous outbreak of the late eighteenth century that had brought down the throne of the Bourbons. All supporters of Napoleon III, and they emphatically included the Jeromes, were in potential danger as crowds of students and labourers invaded the wealthy districts, singing 'La Marseillaise' and hurling bricks through windows. At the same time, war with Prussia was threatened; the Prussian crown prince's decision to place a relative on the vacant Spanish throne offered a challenge to French influence and the

existing balance of power. Given detailed instruction from
Elihu Root at Miss Green's and her present teachers at the
Lycée Coulon, Jennie undoubtedly understood the political
background that led to the present state of France and the
larger dangers ahead.

The day after her sixteenth birthday, 10 January 1870,
the powder keg exploded. The Emperor's fiery cousin,
Prince Pierre Bonaparte, shot and killed the revolutionary
journalist Victor Noir, an idol of the student class; next day,
300,000 rioters, maddened with anger and out for revenge,
charged down the streets (including the Rue Malesherbes
where the Jeromes lived), set fire to houses, drove many
occupants out and beat them, raped maids and humiliated
older women. Hundreds were killed, hundreds more
seriously injured; the Jeromes were placed under curfew,
and it is likely that they only escaped pillage by hanging the
Stars and Stripes out of their windows.

A corrupt, Napoleon-controlled jury acquitted Prince
Pierre of murder in March and more riots ensued; as soon
as it was safe, Leonard arrived and took his family to Nice
and thence to Genoa; they returned to Paris later, to the
now militarily protected Boulevard Haussman.

But there was to be no peace for the family. Another riot
broke out in May, following a failed assassination plot
against the Emperor; once again there were fires, killings
and rapes, the streets littered with broken glass and the dead
and dying.

And then came the whipped-up frenzy of propaganda
against Prussia. Napoleon's attacks on the threatening
Prussian Empire were stimulated in part by his cabinet's
advice that this would have the effect of welding the various
revolutionary factors in a common cause. The ploy worked:
half a million youths rallied to the national flag. But soon
exhilaration changed to despair; Paris was in mourning,
citizens sobbing in the streets, as the young were slaughtered
on the battlefields of Wörth, Weissenburg, Metz, Mars-la-
Tour, Gravelotte and Sedan. At last, the Emperor himself
capitulated and was sent humiliatingly to jail. Cast into

gloom, the Jerome family was faced with a greater horror: the siege of Paris.

The fickle mob, learning of their country's defeat, took to looting and killing again, invading the Palais Bourbon and forcing the rump of the general assembly to proclaim the empire's fall. A new republic was proclaimed at the Hôtel de Ville under a provisional government, with Napoleon's betrayer, the treacherous General Louis Truchu, as president.

Leonard, by now back in New York, sent cables for the family to leave for England at once. They found no help in the US Ambassador Elihu B Washburne, who was profoundly pro-German and was busy assisting not his Francophile compatriots but German residents to leave for home. Jennie, her mother and sisters had to fling whatever clothes they could into steamer trunks, and then, like the Empress Eugénie, flee by train and coach to Deauville on the northwest coast, where they took the ferry to Dover through raging seas. They left almost everything behind: antiques, paintings, even jewellery they forgot in their hasty packing. They barely escaped; within two days, all British and French Channel steamers were stopped.

In Brighton, and then in London, where they put up at Brown's Hotel, the Jeromes found they were far from welcome. The overwhelming mood of press and public was pro-German; the very name Napoleon struck knives in British hearts, decades after the hated, deposed emperor had been exiled and died in St Helena. Thus, Jennie had to have a German governess, instead of a French one, and the family had to face up to a long stay in London, whose climate made them ill.

Despite the blaze of theatrical events that autumn of 1870, most notably the opening of the Opéra Comique Theatre on the Strand, and the extravaganza *Atlanta* at the Theatre Royal, Haymarket, there was little pleasure to be gained. Mayfair, where the shabby Brown's Hotel stood, was built over a vast and leaking sewer, part of seventeen million square feet of uncontrolled London muck. Excrement stopped the drains and ran down the gutters, and dysentery, typhoid and cholera spread, with the constant threat from rat fleas of a return of the Great Plague.

If noise and overcrowding were the curses of New York, they were far worse in London. Jennie, as she ventured into the stinking, squalid city, saw grinding horse omnibuses, hated because they were very filthy and unsafe, swaying dangerously over cobbles; conductors would run alongside, demanding or cajoling pedestrians into stepping in, but most preferred to walk or wade. Armies of street Arabs – ragamuffin children of the poor – ran about yelling in foul language or hammering off the heads of statues in the parks.

That winter of 1870, London must have seemed a potential death trap. Hundreds of accidents were recorded, caused by rain or fog; many people were crushed to death by runaway horses, falling masonry or ill-controlled trains; others were swallowed up in molten factory steel, thrown downstairs in fights, or cut to pieces by flying glass. There were endless abductions, drownings, garrottings; there were an estimated 36,000 criminals in London, 50,000 arrests in three months, and scores of bodies were dragged from the swirling, filthy waters of the Thames. So heavy was the soot from countless chimneys that, to quote the great French eyewitness and social commentator Hippolyte Taine in his book on England, even Nelson on his column was so black with soot he resembled a rat, impaled on a very long stick.

Leonard arrived in Paris to retrieve what he could of the family's belongings from the Prussian forces that now occupied the city. To do so, he had to pose as pro-Prussian, no major task for a Wall Street operator, capable of lying in any emergency. He attached himself to the American colony at Versailles, where the American General Francis Sheridan, who had aided the Prussian Chancellor Otto Van Bismarck throughout the war with military advice, and on presidential instruction, was in charge of American interests in France. Through Sheridan, Leonard was able to retrieve works of art that miraculously had escaped the rioters; in January 1871, he brought them to London and placed them in storage.

That was good news, but there was still the fog of winter; the yellow, villainous mixture of gas and coal dust that invaded houses, flats and offices, making it almost impossible to read or write. No ship could dock, no omnibus could run, hansom cabs had to be led by torch-bearing youths and trains were hours late, their drivers almost blinded by sulphurous fumes; the bleating of foghorns made a mournful obbligato from the river. For Jennie and her family, going to theatres, operas and ballets was a bizarre experience: the actors could barely be made out through the clouds formed by cigar and cigarette smoke and the creeping yellow vapours from outside; the shimmer of gas chandeliers, turned on to the fullest during performances, rendered the proscenium arch no more than a framework for ghosts.

In the wake of fog came torrential rains, making noisome rivers of city streets and spilling the Thames over its banks. Then, at last, the peace treaty that ended the Franco-Prussian war on 10 May 1871 sent the Jeromes happily back to Paris, and their home in the Boulevard Haussman, the following January.

Paris was *en fête*, with unseasonable blue skies and warm sunshine bringing country crowds in gay profusion to the city; the Place de la Concorde was alive with a grand fair, hundreds of brilliantly striped stalls displaying an unimaginably wide range of goods. For children there were exquisitely wrapped bonbons, toys and dolls, and popular puppet theatres, street musicians, romantic comedies and dramas on open stages. A record number of pockets were picked each day, and 3,700 thieves were caught and jailed in a single week.

Then, once again, bad news struck the Jeromes. As they were settling back into the Boulevard Haussman, word reached them from New York that Leonard was in desperate trouble. The stock-manipulating Jay Gould, who had a large holding in Pacific Mail, dumped his stock on the open market, injuring Leonard's already precarious position; a Congressional investigation threatened, and Gould had panicked.

As always in these situations, Leonard left at once for Europe. While keeping up his Paris house, with typhoid raging in London he decided to house his family in the Isle of Wight, so as to be close to the regattas in August and to the Prince of Wales's social circle, revolving around Osborne House. He rented a pleasant cottage, the Villa Rosetta, and soon Jennie grew to love the place.

Once the favourite of Henry VIII, Cowes was from 1815 the headquarters of the Royal Yacht Club, formed by wealthy supporters of the Prince Regent, later King George IV, when Beau Brummel (the notorious dandy who had dared to call George his 'fat friend'), was exiled from society and closed his London clubs to the pro-royal members of the aristocracy.

By 1824, Cowes rivalled Brighton as a retreat for the rich, and by the 1870s it was peerless in its breezy appeal. Napoleon III was a member, and the clubman Sir John Bourgoyne who had arranged the Empress Eugénie's escape from the siege of Paris; the yacht races were a grand spectacle, with the members in dashing blue jackets and white trousers, yachts like floating palaces, and crews tossed in the sea or lashed with a cat o' nine tails if they didn't meet requirements; in the early years cannons were sometimes discharged at a threatening rival team.

In the summer of 1873, Jennie and her parents formed a friendship with the remarkable Hon. Francis Bertie, later ambassador to France. At the time they knew him, he was rising in politics, and became an assistant undersecretary of state in the Disraeli government while he was still in his twenties.

He was a handsome, touchy, fierce-tempered man, noted for his collection of pornography, his passion for lewd gossip that earned him the ear of the Prince of Wales, his taste for gambling, and his access to beautiful women. He was handicapped only by his wife, the plain and charmless Fiodorowna, but she had one supreme advantage: she was the grandniece of the Duke of Wellington.

With Leonard back in New York and the Congressional investigation into Pacific Mail a certainty, a worried Jennie,

Clarissa and Clarita found Bertie an advantage in social climbing. Now that the Franco-German war was no more than a memory, they could, as supporters of the French monarchy, find their place at last; the Empress Eugénie in exile was a friend of theirs and of Queen Victoria's as well.

In August 1873, there was a major event at Cowes: Grand Duke Alexander and his wife the Grand Duchess, heirs to the Russian throne, were in town for the races. At a royal party aboard the guard ship *Ariadne*, Bertie, always with an eye to the main chance, introduced Jennie, then nineteen, to his friend Lord Randolph Churchill, second surviving son of the Duke of Marlborough. And in making the introduction, as Keith Hamilton wrote in his 1989 biography, Bertie would soon be responsible for the birth of Winston Churchill, whom he thoroughly disliked.

CHAPTER FOUR

J ennie saw before her a typical Marlborough: slight, narrow-shouldered, with a heroic moustache turned up at the ends, and pale, almost transparent skin. His eyes were protuberant, burning with a fierce intensity, his smile was warm and seductive, and his rings and jewelled studs suggested an almost effeminate dandyism, corrected by a deep, commanding voice marked by an attractive lisp.

Though 24 years old, he looked like an overgrown boy; his limbs had not the musculature of most men of his age. But there was a powerful and irresistible air of the aristocrat, the landowner and the horseman in his every gesture and every movement of his seemingly fragile but limber body.

Born at that intimidating architectural folly, the family seat of Blenheim Palace, in Oxfordshire, on 13 February 1849, he was only six months old when an older brother, Frederick Winston, died at the age of four. He was educated at Tabor's Preparatory School at Cheam, where he formed a friendship with Nathaniel (Natty) Rothschild, son of August Belmont's closest banking associate in London, who would later be the most profound of influences on Jennie's life.

At Eton, Randolph was, like Leonard Jerome, a rebellious figure; noted for his disgraceful conduct, he at one stage led a gang of hooligans in a charge against the royal carriage of the Prince of Wales and his consort Princess Alexandra of Denmark on their wedding day. He broke the rules by carving his name in his schoolroom desk – it was discovered decades later by the writer and artist Max Beerbohm – taking a pet bulldog into class, and setting the Marlborough coat of arms over the fireplace in his study. He stole sweets from a shop, and strawberries from an hotel, and his behaviour didn't improve when he went to Merton College, Oxford (he was much too poor a student for Magdalen, which demanded very high standards).

He locked a waiter up in the coal cellar, and another in the ice safe; he broke hotel windows, and smoked forty cigarettes a day when even one was forbidden. He fought constant battles with the Don, George Brodrick, who had his eye on the Marlboroughs' traditional constituency of Woodstock, and who never ceased to attack Randolph's parents for running not only a pocket but a rotten borough, a town corrupted by influence. He charged the duke with forcing villagers to vote for him when he was Member of Parliament from 1840 to 1845 and again from 1847 to 1857, and he criticised Marlborough for bribing voters with food, wine or promises of fixed rents. These charges were properly based, but drove Randolph into transports of rage.

Randolph refused to attend church on Sundays, a Jerome-like display of agnosticism that infuriated his parents. He was by no means a scholar. The only book he was known to have read was Gibbon's *Decline and Fall of the Roman Empire*, with its dry account of orgies, murder of Christians, and the destruction of emperors from murder or suicide; the record of a collapsing world that had been expected to last for ever. Randolph may have enjoyed the book's peerless record of dissolution and corruption, but he learned no lesson from its pages; he would remain an Empire man to the day of his death.

At the gala yacht party that August of 1873, Jennie was captivated as completely as any heroine of the French romantic novels popular during her years in Paris. She wasn't drawn to powerfully-built men and slightness and delicacy appealed to her; there was something of a dominatrix in her nature. In turn, Randolph was dazzled by a spirited, unaffected, downright and forthright American beauty of a kind seldom seen in England at the time. Her black hair, brown iridescent eyes, flushed skin and full figure suggested a combination of virgin and sensualist; in short, he was hooked.

Jennie's mother Clarissa was unimpressed. Randolph had neither the physical presence nor the strong personality that she had found in her husband. Younger sons of aristocratic families were notoriously useless, reduced to glorified gamekeepers or rent collectors, good only for riding to hounds or, at a pinch, steeplechasing. When the smitten couple plighted their troth in the correct tradition on a moonlit path the following night, Clarissa was upset. She had in mind a Duke, or at the least a marquess, for her daughter.

Randolph's own father and brother were also upset; neither the photograph of Jennie that Randolph sent the duke in Scotland nor his anxious pleas for an increased allowance proved appealing. Even the assurances that Jennie's father was famous in America and that marriage would end Randolph's time of idleness proved less than exciting; soon, Randolph would add a touch of blackmail, saying he would not stand as parliamentary candidate for Woodstock unless he were granted his wish.

Meanwhile, Clarissa expressly forbade Jennie to write to Randolph, who, back at Blenheim, complained miserably of her silence. Randolph's father, Marlborough, did not at first respond to him, but his brother George Charles, Marquess of Blandford, did, from the Western Highlands. He wrote that pleading with Randolph to change his mind would be like scattering words in a gale or, in a biblical allusion, taking on an army with the jawbone of an ass. Blandford's nature was revealed when he wrote that an affair with a married woman would be acceptable; that marriage for money was also understandable, but a love match emphatically was not. Finding no comfort in that quarter, his nerves shredding daily, Randolph rushed over to Cowes for two days to see Jennie and plead, vainly, his cause to Clarissa, only to leave at once for what he said was a trip to London to buy a locket in which he would place a strand of Jennie's hair. Jennie was touched by the announcement until she was told he was to attend the theatre with two American friends, and she dashed off a very angry letter.

The truth was that he had been summoned to the royal residence of Marlborough House for an interview with the Prince of Wales, which he clearly didn't want to mention since the outcome might be unfavourable. But in fact the prince was enthused by the idea of the match; he had been impressed with Jennie's looks and charm and by her mother's cool elegance, and he probably remembered his encounter with Jerome in 1860 at the New York Academy of Music.

A change in the Duke and Duchess of Marlborough's attitude can be traced from that meeting and they began to have second thoughts: royal approval could scarcely be ignored. The duke began to investigate Jerome through the British Embassy in Washington. He determined that Leonard was an operator, a stock manipulator and had once been bankrupted (in fact he had not), that he also ran a racetrack, and (the ultimate vulgarity) drove a six-in-hand (he didn't). But Marlborough did pick up the strong scent of money.

Jennie heard from her father on 8 September. His letter contained a warning that if anything went wrong with the relationship 'you will make a dreadful shipwreck of your affections'. He knew his daughter: 'I always thought if you ever did fall in love it would be a very dangerous affair.' He had fathered a tigress, and knew it. For such a person, love must be 'way down' or nothing; if 'disappointed' there would be 'untold misery'. But he said he would not disapprove – she could marry anyone so long as he were 'not a Frenchman or any one of those Continental cusses', an odd remark from a man who had spent so many years in Paris.

Then, on 17 September, with Jennie and Randolph getting more frustrated by the hour, Jerome came to the edge of ruin once again. It was Black Thursday: Jay Cooke, banker to the Union in the Civil War, was enjoying a drink with President Ulysses S Grant when he received word that his all-powerful Union Trust Bank, in which Jerome had an interest, had collapsed and that his issue of Northern Pacific Railroad bonds had failed, bringing the stock market down with it. Even the Astors and the Vanderbilts were affected; Jerome was saved only by his ownership of the West 26th Street house, of Pacific Mail ships and the racetrack.

By now, Randolph had received a doggerel poem from Blandford warning him, in a grisly misogynist litany, of the threats of marriage; his own with the ghastly Albertha Abercorn was the cause of much cynicism. He wrote of the horrors of mounting household accounts, perambulators, rusks and the cutting of tiny teeth, as if these were deadly viruses, threatening the very existence of romance; he had three healthy children, but obviously hated and resented them. His was nonsense verse with sinister overtones: the work of a seriously disturbed personality.

As Randolph and Jennie exchanged overwrought, changeable and often panic-stricken letters, the more rational Duke of Marlborough was warming up daily, along with Leonard Jerome. In a highly ambiguous state of mind, Clarissa whisked her daughters back to the Boulevard Haussman; Jerome had by now given his formal consent but the ever-correct matriarch would not approve until the Marlboroughs had finally agreed. Randolph came to Paris and put up at a hotel. The Marlboroughs had failed to discover the effects of Black Thursday on Jerome, and, by now, financial considerations overrode their misgivings. They were badly in need of cash. Beginning in 1862, they had sold thousands of acres in Wiltshire, Shropshire and Buckinghamshire; they were busy that September in disposing of cattle, sheep, chickens and even hunting dogs to Baron Ferdinand de Rothschild. The cost of 88 servants, and of entertaining royalty and maintaining a crumbling palace residence and a house in London were staggering. Whatever Leonard Jerome could come up with would be welcome.

All concerned embarked on a bargain sale that would disgrace a Turkish bazaar. Randolph was being sold off like a racehorse or a prize bull and the sordid negotiations went on for months. Through negotiations with Jerome's old Copperhead team of New York lawyers, Samuel Barlow and Jeremiah Larocque, and the Marlborough solicitor Frederick L Capon, it was agreed that some $250,000 in dowry property would be made to yield an income of $10,000 a year divided between Jennie and Randolph for life; on Jennie's death, half of the capital sum would go to the Marlborough family.

While the horse trading continued, Jennie spent the autumn and early winter of 1873 attending the trial of the decade. Napoleon III's disgraced general, Marshal François-Achille Bazaine, was charged with making treasonable arrangements with Germany to hand over his forces at the siege of Metz, an act punishable by death. Each weekday without fail for three months she set out from the Boulevard Haussman to the Palace of Versailles where the trial took place.

Her interest in the cause célèbre that could have resulted in the execution of a national hero is the first indication we have of a lifelong fascination with courts of justice that would later bring her to attend the famous Steinie Morrison and Crippen murder trials. The fashionable crowd crammed in the mirrored chamber, the sombre judges in black seated on the bench, the tricolour hanging over the embattled jury, the shattered marshal protesting his undying loyalty to France, all made an unforgettable impression. When Bazaine was found guilty and condemned to death by firing squad, there was a profound silence in the court broken only by Bazaine's painful, broken sobs. Later, to general approval, his sentence was commuted to life imprisonment.

At the same time, Jennie became interested in a famous case of wife-killing. She formed a friendship with Gaston, Duc de Praslin, whose father had killed his mother in an outburst of fury, supposedly because she had taunted him over his affair with his children's governess. To save the honour of France, and confronted by possible trial by his peers, Praslin was allowed to swallow poison; it took him several days to die. What Jennie may not have known is that Gaston was the actual cause of the murder: his mother, driven insane by sexual desire which her husband refused to satisfy, had seduced her son Gaston when he was twelve, and the *duc* had found out.

Having procured his father's agreement to the marriage on the promise of running for election at Woodstock in January, Randolph had no alternative but to go ahead with the campaign. He dreaded it; he would have to compete with the old and hated Don at Oxford, George Brodrick, who was still busy slinging mud on the rottenness of the Marlborough-bought parliamentary seat.

When he arrived at Blenheim, he refused to make a speech. To save the day his father imported from London the brilliant young barrister Edward Clarke, then on his way up as future leader of the bar; Clarke was shocked to find Randolph had done nothing, and at a meeting at the local inn, he forced him to talk. When, ill-informed and nervously dishevelled, Randolph fumbled for notes in the inside of his hat, the crowd laughed.

Clarke taught him how to handle question-and-answer sessions with potential constituents, planting hecklers in the audience at the local halls and supplying Randolph with quick and easy replies. Randolph won the seat in late January, by 569 votes to 404. He then, as clearly stated by Clarke in his memoirs, at once left for Paris.

What followed next is mysterious. According to *Burke's Peerage* from 1953 until a revision in 1999, a period of 46 years, Jennie married Randolph in Paris on 31 January, 1874. All Burke's entries for each edition were submitted to families for revision, and certainly Winston Churchill would have authorised the entry. Two possibilities exist. Either a then-secret marriage did take place and was concealed from 1874–1953, or Winston Churchill found out in 1952 that when he was born in November 1874 he was not premature but fully-formed, which meant that he had been conceived in February, and the entry was made to cover the probability of conception out of wedlock.

The present Burke's has declined to respond to two requests by the Churchill medical authority Dr John H Mather on this important matter. All books on Churchill state the marriage date to have been 15 April. And indeed, to legitimise the baby, such a marriage did take place, through the courtesy of the British Ambassador to France, the Marlborough family friend, Lord Lyons, on that date, at the Embassy, as the marriage certificate shows.

Three of Randolph's sisters attended: Cornelia, Baroness Wimborne, the spinster Rosamond, and Fanny Marjoribanks, later Lady Tweedmouth. Sportingly, despite his opposition, Lord Blandford was there, and Randolph's aunt, the Marchioness of Camden; the Marlboroughs themselves, due to the Duchess's illness (on her birthday), were not. The Prince of Wales showed his approval – not shared by the Queen, who detested Randolph – by sending as best man his secretary Sir Francis Knollys.

Jerome gave the bride away. He had to return to New York on the next and fastest ship, however, because the long-delayed Congressional hearing into Pacific Mail was under way that spring. It says much for the continuing corruption of Washington, very much as it is today, that the expensive inquiry with its mountainous documents came to nothing. As in the Union Pacific affair, the more that skilful attorneys uncovered the graft that ruled railways and shipping in America, the less chance there was of anyone going to jail. Jerome and his family could breathe again.

The Churchills left quickly on their honeymoon. Jennie's old friend Lillie Greenough and her wealthy husband, the American banker Charles Moulton, had survived the Franco-Prussian war and were happy to present the couple with their Château de la Petit Val for several glorious days.

The exquisite Louis XV structure, built by a brother of Madame de Pompadour, had an idyllic setting of waterfalls, ornamental terraces, grottoes, greenhouses filled with exotic plants, pavilions and temples, lakes and terraces and hundreds of acres of lawns, making up a picture of tasteful, immaculate elegance. For equestrians like Jennie and Randolph, the estate offered untold delights: magnificent stables housing two dozen prize horses, with 35 stable hands and grooms in round-the-clock attendance. There was no trace of the Prussian military vandalism, when bayonets had shattered mirrors and furniture had been stolen and burned. Moulton had spent millions on the restorations.

In fine spirits, flushed and happy, the Churchills continued to another idyll in Florence and Rome. Returning to England after two weeks of honeymoon, they arrived at Blenheim Palace on May Day, to a great crowd of tenant farmers and villagers, who uncoupled the horses from the carriage and pulled them through the cobbled streets.

Seeing the palace for the first time, and quite unprepared by her husband, Jennie would have been confronted by what the Duke of Shrewsbury had called 'a great quarry of stones above ground', and which Horace Walpole felt 'only from a distance does it resemble a great house'. Blenheim lacked above all things a grand staircase in the main hall, down which the social world could descend in finery at balls and banquets, and it had only one bathroom. The ubiquitous chamber pot, painted customarily with flowers, stood under every bed in lieu of proper plumbing; when the owners of the house and guests arose each morning, maids were ready with steaming jugs of hot water, brought laboriously along endless corridors and up flights of back steps, to allow for washing.

Jennie was in a state of shock. She had to get used to 200 gloomy rooms, many of which were candlelit; half of the staff of 88, of which she would have command, lived in the grounds or village, while the remaining 44 lived in a rookery in the upper floors, maids two to an iron cot in rooms not much larger than a linen cupboard. She had to learn the order of the days from a daunting housekeeper; with her clanging chatelaine of keys, that real mistress of the household ran the servants with whiplash severity. Under the housekeeper was the butler, among whose tasks was ironing the London and Oxford newspapers before breakfast so that not the slightest crinkle would offend his master; and under him were the maroon-liveried footmen and the groom of the chambers, who was in charge of seeing that the latest books were in the library, the embossed stationery fixed in the writing desk pigeonholes, and the curtains opened or closed at the precise moment when daylight increased or began to fade.

The maids were kept in working order: upper housemaids were responsible for supervising the dusting and straightening, while their immediate inferiors were responsible for the fireplaces, which had to be cleaned before anyone rose, and for handling the chimney sweeps. Below that level, at the bottom of the Blenheim barrel, were the scullery maids, who toiled in the kitchen. The dozen cooks were in a class by themselves: Jennie had to prepare for them the menus for them every morning, and when the meals were served, those menus stood by the plates, written by a master scrivener in perfect copperplate.

The grounds staff was necessarily large: the vast acreage of the Blenheim Park estate included stables, goldfish and trout ponds, well-trimmed bushes and trees, and chicken cages. Absolute silence was necessary in the mornings, when the slave army tiptoed about cleaning windows, polishing every piece of cutlery or brassware, or attending to the washing in the steam laundry.

The days were run with metronomic precision: while Jennie was dressed by her personal maid in crinolines, from waist-pinching corset to sweeping skirts, Randolph was dressed by his valet, who then shaved him and groomed his hair. At breakfast, the liveried footmen brought in a long line of silver chafing dishes, with eggs, bacon, ham, kidneys, lamb cutlets dressed with ruffled paper aprons and cold cuts of plump, juicy game. After a light lunch the ladies would take leftovers in hampers to the poor villagers, while the men shot hare or rabbit; embroidered alphabets or Watteau-like country scenes were often the women's afternoon work.

Tea was a major ritual, great groaning trolleys wheeled into the drawing room with Dundee cake, scones, crumpets and muffins, lashings of toast, and countless jars of jam and pots of Devonshire and Cornish cream. Stuffed to the point of indigestion, the family would proceed to rest or walk before a twelve-course dinner, served by flunkeys in powdered wigs and livery, punctually at 8 p.m.

Jennie soon learned the palace's history: Blenheim was an architectural folly, an early eighteenth-century conceit of the dramatist-designer Sir John Vanbrugh, the title of whose play *The Provok'd Wife* applied appropriately to his patron's spouse, the unhappy Sarah, Duchess of Marlborough. She hated the structure, and with good reason. It was begun in 1705, built in Woodstock Park, which Queen Anne had awarded the Duke for his triumphs on the battlefield. Between one and two thousand workmen laboured for three years under the direction of the co-designer Nicholas Hawksmoor and there were fights with stonemasons, carpenters and gardeners. Work was disrupted when in July 1708 Sarah Marlborough made the colossal mistake of accusing the Queen of lesbianism. This could have unseated the duke and duchess for good, but Anne proved tolerant; however, at the end of 1711, the duke's enemies in government brought about his dismissal and exile. After six years, Blenheim was still unfinished, the Treasury refused support, and Vanbrugh was almost bankrupt. The absent Marlboroughs abandoned the structure until 1713 when, returned to England, they started again. The duke being paralysed by a stroke, Sarah sued one workman after another, raged against delays and at last saw the palace she detested completed in 1717. A poem, sometimes attributed to Jonathan Swift, read:

> Thanks sir, cried I, 'tis very fine
> But where d'ye sleep, or where d'ye dine?
> I find, by all you have been telling,
> That 'tis a house but not a dwelling.

Whatever its architectural disadvantages, Blenheim was, with its many galleries, as Hippolyte Taine described it, a kind of English Louvre; a long gallery displayed portraits of successive dukes, while another was lined with cupboards of priceless porcelain. One room contained twelve Titians – voluptuous likenesses of gods and goddesses, they were the gifts of the princes of Italy. Van Dykes, Reynoldses – the treasures went on and on.

Jennie saw in the dining room notorious works by Rubens, stimulating all manner of sexual fantasies in the more susceptible guests while the duke and duchess stood side by side at dinner, carving the joints. In one painting, a woman about to be mounted by a muscular satyr suckled two infant boys; in another, a nude male cavorted laughing and drunk before a naked woman. The *Ansidei Madonna* of Raphael, Van Dyke's famous portrait of King Charles I, Rubens's self-portrait with child and Sir Joshua Reynolds's *The Fortune Teller* were only samples of one of the finest collections in England.

Jennie had little chance to inspect these great works, however, because only four days after she arrived at Blenheim, on 5 May 1874, she was required to attend her social debut: Queen Victoria's 'drawing room', a reception at Buckingham Palace at which the monarch, no longer in seclusion after her husband Prince Albert's death, appeared in person. It was a disaster.

The custom was for a lady of distinction to present a newcomer to the court on these occasions and the Duchess of Marlborough took Jennie. It was hot and raining heavily as the 3,000 guests arrived in their carriages at the noon hour. To make matters even more uncomfortable, the Queen did not follow the timeworn custom of moving among her guests, but sat separately in the Throne Room. The throng of the fashionable set had to stand in long lines to go through the narrow Throne Room door and be presented; many, impatient, hot and burdened with heavy clothes, broke the lines and fought and clawed at each other to obtain a better place. As a result, most visitors lost their jewellery, hundreds of costly dresses were torn and hairdos were reduced to rags. When the strongest entered – and Jennie was among the first of them – she and the others had to climb over concert chairs, nailed firmly to the floor, to reach the space before the throne; court officials bundled the ladies unceremoniously past the Queen in her mourning costume of black silk, black ostrich feathers, black crêpe, and a white veil concealing her face. No sooner had Jennie and a few brave, bedraggled souls curtseyed, than the Queen, shocked by the ragamuffin crew before her, stood up angrily and left.

Worse was to come. The commissioner of police had made the foolish decision that when the reception was over, vehicles could be summoned only in the order in which they arrived, so if anyone ordered his conveyance out of sequence, he would be refused. Because of this rule, the cream of English society had to wait in a now chilly east wind and rain, without umbrellas, perched on steps or walking several blocks to find their carriages. Those who waited had to sit for upwards of three hours as night fell, the wind grew colder and the rain heavier. For an entire week after that, the London *Times* printed letter after letter, usually signed with pseudonyms to avoid royal displeasure, complaining about this ghastly event.

For Jennie, there were compensations: on 12 May there was a brilliant recital by Adelina Patti, followed by a party at which that perpetually sour and complaining star did her best to be gracious; a week later the Duchess of Marlborough gave a party at her house in St James's Square to introduce Jennie to figures of society.

It was important for the Churchills to have a London home, and the Marlboroughs found a house for them in Curzon Street, marred by bad plumbing. Then there was the matter of Randolph's maiden speech in the House of Commons. Most unusually for a wife of that time, Jennie worked on it: a declaration against Oxford being turned into a military garrison, with a consequent threat of rowdyism and a decline of local standards. Randolph made a strong impression. His leader Disraeli approved, and Jennie soon learned she would now be required to entertain the prime minister at home.

Forbidden alcohol by his doctors, Disraeli (later, Lord Beaconsfield) still had to be allowed a feeble fix of brandy and water; champagne drunk around him would prove fatal to his approval of a hostess. And there was the delicate question of his current amour: Selina, wife of the 4th Earl of Bradford. Should she be asked to dinner or not? The conclusion, in view of her married state, and that she hadn't yet admitted the prime minister to her bed, was *not*. But, after all, Jennie found Disraeli a surprisingly charming guest.

As an even more prominent and equally frequent guest, the Prince of Wales was a different kettle of fish. His gross sexual appetite had very often to be satisfied by the introduction of a stray woman to the party, and his gourmand's lust called for a repulsive combination of boiled bacon, oiled kidney beans and boiled truffles; a dismal prospect indeed for Jennie's new French chef. His eyes almost bursting from his head, his cheeks plump and flushed, his voice loud and commanding, the prince resembled some monstrous chuckling baby. Yet for Jennie his nature – cheerful, defiantly hedonistic, all-embracing – had an unsettling appeal.

His mother the Queen disapproved of him, and refused to give him access to State papers, brought traditionally to her in dispatch boxes; she knew that if he got hold of them they would be found strewn and food-sodden on his dining table or crumpled in the tossed sheets of his mistress's beds. To have sex with him must have been the equivalent of being coupled in a stable or pig farm; the results were several randomly sired and bastard children.

Even the leader of the opposition Liberal Party, William Ewart Gladstone, enjoyed the privilege of the Churchills' dinner table; during all the years of parliamentary sniping at each other, he and Randolph remained in a state of secret and guarded mutual respect that would have infuriated their backbenchers if it were known. Gladstone's weirdnesses were legion: the brilliant master of political debate had in earlier years acquired the habit of scouring London slums to find prostitutes, not for sex at a discount as might be expected, but to lecture them on improving their propriety and hygiene. His only means of satisfaction was lashing himself into a frenzy with a scourge of nails. Since he was not a contortionist, this meant he could only attack his stomach, legs and recalcitrant genitals until they bled. In short, Jennie Churchill, innocent, honest, forthright, un-subtle and full of almost excessively bright American ambition, was Alice in London's wicked looking-glass land.

The month of May 1874 was filled with social events. Jennie had to order a new spring wardrobe – just as in New York, she must not be seen in the same dress twice. Spies were out everywhere to advise ladies of society if any of their number had ordered a costume in similar colours; should that be, compromises had to be fought for and reached. The extremely cold spring weather (the tempera-ture falling to minus four at night) meant that Jennie had to buy expensive furs.

On 13 May, Jennie and Randolph were at a Stafford House ball given by the Duke of Sutherland for Czar Alexander III of Russia, who leeringly addressed the newly married twenty-year-old with the words 'here already?' to indicate that she should be at home enjoying the early pleasures of marriage. Jennie was not amused.

Three days later there was the Queen's State Ball for Alexander at Buckingham Palace; after the disaster of the royal 'drawing room', the Queen left the entertaining to the Prince and Princess of Wales. And, in June, Jennie had the excitement of her first Ascot race meeting. At first the weather was hot and the sunshine dazzling; then there was an icy wind and a threat of rain; then heat again and more wind. The *New York Times* reported: '[The tempest] returned in very unpleasant fashion, playing havoc with Ascot toilettes, and robbing the brilliant show of much of its charm. The wind seemed at its bitterest when the scarlet coats of the Royal huntsmen and the whips appeared at the head of the Royal procession.'

Jennie found a new home at Charles Street that, in terms of plumbing, was no improvement on the Curzon Street house: and the gutters ran with excrement after the summer rain. The noise was appalling: organ grinders played loudly and cacophonously outside windows that showed even a glimmer of light, refusing to budge until fistfuls of coins were thrown at them; the German boys' band was an itinerant menace as they slapped broken drums and tootled away on damaged wind instruments; horsemen drew kettle-drum players mounted on a shaky cart; a pianist banged away at a keyboard while mounted on a vegetable truck; and, worst of all, a one-man band played bells, pipes, hurdy-gurdy and brass cymbals while his wife screeched contemporary songs out of tune. And this musical insanity continued all year round, day and night, uncontrolled by police or even the influence of Lady Dorothy Nevill, a constantly complaining neighbour.

Lady Dorothy's grumblings scarcely improved matters for Jennie, who might as well have lived in noisy Whitechapel for all the peace she got and chance to sleep. But Nevill became a lifelong friend. She was a fine botanist, painter and writer, and a direct descendent of the Gothic novelist Horace Walpole, Earl of Oxford – her parson husband had been given a title because the Prince of Wales was fond of her.

In the autumn of 1874, Jennie was in restless movement between Charles Street and Blenheim Palace. Equally rest-less were her immediate family, whom she was scarcely able to get to know on any but the most superficial level. Of this eccentric brood, the most dominating were her brother-in-law Charles, Marquess of Blandford, whose drinking, drug-taking and promiscuity harked back to an earlier century of aristocratic rakehells, and his dreadful wife Albertha, whose childish silly nature caused her to lay booby traps throughout Blenheim for unsuspecting family members.

Albertha had lost two earlier children, probably through her refusal to cut out her social life during pregnancy, and now she had three more whose lusty cries made the Blenheim rafters ring with distressing frequency: Frances, aged three, Charles, aged two, and Lillian, nine months old.

As for the duke and duchess, they were in even more constant motion than the others, taking off to friends in Scotland for fishing or grouse-shooting in season, or cruises in their yacht on the Mediterranean. They had wildly ambiguous characters, at times sweet, attentive and concerned, but more often harsh and imposing. As she grew to know her husband, Jennie was faced with his flaws of personality: his insecure health; his habit of chain-smoking, in a diamond-studded holder, forty hand-rolled Turkish cigarettes a day until his tongue was burned; his effeminate dandyish clothing, with rings, gold chains, diamond buttons and studs à la the younger Disraeli; his irritating deafness; and the strange dark-bronze colour of his skin, resulting perhaps from Addison's disease, a sickness of the adrenal glands. She loved this maddeningly unstable, frantic, overenergised man-boy, but for someone as down to earth, practical and forward looking as herself, he presented her with many difficulties.

By November, Jennie's pregnancy was nine months advanced. She had to conceal from her own and the Marlborough family the fact that she had conceived her child in February, not in April, so she had to make it seem the baby would be premature. She had even gone to the extent of not obtaining a layette of baby clothes and crib, or of making sure an obstetrician would be on call. Instead, in that ninth month she went out in a cart with servants, beating the Blenheim woods for game in a high east wind that had caused many wrecks on the coast, thus deliberately bringing on labour. The ruse worked. And it went on working: countless writers, overlooking the marriage date in *Burke's*, have talked of a premature birth (very dangerous in those days before incubators); few have noted that the child, Winston, was fully formed, of good weight with no health problems and even had a tuft of red hair, all extremely unlikely if he were two months premature.

Winston Leonard Spencer Churchill, named for his father's dead infant older brother and for Jennie's father, was born on Monday 30 November 1874, and was a picture of health, energy and aggression from the outset. Delivered by a local doctor, when the family obstetrician was unable to come from London, he thrived merrily. The letters exchanged between the Marlboroughs and the Jeromes from London to Paris make clear that nobody even then suspected the truth, and they probably never found out.

In late January, bucking the current (and lasting) trend of engaging German, Swiss or more popularly Irish nannies, Jennie settled on Mrs Elizabeth Ann Everest as Winston's nurse. The youngest of four children of a grocer, she was born on 13 February 1834 at Chatham, Kent and, very oddly, was baptised six months later – against church rules of the time. The only explanation is early illness; but by the time she joined the Churchill family shortly after her 41st birthday she was clearly robust, and, despite the pretence of the 'Mrs' (a commonly accepted practice of nannies in those days), she was considered reliable. Her late spinsterhood was not common, though; clearly she was neither pretty nor interested in men. Just as some such women entered lay or religious orders in those days, so others became surrogate mothers, working out their frustrations through loving other people's children. Everest had a good record as a nurse: she had for years been with a Kentish family named Lee, and then with a respected vicar, the Reverend Thompson Phillips at his home at Ivegill, south of Carlisle, taking care of three sons and two daughters from the ages of three to nine. The fact that she had handled so large a brood spoke for itself. But she would never manage to please the Duchess of Marlborough.

History, supported by Winston Churchill's praise, has undermined the feeling, correct or not, in the Churchill clan that Elizabeth Everest was an irritating menace who must at all costs be kept out of the boy's room when he was ill. Most nannies in an English family were gone after children were seven years old or younger. The fact that Everest stayed on long past Winston's childhood, and he would not let her be budged, is unusual; she seems to have served no useful purpose, except as a shoulder to cry on, after he reached adulthood.

Leonard Jerome's failure to see his grandson or attend the christening at Blenheim Palace can be explained by the continuing problem of the Pacific Mail hearings in Washington; but Clarissa's failure can only be put down to her icy refusal to pass up a social engagement, or suspend her Paris salon at which she entertained leading figures of society and the arts. Randolph, forgiving her for her previous opposition, and anxious to please her, wrote her several letters describing Jennie's progress. In one note the duchess, three of whose sons had died in infancy, had said that all concerned had 'tried to ward off the event', but by contrast Randolph expressed pleasure in the baby's successful delivery and good health. Clarissa sent baby clothes and a shawl from Paris; oddly, even by then the Marlboroughs hadn't troubled to supply their own.

Jennie was in Paris with Winston and Nanny Everest in April, when panic swept the city; there was fear of another war as conflicts between France and Germany, fanned on both sides by Russian influence, kept the public in turmoil. In the midst of the crisis, the French government secured Disraeli's agreement to an alliance if Germany should again prove belligerent. As always at that time, the Germans were a threat to European peace.

A continuing presence in Jennie's life was Fanny Ronalds, now the toast of London; tales of her rescue from a pond by Napoleon III had ensured her a lasting notoriety. Still married to Peter Lorillard, who was enjoying his ill-gotten gains as the plumbing authority of New York, she received from him a substantial income; he was busy planning a Gothic castle in Connecticut to house his mistress, and retained custody of one of their two sons. In turn, Fanny, at her house in Sloane Street and despite the presence there of her other son and her daughter, embarked on one of the most talked-about love affairs in England – with the rising Arthur Sullivan, partner of WS Gilbert in creating the most popular comic operas of the day. For years, Sullivan kept a sexual diary, in schoolboy code, of their nightly couplings, to which, through Ronalds, Jennie was privy.

Practising piano and singing for several hours a day, Jennie often joined Fanny in evening musicales, singing Gilbert and Sullivan songs to the captivated delight of the Prince of Wales.

Another and less welcome presence in Jennie's life was the famous male beauty and bully, Sir William Gordon-Cumming. Owner of some 40,000 acres of prize Scottish grouse moor and dashing in his Scots Guard uniform, he was an insolent and ruthless ladies' man who bragged that he had cuckolded half the husbands in London. He wanted Jennie badly, but she was not prepared to share his all-too-busy bed, so he made an effort to seduce her sister Clarita, also without success. He was in Jennie's party when she went to the opening of Gilbert and Sullivan's rollicking *Trial by Jury* on 25 March 1875; given her love of courtrooms, she can only have been enchanted by this burlesque version of a breach-of-promise case. Then something emerged that could have brought the Marlborough family to a real-life court.

Perennially hard up, they had to sell their jewels at auction at Christie's in London, including several that had belonged to Sarah, the dangerous duchess; but, worse, they deceived the auction house in respect of their individual value.

In 1866, a jeweller had provided them with the provenance of each gem; he had singled out those which were fashioned in paste or glass. The Marlboroughs presented the entire collection as authentic, and Christie's neglected to have a new valuation. Only the indispensable *New York Times* got onto this.

* * *

For some time past, Randolph had suspected his brother, Lord Blandford, of having a sexual interest in Jennie, an opinion shared by Blandford's wife, the inescapable Albertha, who still rejoiced in such pranks as replacing soap with cheese in the bathrooms at Blenheim or setting open ink bottles on doors to fall on the heads of anyone entering or leaving.

Blandford, in his customary state of overheated libidinousness, stole a ring from Albertha's jewel case and gave it to Jennie, pretending he had bought it for her. She, thinking it an innocent gift, accepted it. When she showed it to her mother-in-law the Duchess of Marlborough and sister-in-law, the unmarried Rosamond, they were horrified; they at once recognised it as Albertha's, and told Randolph that. He called them liars; he insisted that the ring had never belonged to Albertha; that it was a simple, innocent gift, not a move towards seduction.

The Marlboroughs were furious that Randolph should have accused them of lying; the duchess in tears, they left for London to instead confront Blandford with the theft. Jennie wrote to the duchess, regretting she had been the cause of a feud. In the face of the evidence, Blandford insisted the ring was not his wife's, and Albertha was mischievously silent (no record exists of her response). But the crime and its purpose were clear; the duchess wrote bitterly to Jennie, saying that Randolph had trampled on her affections by his accusations of mendacity, that Blandford was equally a disappointment to her, and that her chief consolation was Jennie, whom she loved, and 'the dear little child', Winston. The ring was returned to Albertha, and the storm died down. But there was far worse ahead.

CHAPTER FIVE

T he new scandal had its origins on 8 January 1871, when Heneage Finch, Lord Guernsey, 7th Earl of Aylesford, married Edith Williams, daughter of the Welsh Lieutenant Colonel Thomas Peers Williams in a spectacular ceremony at St George's Church, Hanover Square in London. They had two children, Hilda, born in 1872, and Alexandra, born in 1875. They had three handsome residences, Diddington House, Packington Hall and a home in London. Aylesford was well over six feet tall, good looking, with massive shoulders and chest, and a strikingly attractive speaking voice. He was constantly unfaithful to his charming and beautiful wife and few women could resist him. In 1875 he was stricken with syphilis, and ordered by his doctors to become celibate; Edith, who was uncommonly lusty, decided that children or no children, she would at once acquire a bedroom substitute. She settled on Randolph's brother Blandford, who was weary of his wife Albertha and ready at this stage for anything.

Edith was not put off by Blandford's pallid cheeks, weak chin, narrow shoulders and exhausted air from his numerous debaucheries; she wanted a man, and he was one – at least biologically. When Albertha found out, she was convinced wrongly that Edith was pregnant by Blandford, and characteristically put a china doll baby under his chafing dish at breakfast.

Despite his syphilitic condition, and his doctor's restrictive instruction, there was no stopping Aylesford as society's favourite stallion. He kept two mistresses in Brighton; he consorted with trollops at the notorious Cremorne Gardens; and he spent many nights a week with Rose, the attractive wife of Charles Dilke, wealthy cousin and namesake of the Churchills' friend Sir Charles, a major political figure. Charles Dilke's Maxstone Castle was a short gallop from Aylesford's Packington Hall; after drunken quarrels between the three principals, Aylesford would carry the unconscious Dilke to bed, then jump into Rose's.

The romps became the buzz of society; everyone talked of Aylesford grabbing Rose at a grouse shoot, singing a lewd song as he fondled her, and Edith's friends beating him over the head with their umbrellas. They spoke also of the carrying on at a brothel in Bognor Regis as black-faced minstrels strummed banjos and women dressed only in skullcaps stroked the men vigorously.

Charles Dilke was no willing cuckold. In love with Rose, and devastated by her infidelity, he tried to drown himself in the Thames; rescued, he threw himself from his coach at a high speed; finally, he cut his throat on 3 August 1877, and saved Aylesford, who hated him, the trouble.

While this was going on, Edith continued her affair with Blandford, and talked of divorcing her husband. When the Prince of Wales took Aylesford with him to India to shoot tigers, she continued her campaign to be rid of him. Egged on by Blandford, who was as eager to divorce Albertha, she wrote to her husband, urging the idea on him. The prince was in support; but he had once taken a fancy to Edith, and had written her letters which, if aired in a divorce court, might cost him his succession to the throne. He ordered Aylesford back to England to make sure they would not be used in the action of which he approved.

Meanwhile, Edith's brother, Colonel Hwfa Williams, a savage Welshman whose idea of fun was jumping on men's chests in bar rooms, challenged Blandford to a duel for seducing his sister; if Blandford should refuse, he threatened to shoot him dead. With murder in the air, Randolph put detectives on watch around his brother day and night. He talked to his brother-in-law, the barrister Edward Marjoribanks, (later Lord Tweedmouth) and to his barrister friend Edward Clarke, as to what could be done; they advised him that the only possible course was to arrange a quiet separation of the parties. He rejected the idea, and so did Blandford; the Prince of Wales must agree to stop the divorce; Randolph, afraid of a family scandal, would accept nothing less. It is safe to say that Jennie, who thought Blandford should be rid of Albertha, deplored such dangerous insistences.

And then Randolph and Jennie had an idea. He would blackmail the Princess of Wales into having her husband block the divorce going through.

Taking with him a helpmate, Lord Alington of Crichal, Randolph arrived without warning at the princess's Marlborough House residence and asked the maid who opened the door for an immediate audience. The maid informed the princess that two gentlemen were in the hall. Asked who they were, the maid mentioned only Lord Alington. Hard of hearing, the princess thought she had said Ailesbury. Lord Ailesbury was a friend of hers, so she had the visitors brought to her at once.

Randolph wasted no time in meaningless pleasantries but came directly to the point. Either the Prince of Wales stopped the Blandford divorce, or his love letters to Edith Aylesford would be given to the press.

With her customary calm in a crisis, Princess Alexandra made no decision on the spot. After her maid had taken her unwelcome visitors to the door, she went to see her sister, the Duchess of Teck, who advised her to see the Queen. Victoria was badly upset by the news.

Apprised of the matter on his way home from India, the prince sent his friend Lord Charles Beresford from naval duty in the Mediterranean to hand Randolph a royal challenge to a duel. It would take place in France or Holland (duels in England had been illegal since 1844). But the prince had forgotten that duels between royal and non-royal persons would, no matter what the location, be disallowed by law.

Randolph refused the challenge anyway, so the prince declared him a coward and a blackguard; it was made clear to the Churchills that they would be banned from society. The prince, who was of course on everybody's invitation list, would never visit a house at which they were received. An emissary, Charles, 5th Earl of Hardwicke, was dispatched to them to convey the royal displeasure; this was an unfortunate choice, since he had serious designs on getting Jennie into bed, and she had, on at least one previous occasion, had him thrown out of her home.

At the beginning of April 1875, with the Prince of Wales still in transit, Blandford set up house in Rotterdam, without Edith, as 'S Seymour, Esq.' He had received no response to the blackmail offer and wrote in frustration to Randolph on 5 April saying that he would thrash the prince, in the traditional terms, to 'within an inch of his life'; Randolph, with Jennie's approval, then took the prince's incriminating letters to the Solicitor General, who ominously announced that if they were made public, the prince would never sit on the throne. In turn, Randolph told Sir Charles Dilke that he held 'the Crown of England' in his hands.

He took a ship to Holland to try and settle his brother's nerves while Jennie stayed at Charles Street, her own nerves shredding rapidly. She suffered through tortured days and sleepless nights; threatened with social ruin, she would sit in an armchair for a moment, then jump up and prowl around like a caged tigress. She would decide to talk to Hardwicke, then, remembering his busy hands, desist; her only escape was going to the opera with Edward and Fanny Marjoribanks.

Meanwhile the prince tried unsuccessfully to appease his mother by denying an affair with Edith Aylesford, that she had been 'too great a fool' for him to want her as his lover.

And then, at long last, he was back in London on 12 May to tackle the matter that threatened his entire future. He put a brave face on it by attending the Opéra Comique Theatre that night – as if nothing had happened; he was given a standing ovation and afterwards appointed Lord Hartington, the future Duke of Devonshire, to settle the matter once and for all. Hartington could influence granite. He persuaded Edith to agree to a private separation, rather than a public divorce; Blandford would leave the country with her and access to the children would be shared. Jennie and Randolph would remain banned from society; by royal command they would leave at once for America. The Marlborough parents would also be exiled. In Randolph's presence, Hartington burned the prince's letters in his fireplace.

Only two people stood firm with Jennie and Randolph in their plight. The Irish-born playboy and Jennie's future lover, John Delacour, told the Prince of Wales he would let no man choose his friends; eventually, that statement would cost him a knighthood. The American socialite Consuelo Yznaga was also loyal; she had been a fellow pupil of Jennie's at Miss Green's School for Girls in New York. Leonard Jerome loved her and her parents, and was to arrange her marriage to George Victor Montagu, Lord Mandeville, the future Duke of Manchester, who had vast estates surrounding his Kimbolton Castle in Huntingdonshire; the couple married at Grace Church, Broadway, New York on 22 May 1876. Jennie sent a loving cup, Jerome gold bracelets and James Gordon Bennett a locket studded with diamonds and emeralds. Arrived in England, Consuelo announced she would brook no nonsense from the Prince of Wales, who henceforth refused to receive her. She responded by not including him in her guest lists – until both of them relented, just under a year later.

Jennie and Randolph sailed for America in July; they were accompanied by an amusing bachelor, Harry Tyrwhitt-Wilson, member of a distinguished family that produced the composer Lord Berners. The diminutive charmer had long appealed to them both and, as equerry to the Prince of Wales, he might be handily placed to bring about a reconciliation. But he took a considerable risk of incurring the royal displeasure in travelling with them.

New York was noisier and more crowded than ever, the deafening din of the Third Avenue Elevated train's construction providing an ordeal. Jennie found her father exhausted, aged; severely affected by the successive debacles of the Union Pacific and Pacific Mail, betrayed by Jay Gould, he had for some time barely been able to pay Randolph's and Jennie's shared allowances, and there had been conflicts over that. The couple's visits to Jerome Park, the Saratoga races and the Philadelphia Centennial Exposition scarcely provided Jennie with compensation for the suffocating, thunderous heat broken by electrical storms and the painful thought of disgrace in London society. The Churchills were miserable in New York.

During the couple's absence, a heaven-sent opportunity arose to get the Marlboroughs out of England. Ironically, Albertha Blandford provided the solution; her father, Lord Abercorn, would be returning home soon from his post as Viceroy and Lord Lieutenant of Ireland, leaving vacant an unenviable appointment that Marlborough had sensibly refused before. Under pressure, the duke and duchess agreed to this inconvenient exile, which would leave the management of the Blenheim and other estates in questionable hands; not to mention the costs out of their own pocket, scarcely to be met by the secret viceregal allowance from the British government of £21,000 a year.

The Churchills returned from America to find Blandford in an hysterical mood; forgetting he had instigated the blackmail plot in the first place, he had written to Marlborough accusing him and Randolph of a conspiracy to prevent his divorce; an abject apology followed. Distraught and disturbed to the point of madness, he had refused to leave the country as he had promised. The musical beds went on: he still slept with Edith; Lord Aylesford with Rose Dilke. Meanwhile, a post had to be found for Randolph abroad. It was decided he would occupy the artificial role of private secretary to his father in Dublin; after much argument he was allowed to keep his Woodstock seat in parliament – which at least gave him a tenuous foothold in politics, and would allow for frequent visits to England.

It was customary for lord lieutenants and viceroys, whether of India or Ireland, to have an audience with the Queen before assuming their appointments. Thus, she would receive the Duke and Duchess of Marlborough at Windsor Castle before their departure for the post in December 1875. As it happened, she was fond of them and, unlike the Prince of Wales, did not condemn them for their role in the Aylesford crisis. It was, however, an uncomfortable audience. The Marlboroughs were racked by strain, distressed and wretched; only their daughter Rosamond, who accompanied them, was in reasonably good spirits. The Queen was sympathetic, up to a point, and no mention was made of the painful matter in hand. Unfortunately, she tried to lighten the occasion by referring to a custom of Dublin Castle: a grisly welcome ceremony at which every society lady would be kissed by the new Viceroy one by one. After that threat or promise, the duchess took, quite unwell, to her bed.

And now there was the prospect of Ireland: that agrarian appendage of Britain, constantly threatened by national liberation movements that called for displays of violence. In 1801, the Irish parliament had been abolished following a people's uprising; in 1845–47, one million people died in the great famine, for which the British were blamed. In the next few years, over a million left Ireland for America; the rise of the landlords, who evicted anyone who refused to pay increased rent, caused further dissent. By 1867, 38,000 owners controlled 586,000 tenants and 8,209,549 acres of land. There were repeated calls for revolution by Fenian terrorists.

Neither the Marlboroughs nor the Churchills would be welcome in Dublin. Aggressively anti-Catholic, and hated in Ireland for that, the Duchess of Marlborough was also the daughter of Lord Londonderry, an unpopular landowner there, whose tenants were evicted at the drop of a silk hat. The duke's – and Randolph's – attacks on Home Rule eclipsed any degree of paternalistic sympathy for Ireland they were credited for.

When Jennie arrived in Dublin with Winston and Mrs Everest in December 1876, she herself faced unpopularity as a supporter of the Irish Protestants, the Ulster Orangemen's who wanted permanent assurance that Home Rule (to which Jennie was opposed) would not crush them through a Catholic majority. But that was the least of her problems. As an American, she was an object of hatred because of the American beef scandal, which had brought Fenian opposition to the edge of revolution.

Day after day, ships arrived from New York with cheap beef, cured and packed by the ton, throwing into panic the farmers who in the past two years had turned from wheat to grazing land in the face of promises from Whitehall that England would guarantee them purchases by the well-to-do, and that a protective tariff would be set up. It wasn't, and the British importers had obtained cut prices from the meat-packing barons the Armours and the Swifts of Chicago for enormous profits. To make matters worse, because the British landowners had not supplied barns or blankets, the cattle in Ireland had frozen or died of pleurisy in the savage winter weather.

And, as if the situation weren't bad enough, the Churchills befriended the most hated man in Ireland: Thomas Henry Burke, the continuing undersecretary, who effectively ran the country with the viceroy as figurehead.

As agnostics, Jennie and Randolph had reluctantly to attend twice-daily religious services at Dublin Castle. Even more disagreeable was the presence of Sir Bernard Burke, the undersecretary's unrelated namesake, master of castle protocol and editor and son of the creator of the labyrinthian *Burke's Peerage, Baronetage and Knightage*.

This plump and pompous popinjay, the very image of self-satisfaction from his smarmy smile to his smartly shod feet, had been in office, to everyone's annoyance, since

1854; with irritating effeminacy he had laid down the rules of etiquette, precedence and deportment that even extended to the aristocracy and religious leaders who had the temerity to enter his domain.

Not content with making everyone's life a misery, as Ulster King of Arms the ageing despot extracted fees for supplying family histories and heraldries; from the moment the Marlboroughs and the Churchills arrived, he announced that at the first reception, when the duke would unhappily have to kiss the ladies, only women who were married and of high station would be admitted.

Jennie and Randolph obtained relief in January, when the great Henry Irving, the leading star of theatre, appeared at the Dublin Theatre Royal in his sombre production of *Hamlet*. Unlike Jennie, Randolph followed the aristocratic habit of turning up late and talking through the performance. He arrived after the first act and his ignorance was such that he had no idea what the play was about. After the second act was over, he strode into Irving's dressing room, brashly insisting on knowing what would happen at the end, because, he said, he might not be able to stay until the final curtain. Irving asked him if he really didn't know; Randolph replied in the affirmative.

At this Irving turned on him, threatening to punch him, and berated him with all of his famous fiery eloquence. Then, with amazing skill, the star provided a played-out, potted version of the remaining acts in fifteen minutes. Chastened for perhaps the first time in his life, Randolph more or less humbly apologised, rejoined Jennie, and saw the performance to the end. Next day he bought a Shakespeare collected edition and read every play in full, returning each night to see Irving and give recitations the actor could certainly have done without.

Soon after, the Marlboroughs held their first 'drawing room', an imitation of Queen Victoria's; Sir Bernard Burke excluded tradesmen, tenant farmers or merchants, who formed a battalion, shivering in the snow outside the castle walls, protesting as the family arrived.

Disaster followed: in order to obtain warm relations with Roman Catholic leaders, including bishops, the duchess and Jennie sent out invitations to a select number without referring to Sir Bernard Burke; for once, they should have consulted him. The invitations were delivered in the second week of Lent, the time of Catholic fasting.

With mostly empty places at the table, the two hostesses were mortified; Burke's gloatings can only be imagined. The duchess made matters worse; she sent messages to the editors of the Dublin newspapers, begging them to publish nothing of the gaffe. They failed to oblige.

Yet another faux pas marred that winter of discontent. The investiture of the Order of St Patrick in Dublin Cathedral should, as a diplomatic move, have been accorded to a Catholic peer; but Jennie, concerned with the objections of Consuelo Mandeville's future parents-in-law to their son marrying an American, decided to help her out. She persuaded her father-in-law to give the award to the Duke of Manchester – he did own Irish properties, but was not much liked as a landlord.

With great boldness, Jennie had the Marlboroughs invite her nemesis the Prince of Wales to the ceremony, but it was too blatant an attempt to rekindle royal favour and he refused to attend. Queen Victoria, however, kept her affection for the Marlboroughs, and sent her son the Duke of Connaught instead.

At the investiture on 24 March 1876, Jennie, seeking simplicity and hating ostentation, upstaged the local noble-women who were festooned with jewels; she wore none, thus stealing the show. That same week it was leaked to the press that while Randolph had announced he was acting as his father's private secretary for nothing, he was actually in receipt of £800 a year. Since if he took money he would have to surrender his seat in parliament, he had to cancel the sinecure.

Jennie, with Randolph often absent in England, tried to work off her loneliness with frequent visits to fox hunts; she was put up in castles and mansions while Everest took care of Winston in Dublin. Meanwhile, in August, *Truth*, Henry Labouchère's London gossip sheet, announced that Randolph had bought a house in St James's Square and had sold his society guest list to a tenant.

Then, on 17 September, at the Woodstock Agricultural Show, Randolph made his worst blunder to date. Based on his and Jennie's observations of conditions in Ireland, he launched, with her approval, a violent attack on the British rule of centuries, raging on about tyranny, oppression, suppression of voting rights, disenfranchisement and neglect of education. The speech horrified the Marlboroughs; the duke wrote to a friend, Sir Michael Hicks Beach, that Randolph was clearly mad or drunk. The fact that all he said was true made matters worse. He was, like Jennie, a Whig in Tory disguise.

He maddened even the Irish MPs, as his approach remained paternalistic rather than democratic. He saw the Irish as unhappy children who would be stranded without parental guidance; to give them their own government would be like handing a cannon to a twelve-year-old. That Jennie was against him in this attitude speaks for her American democratic spirit; her father had grown up a Whig, after all; she hated the oppression of Ireland, even though she still opposed Home Rule.

Randolph wanted to pre-empt Gladstone at the next election by using the same arguments Gladstone would use on the Irish issue. And at the same time, the Marlboroughs set out to trump Gladstone's aces: he wanted to give amnesty to Fenian prisoners, so Marlborough did. The duke pushed Irish education bills through parliament – they had been high on Gladstone's agenda. Gladstone talked of freeing the insurrectionary Michael Davitt after seven years' hard labour in Dartmoor Prison – Marlborough freed him. When Gladstone came to Dublin the duke, the duchess, Jennie and Randolph gave him an elaborate luncheon at Dublin Castle which scarcely improved his spirits.

*   *   *

By 1877, anti-British feelings in Ireland ran higher than ever; the failure of the potato crop, and militant activity by the terrorist John Devoy, were further threats to Jennie's peace of mind. On 2 April 1878, a friend and host of the Churchills, the Earl of Leitrim, who had evicted a widow from her cottage for not paying an increased rent, was shot and killed by angry members of the Fenians near his house in County Derry. Then the following month, Jennie had news from London. The Aylesford scandal had re-emerged.

Aylesford, in the wake of Charles Dilke's suicide the previous August, wanted to marry Rose, Dilke's widow; Blandford still wanted to marry Edith Aylesford. The rivals entered into collusion: Aylesford filed for divorce, naming, with his approval, Blandford as co-respondent. The divorce was denied on the grounds of a two-husband conspiracy.

Soon afterwards, Aylesford tired of Rose Dilke and left for New York, where Jerome's old nemesis Jay Gould took care of him. With a personal physician, a personal meat-cutter and butcher and a personal spiritualist, the embattled nobleman went of all places to Big Spring, Texas, where he bought 40 acres of land, put his family seal on 300 head of cattle, sported a Stetson, built a wild-horse corral and marble slaughterhouse and, when refused entry to a local hotel as a drunk, bought it and moved in permanently. He died on 3 January 1885, after throwing down a quart of rum and a half-gallon of whisky in a day.

Blandford moved with Edith to Paris, and together they had a son, Eugene, who was born out of wedlock. It was two years before Albertha finally got a divorce.

In the summer of 1878, Jennie was in London to attend several performances of her beloved Minnie Hauk in *Carmen*, a part her old friend played with extraordinary sharpness, savagery and attack. Afterwards, there was a party at which more than one impresario offered Hauk an American tour. Jennie joined the storm of laughter when she replied that she had just come from one, and had been seasick all the way.

Randolph had grown increasingly impatient with his Conservative leader Lord Beaconsfield, formerly Disraeli, whom he considered a decrepit old fogey of politics and whom he had dreams of eventually replacing. This was a case in which Jennie disagreed with him: she clearly felt that party loyalty and consolidation were essential. To show her independence of spirit, she defied him on 15 July by appearing to cheer Beaconsfield's speech at the Wellington Riding School given after he had signed, despite illness, the important Treaty of Berlin, intended to bring peace to Europe. She would never forget the prime minister's eloquent attack on Gladstone, saying he was 'gifted with an egotistical imagination that can at all times command an interminable and inconsistent series of arguments to malign an opponent and glorify himself'.

In February 1879, the Duchess of Marlborough embarked on a fundraising campaign to assist the poor and starving of Ireland; Randolph dropped everything to help her and Jennie sent begging letters to everyone she knew with money, and some £135,000 was raised.

It didn't help: that month, 10,000 smallholders and Fenians met in the light of flaring torches in the central square of Irishtown, County Mayo, calling for revolution. Named an enemy of the people was Randolph and Jennie's friend, the Irish Solicitor General Gerald FitzGibbon, whose application of the law, though often just, was very fiercely resented.

And in the troubled summer that followed, Jennie became pregnant for the second time. Ralph G Martin, most recently (and cautiously) echoed by the distinguished Churchill biographer Roy Jenkins, suggested that the father was John Strange, the future 5th Earl of Roden, on seemingly no better evidence than that Strange was allegedly godfather of the child (he wasn't), and his name was accorded to the baby at birth.

The father can only have been Randolph Churchill. The 56-year-old Strange was absent at the time of conception, May 1879; he was in the South of France, at the town then called Mentone, gravely concerned over the illness of his nephew the 4th Earl, who died on 9 January 1880, of consumption, leaving Strange with the burdens that came with his inheritance of the title. He was also preoccupied with arrangements for his daughter Violet's wedding to Sir Reginald Proctor-Beauchamp on 7 June of the same year; he did not act as John Strange's godfather, as the present Earl of Roden confirms.

Why then was the boy, born on 4 February 1880, named John Strange Churchill? Because Roden was an intimate friend of the Duke and Duchess of Marlborough; he was a visitor to Blenheim when Jennie first arrived there in early May 1874, and he had accompanied the family to the ill-fated Queen's 'drawing room' at Buckingham Palace. Later, he became co-executor of the duke's will, a sure sign of intimate friendship and trust. Further disproof of the fatherhood theory may be seen in photographs of John Strange's son John: he was an exact double of his brother Winston. John Strange himself resembled earlier Dukes of Marlborough.

There is an odd addendum: John was not baptised. The only possible reason is that Jennie and Randolph, agnostics both, and dreading the publicity and pageantry that Sir Bernard Burke would insist upon, felt a christening was unnecessary. They were also packing hurriedly to leave Dublin with the Marlboroughs at the end of the viceroyalty to escape possible assassination, and their baby could be in danger, along with Winston.

An angry crowd of Fenian-led dispossessed tenant farmers attacked the Marlborough coach, in which they were riding to the wharf, with rotten eggs and vegetables. It was a horrendous conclusion to years of discomfort.

Back in London, Jennie, Randolph, Everest, Winston and Jack (as the new arrival would always be known) moved into their formerly leased house at 29 St James's Place. Soon afterwards, Jennie had a horrifying experience, related in a letter written by her grandniece, Anita Leslie, decades later to the mother of the present Earl of Roden; drawn from an account by a contemporary, it was excluded by Leslie from her 1969 biography of Jennie.

Thomas Boscawen, 7th Earl of Falmouth, was known popularly as 'Star', because of his impressive looks, worthy of a leading figure of the stage, and his melodramatically virile habit of twirling his moustache while speaking to a beautiful woman. He was captivated by Jennie, and decided to add her to his long list of conquests, but on a visit to her house she resisted him; in his fury and resentment he raped her on her drawing-room floor. Later, incredibly, she forgave him, and called him 'Star' to the end.

Soon after this traumatic incident, Jennie for the first time, at the age of 26, became deeply committed to politics. Leaving Winston and Jack to the care of Nanny Everest at Blenheim, she joined Randolph in throwing all of her formidable charm and energy into removing the old regime from the Conservative Party; she no longer held a candle for Lord Beaconsfield. The poverty of Ireland, the horror of the eggs and vegetables thrown at her conveyance as she left Dublin, the murder of Lord Leitrim, made her as impatient as her husband with the anti-Irish ignorance and complacency of the Conservatives to whom she belonged.

This should have been the time for Randolph to cross the floor of the House of Commons and join the Liberals, but again, no doubt to Jennie's disappointment, he couldn't do so while holding the seat at Woodstock. And to him and Jennie, Gladstone was also an old fogey, no better than Beaconsfield in many ways. In truth, they both wanted Randolph to be prime minister (he would have been the youngest since William Pitt the Younger in 1783), to completely revise Empire politics in favour of better Irish (and Indian and Egyptian) conditions, without losing paternalistic control by granting Home Rule, which both Randolph and Jennie opposed.

The 1879 agricultural depression in England, the worst in many years, the failure of trade agreements and the unpopular Zulu and Afghan wars had left the government in tatters. Strikes in the Midlands gave Gladstone all the ammunition he needed. Beaconsfield had grown indolent, careless of administrative detail; his cabinet was a shipwreck of its former self. In spring 1880, a general election was called.

Fearful of losing Woodstock, Randolph rushed to Blenheim with Jennie to confer with the duke and duchess, who remained furious at his attacks on their own party; every word he uttered undermined any effect he might have. Naively, Randolph was shocked to find his constituents embittered by his infrequent visits during the previous four years. Ducal agents had stripped them of benefits, failed to support them in the recent crop failure, and utterly failed to wage war on bug blight, infestations of predatory birds and foot-and-mouth disease; and at the same time those agents had increased rents shamefully.

Throughout the campaign, Jennie was at Blenheim and on the local hustings, bringing glamour to every meeting. She found the Duchess of Marlborough, who had been so friendly when they had worked day and night on the Dublin relief fund, quite suddenly her enemy. Despite her appearance of formidable, even frightening self-confidence, the duchess was in fact fragile, wayward and unpredictable. Her loss of composure during the affair of the Blandford ring, the merest statement that she was a liar having her in total disarray, and her shaken and unhappy appearance before the Queen before going to Ireland, indicate that she was painfully oversensitive; and now, it seems, she laid on Jennie the charge of being in favour of the Irish peasantry in the wake of murders of her friends in that country.

On her side, Jennie, always confident, direct and utterly American, was exasperated by the duchess's hauteur and icy criticisms. With a touch of vanity, she wrote to her mother in Paris that the basis of the duchess's hatred of her was that she was prettier than her sisters-in-law: 'Everything I say or wear is found fault with. It is rather like a volcano.'

Largely through Jennie's efforts, Randolph won the Woodstock election by sixty votes; it helped that his opponent, a nonentity named William Hall, had no strength and Randolph, in his customary role of the pot calling the kettle black, denounced him for doing the very thing the Duke of Marlborough was doing: forcing the voters' support in return for promises and bribes. So great was his eloquence – Jennie once again worked on his speeches – that he managed to praise, and get away with it, the unpopular British campaigns in Afghanistan and South Africa as fine displays of imperial might; he attacked his Irish friends in parliament with charges of Communism and nihilism on the issue of Home Rule. But it was a hollow victory, in which he abandoned his quasi-Liberal ideals.

In London, the Churchills were still excluded from royal society; when told there were threats against her life, Queen Victoria replied that she had no idea who might be threatening her, 'unless it is Randolph Churchill'.

Gladstone became Liberal prime minister in April 1880; with Beaconsfield finished – he died soon afterwards – the Churchills had to form a splinter group within the Conservative party, a cabal that would light a fire under the traditional old men who were bringing it down. Oddly, they chose as members of this so-called Fourth Party certain maverick figures who were also scarcely young.

Their first selection was the wealthy Sir Henry Drummond Wolff. A convert from Judaism to Christianity, he kept a foot in both religious camps; he was a man of warm and generous character, humorous, with twinkling, bulging eyes.

He had first been a missionary, then a diplomat of sorts; he had travelled extensively abroad, with enough dirt scraped up on colonial affairs to make any government feel uncomfortable. As Member of Parliament for Portsmouth he had a firm grip on maritime matters; his forked tongue could be relied upon in parliamentary debates and and he was a popular clubman. Mention the China tea trade, the activities of the Sultan in Constantinople, or the emirs of West Africa, and he was sure to have something pertinent and pungent to say. His only weakness was for soothsayers and palmists, whom he believed could foretell the future; since they predicted only glory for him, that was understandable.

The next Fourth Party member was the lawyer Sir John Gorst. He was the exact opposite of Wolff: pale, still, cold, apparently devoid of emotion, he was utterly without sex appeal. He was a creature of pure reason, whose thin, unmuscular body was, like Sherlock Holmes's, a mere appendage to his brain. And his brain was phenomenal: brilliantly clever and polemical, he could destroy an enemy with one short, piercing phrase. Like Randolph and Jennie, he was an agnostic, and that was very appealing to them.

A third man was not so much a member of the Fourth Party as an uneasy addendum. Arthur Balfour, nephew of the Marquess of Salisbury (later Randolph's nemesis), was an odd bird in this newly formed political peacock brood; he was humorously dubbed 'Postlethwaite' by Jennie and Randolph. He was a spiritualist, or rather one who sought to prove the world of spirits, and later became President of the Society of Psychical Research. In 1875, he had fallen in love with Gladstone's niece, May Lyttleton, who had died of typhoid fever one month after they announced their engagement. In agonised grief he began consulting mediums to conjure her up from the black Styx of death; in some form of madness, he blamed Gladstone for her demise and devoted himself to attacking him whenever possible. If only he had not been shaky and unreliable, he would have been an ideal recruit to the Fourth Party, but he was too often absent at seances.

A further addition to the Churchills' conspiratorial hideout at St James's Place was not a member of the Fourth Party: the ferocious Henry Labouchère, wealthy joint-Member of Parliament for Northampton and publisher and editor of *Truth*, the very popular social and political gossip-sheet magazine.

He was of French origin and his cold, rational detachment from British political affairs showed the application of a foreign, basilisk eye. An agnostic and a sceptic in everything, he used chain-smoking as a literal smokescreen; he kept the House of Commons on its toes, when he dashed from his seat to the smoking room to take a puff or two of his hand-rolled, Randolphian black Turkish cigarettes. He was famous for his quips: he said of Gladstone that he didn't mind the prime minister having an ace up his sleeve; he only objected to his assertion that God had put it there.

Disgraced at Eton and sent down from Trinity College, Cambridge, for cheating in an examination, he spent much of his life losing money at the racetrack. He worked as a circus roustabout, fought duels and played roulette with equal enthusiasm, and was caught buying votes. Tall, stoutly built and flaring in his tempers and approvals, he was a vision few would forget.

Yet another supporter of the Fourth Party was the rubicund Irish politician Justin McCarthy; Randolph admitted to him, at this outset of a serious political career, that he knew nothing; that whatever he had learned at Eton and Oxford had long since been washed out of his mind; and that with Jennie's aid he was only now reading the Roman classics, starting with works by Horace.

Randolph and McCarthy would tease Labouchère, who was always looking for items of gossip for his *Truth*; they would stand in the lobby of the Commons, whispering about nothing, with furtive looks as if they were sharing in some great government secret. Then, when Labouchère came to them eager for gossip with pencil in hand, they would laugh in his face.

The Fourth Party needed targets, and for the first of these they had no distance to go. The Churchills' next-door neighbour at St James's Place was Sir Stafford Northcote, leader of the House of Commons, whom both Jennie and Randolph hated as the ultimate old fogey who was dragging the party down.

Northcote was everything Jennie despised in a man: flabby, white-faced, with the nervous disposition of Lewis Carroll's White Rabbit; his watery blue eyes were another annoyance, along with his air of complacency, cheerful mediocrity and bland, inoffensive charm. To tigers like the Churchills, he was a sickly old idler ready for the taking.

And Randolph was jealous of his erudition. Northcote's favourite reading was Sir Walter Scott's *Count Robert of Paris*; he admired Tennyson, whom Randolph deplored; he despised Thackeray's *Vanity Fair*, which Jennie loved, because its anti-heroine, Becky Sharp, was 'a wanton strumpet'.

Another target of the Fourth Party was Charles Bradlaugh, joint-Member with Henry Labouchère for Northampton. He had a magnificent, daunting presence: a huge head, like that of Danton of the French Revolution, a thick neck, enormous shoulders, and an athletic, big-boned, perfectly proportioned frame. Refusing to wear moustache or beard, he offered a face devoid of pretentiousness, ornament or disguise; his voice rang out in the House of Commons with thunderous force. All but the most powerful boxer's fist would break on his jaw. To his unpopularity could be added his support of the mystic Annie Besant, his belief in contraception, and his hatred of the Queen. He proved an ideal target for the Fourth Party, which, ironically given Randolph's agnosticism, assumed the mantle of Christian righteousness in attacking him.

Bradlaugh liked to shock the religious: a teetotaller for a while, when he was informed that Jesus liked wine, his response was that such an attitude implied very poor taste.

On 24 May 1881, Jennie saw to it that Randolph had his first major breakthrough in the Commons. He attacked Bradlaugh directly, making himself famous overnight. It was understood that on election to the House all new members must swear their affiliation in the oath of office, placing a hand on the Bible and swearing their allegiance to the church and monarch. When his turn came, Bradlaugh thunderously refused, stating that he was an atheist and that the terms of the oath were unacceptable to him. Randolph denounced him with a fiery eloquence that brought cheers from both sides of the house; he stamped on Bradlaugh's inflammatory and seditious pamphlet 'The Impeachment of the House of Brunswick', an attack on the royal family's historical corruptions and intrigues.

As Jennie left the Commons that afternoon, members and their wives rushed to congratulate her, as if she herself had done the trampling; everyone in London knew by now that she was the power behind Randolph's every move, the only significant woman in English politics apart from the Queen.

And so, with Jennie's great support, Randolph was launched on his great political career. She was often present in the ladies' gallery as he appeared in his favourite seat, below the gangway and directly facing Gladstone, who sat on the Treasury Bench. At question time, nagged with irritating and often pointless charges to which he could not at once respond, he let his monocle fall, toyed with the Maltese Cross ring Jennie had given him, called for a brandy and soda, drank it down, walked to the smoke room for a puff on his hand-rolled Turkish cigarette, then returned, stroked his stockinged legs, observed his face in the mirrors of his highly polished shoes – and made his response. His baby-blue coat, an imitation of Beaconsfield's when young, stood out like a flag against the black uniformity of his fellow parliamentarians – until Gladstone, with mischievous humour, assumed the same colour, and everyone laughed.

Although Gladstone secretly admired Randolph as a surrogate Liberal, he was the very devil in opposition in a debate. He would arrange question time at the dinner hour, when most members were out eating and quaffing; he would fix Randolph before an almost empty house with so glassy a stare that even this obstreperous young member would be crushed. Once, in the middle of a stinging Gladstonian sally, Randolph fainted and had to be carried out by Sir Henry Drummond Wolff.

The Fourth Party, led often by Wolff, met every Sunday for conspiratorial conferences, first for lunch at the London home of the Churchills' former neighbour, the fussily charming Lady Dorothy Nevill, then at the house of Mary Mackenzie, wife of Sir Francis Jeune, and then in the evening at St James's Place. There, determined not to be overhead by Sir Stafford Northcote next door, or by spies who might come disguised as tradesmen, they talked in whispers, plotting the downfall not only of Gladstone, but of Northcote as well.

And in the midst of this activity, Jennie embarked on the most serious love affair of her life.

CHAPTER SIX

It has been said that Jennie met Count Carl Kinsky zu Wehinitz u Tettau in London for the first time in 1881; but in fact they must have run into each other in Ireland when, with his father Prince Ferdinand, Kinsky had been in the personal entourage of Jennie's friend the Empress Elizabeth of Austria, whose passion for foxhunting took her, despite death threats, the length and breadth of the Emerald Isle. Now, with the Empress in England, Kinsky was a member of the hunting set at Pytchley, near Cottisbrooke, and at Melton Mowbray; although Jennie was still officially banned from these equestrian centres, she was often admitted to them when the Prince of Wales was tied up in London, Sandringham, Balmoral or abroad.

Born in Vienna on 29 November 1858, Kinsky was, at 22, Jennie's physical type: five-foot-seven, slight, with an exquisitely proportioned physique, and a fine seat on a horse, he was handsome, with clear blue eyes, neatly trimmed military moustache and cheeks flushed with health. And, though he was far more muscular and virile, like Randolph he was stamped with the mark of the aristocrat; eighteen years later, he would inherit the title of Prince Carl Kinsky. Jennie fell in love with both his looks and charm.

Calm, confident of his sex appeal, and devoid of neuroses, he was a temperamental contrast to Jennie's husband. When he walked into a room, women undressed him with their eyes: for Jennie, he was a major catch. His family, of the ruling class of Austria-Hungary, could be traced back to 1326, when King John of Luxembourg raised Balthasar, Wilhelm and Johann Kinsky to the rank of barons for their military prowess and gave them membership of the ancient Order of Teutonic Knights. The family provided political advice to one king after another; when Jennie met him in London – the exact occasion is unknown – Kinsky was already a court favourite, and an intimate friend of Crown Prince Rudolph, the ill-fated heir to the Austro-Hungarian throne.

With vast inherited estates in Bohemia, a Chancellor of the Austrian House of Peers, Captain of Cavalry, and wealthy beyond calculation, he was a supreme catch of European society. His life was horses, diplomacy and espionage; his files in the Vienna Straatsarchiv, opened recently for the first time, show that he was active in Paris, London, Brussels, Vienna and St Petersburg as a secret agent; he was appointed special attaché in England to the embassy secretary, the spy-cum-diplomat Count Constantin Dumba.

A racecourse jockey from the age of sixteen, he was one of the finest riders in Europe, trained by the Masters of the Austrian Royal Horse, the British brothers Rowland and Jack Reynolds. In tight-fitting cavalry uniform, coaxing his favourite steeds to win steeplechase after steeplechase, black hair tossed in the wind, flashing smiles at the women spectators, he was something to behold. His best friend and mentor was one of Jennie's ardent admirers, Captain William (Bay) Middleton, with whom he shared a hunting lodge near Leicester. Jennie would meet the two men in 1881 at Combermere Abbey in Cheshire, where she saw them negotiating to buy the handsome mare Zoedone at a country sale; though unsuccessful at first, Kinsky later bought the horse and ran her at the Grand National.

Jennie could scarcely have Kinsky to her home, with Randolph there and with her children, nanny and a large staff; it seems that they met mostly in the country, at places where the Prince of Wales would seldom be seen; the most likely location for their nocturnal trysts was the Bay Middleton hunting lodge.

Meanwhile, on 2 June 1881, Jennie's sister Clarita had been married – without the Churchills present – to the adventurous and foolish international speculator Moreton Frewen at Grace Church in New York, where both were visiting. He was good looking, of decent family, but a brainless and indigent pipsqueak, always coming up with absurd money-making schemes that drained what little income he had. He was emphatically a cad; he hated Jennie and her mother, whom he rudely dubbed Sitting Bull, in reference to her imaginary native American origins.

On 26 April 1882, the Churchills set out for New York; Leonard had again been negligent in making the payments he had guaranteed as part of the dowry; he had moved back into the West 26th Street and Madison Square mansion, which he had claimed he had sold to enable the allowance; in fact he had only leased and mortgaged it. They sailed with the Duke of Manchester, Consuelo's father-in-law, who remained grateful to them for engineering his Order of St Patrick six years earlier. It was a rough crossing; transatlantic weather was the worst it had been in twenty years.

They arrived to severe conditions: electrical storms, one after another for days on end, made it impossible to leave West 26th Street. The streets ran with liquid effluent and anyone going for a walk had to roll up trousers or raise skirts; sewers ran over and there were the usual outbreaks of typhoid.

And to make matters worse, there was very bad news from Ireland. Two days after the Churchills arrived, their old friend, the undersecretary Thomas Henry Burke, and Lord Frederick Cavendish were stabbed to death by Fenians in Phoenix Park, just a stone's throw from Little Lodge, where Jennie and Randolph had lived. The assassins were caught, but there was the shock that the Churchills' friend Charles Stuart Parnell, as the leading opponent of British rule, was accused of instigating the crime. Later, forged notes allegedly written from him as authorisations for murder would be used against him; it would be years before his name was cleared.

Devastated, the Churchills left New York only thirteen days after they arrived, returning to London without any guarantees from a broken and aged Jerome that he would be able to send them any more money in the future; he was finally selling the mansion he had just reoccupied to the Union League Club, which had leased it previously.

No sooner were the couple in London, settled in a modest cottage in Wimbledon (they had been forced to let St James's Place for lack of funds), than they had more problems. Fanny Ronalds was frantic; she was, she said, pregnant by Sir Arthur Sullivan. That would mean social ruin and impoverishment, since her husband Peter Lorillard might cut off her income; what could she do? There was talk of her going to an abortionist, which she did. The quack told her to wait another month, to see if she missed a second period, and fortunately she did not; there had been a simple gynaecological problem and everyone could breathe again. But Jennie's stress, in her present shaken condition after New York, was very severe indeed.

It was only briefly lessened; Fanny soon announced in tears that Sullivan had another, and younger, mistress. There was nothing she could do and he continued, while composing the comic opera *Iolanthe*, to commute between beds.

At seven years of age, Winston was increasingly a handful – noisy, bumptious, a tiny egomaniac – but contrary to published statements, Jennie and Randolph were very good to him. They kept him mostly at Blenheim, where he had magnificent grounds to run about and play in, and in addition to Nanny Everest, he had lackeys to do his bidding.

Jennie sent him tin soldiers until he had a virtual army and a papier-mâché castle to billet them in, so he could play war games to his heart's content. The Duchess of Marlborough rejoiced in giving him lessons at her knee; whatever she thought of Jennie she never ceased to love the child. He had a pony, Rob Roy, that he could canter freely, and he adored his baby brother Jack.

Life for him was bliss; although the Churchills, with House of Commons commitments, were not often at Blenheim, no child was more thoroughly spoiled.

During that summer of 1882, Jennie and Randolph were concerned over the critical situation in Egypt, where nationalist insurrection against British colonial rule was a major threat.

Randolph, through his school friend, Natty Rothschild, knew that Gladstone had substantial investments in that country, particularly in the Suez Canal and in cotton shares, and that his motives for assuring absolute power there were mercenary as well as political. Britain must at all costs retain the passage to the Orient through the canal; rebels might seize it at any time, thus ruining countless investors in the City of London, as well as Gladstone himself, most of whose portfolio was Egyptian.

Annoying Rothschild, and most of the Conservatives as well as the Gladstonians, Randolph, Jennie and the Fourth Party, with insolent daring, backed the anti-British Arab nationalists in Cairo. Their audacity can hardly be overemphasised, since they were working against the very thrust of Empire, and the specific wishes of the Queen. Egypt's recent history infuriated the Fourth Party: they hated the control of the Cairo puppet administration by the British Resident and Consul General Sir Evelyn Baring of Barings Royal Bank, by the Rothschild Bank and by the interests of Sir Ernest Cassel, investor for the Queen and the Prince of Wales.

Therefore it was in outright defiance of the royal family and the present government that the Fourth Party, headed by Jennie and Randolph, gave moral and financial support to the Egyptian rebel nationalist Ahmad Arabi Pasha against the puppet ruler Khedive Tewfik, a willing tool of White-hall. A riot in Cairo, allegedly engineered by the Khedive to secure military support from England, brought the situation to boiling point; on 11 July, Admiral Sir Beauchamp Seymour bombarded and invested Alexandria; soon after that, Sir Garnet Wolseley crushed Arabi's forces at the battle of Tel el-Kebir. Randolph rushed funds to Arabi's defence when he was put on trial and he made such a fuss that the rebel leader wasn't hanged, but merely deported to Ceylon (now Sri Lanka). Years later, when he was Secretary of State for India, Randolph unsuccessfully tried to bring Arabi back to Egypt.

In July 1882, in the midst of this embroilment, Jennie found a new house at 2 Connaught Place. She soon discovered that her silk wall panels were ruined by the poisonous air, so she replaced them at great expense and insisted on installing electric light, a novelty in London, obtained from a dynamo in the cellar. This tended to be unreliable, often plunging the house into darkness. Meanwhile, the Churchills learned the news that Gladstone, through the successful war in Egypt they had opposed, had raised the value of his Suez Canal-Rothschild stocks from £38 to almost £100 each, making him a very rich man. Natty Rothschild had made an additional million-pound investment in Canal bonds that hugely increased his firm's wealth. General Charles G Gordon, so often thought to be beyond reproach, was also well stocked with Egyptian investments; he would later be advanced as much as £10,000 pounds (worth a million and more today) to buy off his arch enemy, Arabi's nationalist successor, the Moslem fanatic Mohammed Ahmed Mahdi. He didn't succeed.

The Churchills had more enemies than ever over Egypt. Manipulation and coercion would have worked better but subversion was not their style. They seemed to have a perverse thrill, when faced with adversity; they manned the battlements at 2 Connaught Place and to hell with the consequences.

They had a spy in the liberal camp: M Maltman Berry, later a friend of George Bernard Shaw, who had worked for Karl Marx. An aggressive anarchist, he edited an anti-royalist newspaper in London called *Freiheit*; he was, with the Churchills, in league with the seditious radical Henry Hyde Champion, who for years fomented strikes and riots in English industrial towns, until in 1894, much to everyone's relief, he fled to Australia one step ahead of the police, and stayed there for good.

Yet another Fourth Party spy in the enemy camp was Cyril Flower, later Lord Battersea, who was married to Constance Rothschild, Natty Rothschild's niece. Gladstone unwisely trusted this treacherous butterfly, who leaked vital information to the Churchills.

On 3 November 1882, at Jennie's insistence, Winston went to school for the first time: to the Reverend HW Sneyd-Kinnersley's St George's, at Ascot; this was convenient, because it was close to Jennie's favourite racecourse. A great deal of fuss has been made about Winston's ill-treatment there; but bullying by other boys and frequent spankings by masters were absolutely standard in Victorian times, and Winston was an arrogant and troublesome child. The Victorian parental attitude was that life was an obstacle course, brutal and endlessly challenging, even for the rich and privileged, and that a boy should learn early to be a man. This meant taking his punishment for his misdeeds without complaining, defeating all comers with kicks and fists, studying diligently day and night, and playing hard at cricket, rugby and soccer, training in rain or snow-swept play yards without complaint. Jennie supported this policy; she must have remembered Lucy Green's rigorous training; though resenting it at the time, she had learned its value later on. That early education had put steel in her soul and she wanted her son to be made of steel as well.

To Jennie's delight, Randolph grew more famous every day. Members of the House of Commons no longer took their dinner hour to vacate the chamber at question time;

they gobbled their food in the Members' Room and rushed back to see him display his arrogance and sword-thrust humours. He was the most exciting young presence in parliamentary debates in decades, and Jennie was there to cheer him in the ladies' gallery day after day.

Cartoonists in the press portrayed him variously as Puck, a court jester in cap and bells, a sulky-eyed pug dog and a mongrel pup let loose at the Derby with a kettle attached to its tail. The traditional Conservatives in the House, afflicted with boredom, laziness and ineptitude, were thrilled by his onslaughts even though they suffered from them; as for the Liberals, even they had to admire his invective. He called Gladstone a 'purblind and sanctimonious Pharisee' and he referred to the aged Birmingham radical John Bright as a 'senile and infatuated hypocrite'; like an alchemist, he translated the basest cajolery into rhetorical gold.

He talked of the colonial British government in Egypt, India and Africa as 'wading in blood', adding that 'from massacre to massacre they march; their course is ineffaceably stamped upon the history of the world by an overflowing stream of blood'. He talked of the Liberals as a gang of political desperadoes, a legion of foul fiends, and a mob of ill-mannered sinister machinists; they were 'poltroons and traitors, transparent humbugs'. It was as if a series of lightning bolts had struck the sombre chamber of the House of Commons; youth had at last been heard in this all-too-hallowed hall, and Jennie was delighted by his success.

Neither she nor Randolph was in good health in late 1882; before and after the trip to New York, Randolph had suffered from an illness that involved coldness and numbness of the extremities, and attacks of weakness and fainting after hot applications or baths; this has been diagnosed by the physician and Churchill medical historian Dr John H Mather, as Raynaud's disease (today, Raynaud's Syndrome), a sometimes recurrent illness that normally afflicts young women in their teens.

Jennie was vigorously healthy until the winter, when the poisonous air of London's West End, carrying with it the usual amount of pestilence, finally struck her down. Meanwhile, Randolph, seeking relief from his own condition, had gone to Algeria; typically for Englishmen of his class and time, he was quite prepared to miss Christmas with his family, enjoying the dry climate and the balmy pleasures of the Arabian nights.

On 17 December, Jennie first suffered a feverish condition that was later diagnosed as typhoid but in fact, from contemporary evidence obtained by Dr John H Mather, was the less serious condition of paratyphoid, an illness that was little understood at the time but also involved high fever and possible risk to life.

She was exhausted; never one for half measures, she had flung herself into decorating and furnishing 2 Connaught Place, dredging up some items from deep storage, buying others she could ill afford from antique stores and replacing expensive wallpaper and panelling ruined by sulphur fogs. At the same time she was trying to get her father to renew their dowry income, commuting to nights with Count Kinsky while keeping her husband guessing, making visits to Paris to fend off or encourage such ardent suitors as the diplomat and author the Comte de Castellane, or taking a train to country estates as a freeloader when the Prince of Wales might at any moment arrive. Then there was the preparation of Randolph's speeches with him for the debates in the House of Commons, and the reading of every newspaper, ironed by servants, to keep up with the latest political developments. On top of all that, on the family front she was giving small dinner parties to friends, her numerous sisters-in-law and cousins; settling her younger sister Leonie's random romances; and dealing with correspondence from Clarita, who had plunged into the life of a pioneer of the American wilderness, and whose husband, the dreaded Moreton Frewen, was suicidally involved in speculations.

Her affair with Kinsky had been especially difficult to sustain. Carrying on illicit sexual relations in the mid-nineteenth century would challenge anyone: servants had to be virtually locked up in attic or cellar to stop their keyhole-peeping and prying; husbands and wives had to be firmly located at outside businesses or entertainments or with lovers of their own; and then, once the bedroom battlefield was open, there was the challenge of removing endless overskirts, bodices, stays, corsets and bloomers, with nothing left so crumpled that it would set tongues wagging in pantry and kitchen. The gentleman would have to rid himself of coat, cravat, starched shirt, studs, numerous buttons and long and encumbering underwear; in winter, a fire would have to be lit and brightly crackling, so the amorous combatants would not be chilled. At last, after what amounted to a military dressage in reverse, the naked couple could happily conjoin. But not before a primitive condom in the form of an animal-gut device had been stretched over the erect male member, and milady had inserted an object that in some cases is reported as being a golden orb, in others the merest sponge.

Laid up at Connaught Place, with Winston kept ignorant of her condition at Blenheim in the keeping of the mollycoddle Everest, Jennie was taken care of by Leonie and Clarissa, who reluctantly arrived from Paris. From her sick bed, in pencilled scrawl, she wrote to Randolph in familiar terms about the drawing-room redecorations, for example; all of her letters were written in breathless telegraphese, with dashes replacing the punctuation she had presumably learned at Miss Green's and in Paris. A visit from a now-friendly Duchess of Marlborough brought dubious consolation, and when the Queen's physician Sir William Gull came to see her, she knew she was, after years, at last back in royal favour. He would never have dared attend her had the Prince of Wales disapproved.

Gull, who would later be falsely accused of complicity or worse in the Jack the Ripper case, had famously saved the Prince of Wales from typhoid in 1871, urged on by a frantic Queen Victoria, who had lost her husband Prince Albert to the foul contagion from the various royal drains; to Jennie he applied the same repulsive cure of brandy, milk and jelly that had saved Wales's life.

Her invalid's letters to Randolph are touching, remarkably well written and energetic in view of her condition. Writing to Algeria which, despite rebel activity against the French, appears to have had a postal service superior to London's today, she kept him abreast of every symptom and improvement; she told him not to worry, a useless instruction in the circumstances. When a letter was delayed, she telegraphed, and he telegraphed back. She sat up, poring characteristically over maps of Algeria and books of geography, determined to keep track of him as he moved from one obscure village to another. At last, he reached the South of France, where he was in an agony of stress; but his Fourth Party colleague Sir Henry Drummond Wolff brought him encouraging news of Jennie's condition from London. He met his other colleague Sir John Gorst in Nice and, by mail, he fretted to Jennie about poor little Winston himself not being well; was this the unloving father portrayed in numerous books?

On 3 January Jennie wrote to him, saying she felt wretched that Randolph had been so worried, but that she was glad he was in Nice. She told him that her temperature fluctuated and she couldn't walk; that she often became depressed; that bills were pouring in from wine merchants and furniture suppliers; and that she was a bag of bones on the royal diet of milk, brandy and jelly.

All she could think of was joining Randolph in the South of France; she made no suggestion he should make the journey to London, when he was ill himself. Nothing illustrates her optimism, strength and determination better than these loving letters. She was amused by the fact that her mother-in-law the duchess had engineered the wedding engagement of Randolph's 27-year-old sister Georgiana to the 21-year-old 4th Earl Howe. ('They call your mother the Baby Snatcher,' she wrote to her husband.)

Randolph scribbled of his relief at her improvement, and correctly suspected the Connaught Place drains had done her in. He sent Sir John Gorst to see her with the message that he would meet her in Marseilles and they would enjoy the Riviera together. He also sent her a sterling silver oyster knife; Jennie loved oysters.

On 14 January she was able to take a hansom cab ride with her sister Leonie. Meanwhile Randolph, at the Villa Carmen in Monte Carlo, was again ill in heavy rainstorms. There was talk of his having syphilis, but he had no symptom of the disease and no indication of even a minor venereal ailment. His mind was unclouded, as sharp and belligerent as ever; his health, apart from recurring spells of Raynaud's disease, adequate; his body showed no loss of weight and there were no telltale rashes on his skin. His letters were not only coherent but brilliant, and his behaviour erratic but not irrational; eccentric but not demented. His sons were healthy, bouncing boys; Jennie was not infected. In short, the syphilis theory is nonsense and no indication of it would be seen in later years when another, and more terrible, illness would take hold.

As it turned out, Jennie, upon her recovery, did not go to the South of France, and Randolph returned in good spirits. It is likely that the fact she had suffered a life-threatening illness caused some softening of the Prince of Wales's heart. On 15 March 1883, the political figure Sir Henry James persuaded the prince to attend a dinner party at his house at which the Churchills were also guests. *Vanity Fair* magazine almost ruined everything by printing that 'although Lord R. feels much satisfaction at being again on friendly terms with the Heir-Apparent, he does not propose to become intimate with all the Prince's friends' but Francis Knollys, the prince's secretary, wrote to Sir Henry telling him to reassure Randolph that the prince did not hold him responsible for such careless and irresponsible reporting, whereupon the Churchills' old friend and neighbour, Lady Dorothy Nevill, also gave a party for them and the prince.

On 30 March Jennie was at Aintree, near Liverpool, to see Carl Kinsky ride his magnificent mare Zoedone in the Grand National, which she never failed to attend. It had been pouring with rain for five days and the course had turned to liquid mud, threatening the horses' hooves and making riding difficult.

In his dashing white-and-red colours with a bright-red sash from shoulder to waist, Kinsky made a striking impression; and Zoedone, superbly trained by Kinsky's friend Roland Reynolds at Parbuce in what is now the Czech Republic and run in various tests on English soil, was more than equal to the contest.

There was no heavy betting on the mare, but Kinsky rode her splendidly over the newly heightened fences and the notorious Becher's Brook to a startling victory of ten lengths that had his supporters in ecstasy.

Jennie returned to London in time to join Randolph in an attack on Sir Stafford Northcote, whom they continued to despise, as leader of the House of Commons. They called him the Goat; when in a fake gesture of conciliation they invited him to a dinner party they set a Dresden china goat on his table; recognising their term for him, he left at once. His physical weakness – he suffered from a heart complaint – only increased their contempt for him. And now, to the Churchills' unreasoning prejudice and fury, their old enemy Northcote would be in charge of unveiling a statue of the late Lord Beaconsfield in Parliament Square.

Randolph wrote two angry letters to *The Times*, the first anonymously, the second signed, attacking the choice of Northcote. In that second note he lost his head completely, attacking the Tory party head on. When he walked into the Commons on 2 April, he was greeted with a chilly silence from both sides, while Northcote was cheered to the echo. Randolph laughed off the humiliation but he was horrified when his fellow Fourth Party colleagues, Gorst and Wolff, signed a document offering support to Northcote as leader.

In May, Randolph published an article in the *Fortnightly Review* fiercely attacking Northcote yet again. The article at least had the benefit of swaying Wolff, who turned up with congratulations at the Churchills' the night after it appeared, only to enter a small domestic quarrel. Jennie ran in during the discussion saying how excited she was to have found two painted panels, covered in London grime, in an antique shop; cleaned up, they would be a bargain at three hundred pounds. Pressed as always for money, Randolph dismissed the idea out of hand, refused to listen and told her to leave the room. She was furious. Later, the panels sold for more than twenty times the amount she would have paid for them – a fact she never forgot.

In honour of Lord Beaconsfield's memory, and to celebrate the statue's unveiling, all members of the Conservative party wore, for a whole week, the late prime minister's favourite flower, a primrose, in their buttonholes. Sir Henry Drummond Wolff suggested that he and Randolph, with Jennie and the Duchess of Marlborough as leaders, start up a Primrose League, a Conservative society of men and women who would wear the flower as an emblem, and carry out a less-malicious anti-Liberal policy in a manner that would quell the hatred so many felt for Randolph and his more irrational criticisms. Randolph agreed, Jennie and the duchess were delighted, and the Primrose League soon became famous.

Jennie was in Dublin in May when her fascination with murder and murderers, expressed in Paris when she became obsessed with the Praslin case, resurfaced. She ran into one of the assistant wardens of Kilmainham Jail, who offered to have her come there and meet the Phoenix Park assassins, killers of Burke and Cavendish.

The killers were members of the terrorist group known as the Invincibles, and their target had only been the under-secretary Thomas Henry Burke, whom they correctly saw as a betrayer of the Irish. Lord Cavendish had not been an intended victim, but his presence as a witness made his brutal knifing necessary. The killers included Joseph Brady, a 25-year-old labourer, Tim Kelly, also a labourer, Patrick Delaney, and Thomas Caffrey. They had been informed on by James Carey, an Invincible who obtained a pardon by giving queen's evidence.

The ghastly voyeuristic visit involved lining up the killers in their prison garb in a room where Superintendent John

Mallon of the Dublin police questioned them meaninglessly so Jennie could look them over. Mallon lied that she was a member of his own family. When nineteen-year-old Tim Kelly turned to leave, he pleaded with Jennie to give help to his wife if he should be hanged. Shaken, she said she would, but there is no evidence that she did.

She was shown the maggoty meat pushed through narrow grilles for the prisoners to eat; she was shown James Carey, the informer, held for his own safety in a comfortable room; he glared at her in anger like a bear in a zoo. As she continued the tour, a man came up and told Mallon that the Inspector General of Prisons was on his way through the gate and if Jennie were seen, in defiance of prison regulations, and without an authorisation signed by the viceroy, Mallon would be punished.

She was rushed into an empty cell while the Inspector General walked past, and she languished there for twenty minutes in total darkness, rats scurrying about. Luckily the inspector didn't look through the bars, or he would have seen a famous lady, dressed in the height of fashion, sitting inside. At last the footsteps died away and she could make her escape; she left exhausted and depressed. The experience, begun as a heartless jaunt, left a deep impression on her; seventeen years later it would influence her in having Winston Churchill, as home secretary, instigate prison reform.

Jennie celebrated the fourth of July, Independence Day, at Blenheim with several of her American circle, including Fanny Ronalds, Lily Marlborough, Consuelo Manchester and Leonie. Randolph was in London, staying with his father; they took dinner together.

Next morning, the duke's valet came to wake him up, prepare his toilet and dress him, only to find him dead on the bedroom floor. Jennie rushed to London, where Randolph was inconsolable; the duchess also was devastated with grief. On 10 July a special train was commandeered to take family and friends from London to the funeral; a hundred mourners accompanied the heavy oak coffin on its short, sad journey to Blenheim Palace.

A silent crowd in black, with black flags, greeted the many members of the nobility; 3,000 filed past the catafalque in the Palace hall; the religious service at Woodstock parish church was accompanied by a full choir singing 'I Heard the Voice of Jesus Say' and 'Thy Will be Done'.

Perhaps the most astonishing presence at the funeral breakfast was the inescapable Albertha, wife of Blandford (who had abandoned Edith Aylesford after the birth of their illegitimate son in Paris). Although Albertha's marriage was officially dissolved in 1880, she could hardly resist becoming the duchess and staying on to queen it over the palace and vast estates. The Dowager Duchess of Marlborough was furious, and not least when the most vulgar floral wreath placed on the coffin was marked 'From Goosie', Albertha's nickname.

Jennie and Randolph had to face the prospect of the dissolute drug addict Blandford inheriting the dukedom. It soon turned out that the Marlboroughs were deeper in debt than ever; the sale of the famous Sunderland Library with its priceless first editions, which Jennie never ceased to regret, followed by complete sets of Meissen, Spode and Minton china at Christie's, had failed to meet their obligations. Even the family jewels in their famous red plush velvet boxes had gone, along with an almost priceless Marie Antoinette table. The new Duke was soon to sell a great deal more and turn the famous Titian Gallery into a fruit and orchard hothouse. He would remove the maids from their upstairs rookery and replace their rooms with a chemistry, metal and chemicals laboratory where he conducted mysterious experiments. The staff and guests would get used to being awakened by explosions and puffs of smoke from the windows in the dead of night.

Soon after the funeral, the Churchills made a shocking discovery at Connaught Place. Supervising electricians who were repairing the basement dynamo and pulling up the cellar floor found large piles of bones, and the stench made the senses reel. Jennie made enquiries and found that the house had been built over Potters' Field, where the hanged criminals of Tyburn Tree had been flung. She had the bones removed, whereupon disturbances in the night, which she sensibly put down to the drains, were interpreted by her staff as the angry spirits of the dead.

On 12 August 1883, Randolph wrote to his brother the duke, begging him not to sell any more heirlooms; but already the Christie's cataloguers were listing more paintings at Blenheim. Blandford had been unable to raise money, as his father had left him nothing; and when the story leaked that his father had uncertain health and might predecease his mother, he was refused bankers' loans that might have been guaranteed against her death. (And the same went for Randolph.)

The Churchills took off on holiday to Europe in August. It was typical of their disregard of money that they would embark on this expensive trip when they were both desperate for ready cash.

At the famous watering place Bad Gastein in the German Alps, they met Chancellor Otto von Bismarck, who was taking the cure. It is possible that the meeting was not accidental, as it has previously been described; it was essential that the British be informed of Bismarck's intentions. Bismarck had decided to expand the Empire and the Germans were threatening British interests in Southwest Africa. It is likely that Count Kinsky engineered the encounter, and it can scarcely be a coincidence that Emperor Wilhelm II of Germany was also present.

The regimen with two German leaders in town was fascinating: Wilhelm, who had visited Bad Gastein with only two exceptions every year since 1863, literally took over the town with his retinue of servants and cabinet members. Both he and Bismarck rose at precisely seven-thirty each morning, bathed, and were dressed by their valets; they walked from eight to ten then enjoyed an ample lunch, the Kaiser always eating boiled crab. Then from two-thirty to three-thirty the cabinet, both military and civil, joined their leaders in conference. One royal habit was insufferable to the Churchills: instead of the custom of afternoon tea, dinner (only three hours after lunch) was served at 4 p.m. Both careful eaters, Jennie and Randolph had to struggle through soup, fish, boiled beef, two cuts of roast lamb, heavy pudding and fruit all washed down with Rhenish wines at what should have been teatime. Bloated and sleepy, Jennie and the other ladies repaired to the drawing room while the men enjoyed brandy and cigars; at least this was as it would be in England. Late at night, Bismarck and the Kaiser offered to those still standing poached eggs, potted meat, strawberries, ices and, as a nightcap, the very best champagne.

Soon after the Churchills' return to England in late August, the Duke of Marlborough's will was read aloud to family and friends at Blenheim. The 5th Earl of Roden was co-executor with the Duke of Roxburghe. The estate was valued at £146,000 pounds (about seven million pounds today); the duke left £2,000 (about £100,000) to the duchess, along with the jewellery, plate, horses, carriages, wines, furniture and pictures at their house in Grosvenor Square, and whatever she should select of the furnishings and paintings at Blenheim; he did not leave his homes to her – or to anyone – but she would automatically inherit them. Her 'unmarried daughters' (all were married now) would divide £10,000 between them; the rest of the cash they would receive when the duchess died. All land in other counties was to be sold, and the proceeds held in trust for the duchess. Needless to say, given the folly of such a testament, with no mention of sons, married daughters or sisters, the will was in the courts for years; if Lady Marlborough had not inherited money of her own, from the Londonderries, she would have been seriously out of pocket.

In the twenty-first century, when youth is king and a child can hold the floor at family debates, the sight of a 34-year-old firebrand with a 29-year-old wife appearing on public platforms to unseat a party leader would not attract notice; but in 1883 it was an astonishment. On trains in all weathers, crammed with their supporters in first-class carriages filled with cigar smoke and animated conversation, the Churchills were on the rampage. Randolph was determined to head up the National Union of Conservative Associations as one bold step towards becoming party leader and, most improbably, prime minister.

This somewhat egregious organisation, whose name exceeded its actual importance, acted as a reorganising body, rendering the party machinery more popular and efficient. In order to seize control of it, Randolph had to make peace with the enemy. Northcote, as leader of the Commons, had to be coddled; too much of a gentleman to be the normal indecent politician, he forgave the Churchills the goat figurine placed before him when he dined with them, the insults heaped on him for years, and joined them, bent always on the interests of his defeated and disorganised party. In December 1883, Randolph, with Jennie in London, delivered a triple blow: three speeches in the provinces. In the first of these, he attacked Gladstone's onslaught on Egypt and praised the exiled Arabi, but he dared not mention Gladstone's investments in that country, or those of his mother's London neighbour, the royal financier Sir Ernest Cassel. In a second speech, he attacked the new proposed Reform Bill, on which so many of his party had laboured hard and long. And in a third he tried to slaughter Gladstone by comparing him with household products like Colman's Mustard and Horniman's Pure Tea. He accused him of chartering a transatlantic liner for his personal use; of cutting down trees as a destructive hobby ('The forest laments, so that Mr Gladstone may perspire') and he described the prime minister receiving a working-class delegation at his country estate of Hawarden, surrounded by the rotting trunks of once noble trees.

The attack was the ultimate in cynicism; Randolph wouldn't have wept if he had seen a birch grove burn before his eyes. But seditious ridicule worked wonders on his fellow Conservatives; even though he came up with no concrete plan for tariffs to protect the Midland industries he so sternly described as ruined, he made audiences laugh, and he was immensely popular as a scourge. He was widely supported when he announced he would run for Birmingham against the mangy old tiger John Bright at the next election.

Jennie could not always be with him on the campaign trail. Given her fondness for Rothschilds and Cassel, both Jews, she must have disapproved of the anti-Semitic remarks he uttered in attacking them when he pursued the issue of Egyptian exploitation.

She had much to preoccupy her, though. Winston's education, virtually ignored as well as deplored by Randolph in his headlong pursuit of power, was not yielding results: the reports from St George's School, prepared between vigorous applications of the cane, were discouraging. She was shocked to find that his spelling was bad, his composition feeble, his diligence nonexistent; he was naughty, weak in geography, elementary in drawing, and (a comic touch) 'rather greedy at meals'.

Only in January 1884 were the reports somewhat milder; but by April his conduct was described as 'exceedingly bad; he is not to be trusted to do anything'; he was 'a constant trouble to everybody, and is always in some scrape or other'. He was thus firmly in line with his father, and his grandfather Leonard Jerome. And the canings went on and on.

In addition to pushing her son into better behaviour and shows of ambition, Jennie had to deal with a tricky personal situation. Still sleeping with Kinsky whenever she could, she found him in almost daily meetings with his horse-owning and foxhunting partner, the dashing Captain 'Bay' Middleton, who in turn, in what amounted to a *ménage à quatre*, was enjoying the favours of the beautiful Blanche Hozier, daughter of the Earl of Airlie.

On 28 September 1878, Blanche had married the possibly impotent sadist Colonel Henry Hozier, who detested the idea of children, and never had her to his bed. She needed an immediate substitute, and it is probable that Jennie found it for her. Middleton eminently filled the bill: what could be a more enjoyable bantam cock than a member of the 12th Lancers (Jennie's future lover John Delacour was a member of the 11th)? With his tight-fitting uniform showing off every aspect of an imposing figure, his thick black hair, melodramatically smouldering eyes and unique way with a horse, Bay was the finest equestrian in England.

Jennie and Blanche, never fond of prankishness, could even put up with the Kinsky–Middleton japes: these over-grown schoolboys would get on all fours at parties and growl at each other in imitation bear fights; they would pelt each other with lemons, at one house breaking a cabinet and smashing a set of Meissen china; they wrecked the London Café Royal in a free-for-all with sticks; and they attacked a billiards champion by cutting off his coat tails.

In July 1884, however, Blanche became pregnant by Middleton; this could have ruined her had not her husband, whose older daughter also resulted from an outside affair, stepped in and declared the child his own. Propriety, and a desire to appear virile, worked wonders. The Middleton child later became Jennie's daughter-in-law, Clementine, wife of Winston Churchill.

Jennie made no secret of her affair with Kinsky, in spite of her husband's political aspirations and the need for fake respectability; the press oddly left unmentioned her stay with the count in Paris on 2 June, where they were joined by the Prince of Wales, James Gordon Bennett and Sir Henry James at a party at the Café Anglais; or her bold arrival with Kinsky at the House of Lords on 18 June to hear Blandford as Duke of Marlborough appear in a debate at the House of Lords.

Jennie's younger sister Leonie had meanwhile fallen in love with an unimpressive painter and heir to 50,000 Irish acres in Counties Monaghan and Donegal named John Leslie, the son of a baronet whose ill-treatment of the peasantry was depressingly predictable. Unlike Moreton

Frewen, who was ineptly running a property in far-away Wyoming, the Leslies had money; their castle, romantically situated on a lake, was filled with art treasures.

To add to John Leslie's romantic image there was the belief that he was descended from King George IV and his mistress Mrs Fitzherbert; and to add to Leonie's there was the unfounded rumour she was the mistress of the Queen's son, the Duke of Connaught.

Jennie was in New York briefly for Leonie's wedding at Grace Church, New York, on 2 October 1884; she took the next ship back to England to be with Randolph on his first campaign to win the Birmingham parliamentary seat from John Bright.

Needing a supporter and helpmate, they conjured a genie from a bottle: the huge and daunting Colonel Fred Burnaby, a friend of Bay Middleton and Carl Kinsky. Six-foot-four and 230 pounds of muscle, he had a 44-inch chest unexpanded, a fact he never ceased to mention as he, quite against the etiquette of his time, would strip off his shirt and vest and display his swelling pectorals to anyone who cared to watch – and many who did not.

His feats were legendary: he was famous for having eaten an entire roast goose at one sitting; for hurling a fellow passenger out of a train carriage door when he disliked his conversation; of carrying a pony (some pretended it was two) up flights of steps at Windsor Castle to bring it whinnying to the Queen; and of holding a 170-pound barbell at arm's length with one hand and bending pokers in half. He had crossed the Channel by hot-air balloon, ridden 6,000 miles through the Middle East on a donkey's back, fought with rebels in Spain and with Cossacks on the Russian Steppes, been with Gordon in the Sudan and had enjoyed stunning success as a travel writer.

On 13 October 1884, Jennie arrived with Randolph and Colonel Burnaby at Birmingham; they were joined by Sir Stafford Northcote, as weakly compliant as ever.

The Liberal Joseph Chamberlain was behind what happened next. He issued some 100,000 forged tickets to the

Conservative rally at Aston Hall and Park to any Liberal youth who would protest and riot, and free railway tickets to rowdies from out of town; every man ready to come was issued a Gladstone badge. When the mob, armed with sticks and cudgels, poured in off omnibuses and trains, Randolph ordered the park gates closed and locked; but the rioters, screaming with anger, were not to be stopped. They had been issued with ladders for such a contingency and they flung them against the stone walls, clambered up and dropped down the other side, brandishing their weapons.

They burst into a tool shed, seized planks and charged the police squad; many broke through and hurled rotten vegetables, chairs and fruit at the Churchills, Burnaby and Northcote. Two men lifted Jennie bodily, and began pulling off her dress; another raised Randolph in his arms. Burnaby levelled them with mighty blows of his fist; temporarily awestruck, the crowd shrank back as the colonel, laughing at their discomfiture, leaned up against a lamppost and coolly lit a cigar.

But after a few moments the crowd screamed again, and Jennie and her companions fled into Aston Hall and the police locked the doors. It was useless; the mob broke them down. Randolph rushed Jennie into a back room, then stood with Burnaby and spoke to the ringleaders, who drowned him out with a shouted 'Rule Britannia'.

Randolph urged them to stop this nonsense, and join him in 'God Save the Queen', but they refused, and he and Burnaby were forced to run for their lives. Jennie joined them in headlong flight through the back garden to a skating rink where another mob greeted them; it was only when more police arrived that they were able to reach their hotel, their clothes torn, Jennie and other female supporters in tears of anger and fright. Chamberlain achieved his purpose: Randolph would lose the election next year. In December, he left for India.

Shortly after Randolph's departure, on 3 December, the London *Times*' editor asked Jennie if she was furious at his paper's recent article attacking her husband. Her reply was typical: 'Not a bit. I have ten volumes of press cuttings about Randolph, all abusive. These will only be added to them.'

Meanwhile, Winston had left St George's and gone to the Miss Thomsons' School at Brunswick Road, Brighton, where he was much happier. Jennie's choice of a school run by siblings reflects her continuing memory of Miss Green's on Washington Square; Lucy Green had been greatly assisted by her sister Mary. But the Miss Thomsons' School was a far less strict establishment.

Randolph wrote to Jennie consistently on his trip: the Suez Canal, much of it owned by Gladstone through the Rothschilds, he dismissed as a 'dirty ditch'; describing the burning of the dead at Benares, he mentioned their expectations of heaven, no matter how rascally they were. Gladstone, he added, should be similarly burned; it would be his last chance for Paradise. In India, he met, with pleasure, the grand commander Sir Frederick Roberts and formed a lifelong friendship with Lord Dufferin, the incoming viceroy, while deploring the departing one, Lord Ripon. He was horrified by the poverty of 250 million people and dreamed futilely of ameliorating it. He was shocked by the ignorance and complacency of officialdom and disturbed by the potential threat of insurrection from the Moslem faction; the rift between the administration and the needs of a great and suffering people troubled him greatly.

The highlight of his trip was the military display arranged for him by Roberts in Delhi on 18 January 1885. As he watched on a specially erected platform with Roberts and Dufferin, 35,000 troops in full dress uniform marched and formed squares in front of the city's walls. A 31-gun salute startled ravens and vultures from the battlements, followed by a great burst of thunder and flashes of lightning. For four hours, drenched to the skin, the troops continued their parade. It was a sight Randolph would never forget; he later said that without India, England had no meaning. And, to cap everything, he brought Jennie home a Bengal tiger skin.

Two tragedies occurred during Randolph's absence: the Earl of Aylesford died of drink at Big Spring, Texas and, far more importantly to the Churchills, their beloved Fred Burnaby, hero of Birmingham, perished in the Sudan.

Hungry as always for adventure, he had barely recovered from the Aston Park riot when he enlisted with Sir Garnet Wolseley's military force to relieve General Gordon, who was under siege from the Mahdi in Khartoum. Although he knew Burnaby was lacking in tactical military knowledge, and was chiefly recognised as a soldier of fortune, Wolseley had rashly made him second-in-command of the relief force when the Mahdi confronted it at the oasis of Abu Klea. Burnaby was in command of a moving square of foot soldiers, cavalrymen and a contingency of bluejacket seamen.

The purpose of a square was to remain intact; Hussars and cavalrymen provided a protective shield, and no man must break the square as it would leave a possible entrance for the enemy. With shocking irresponsibility towards his men's safety, and hellbent on glory, Burnaby broke the square and rode headlong against the dervishes; within minutes, he was hacked to death. The Mahdi's men cut deep into the square and left almost nobody alive; Burnaby might as well have murdered the force for all his bravado did for it. A military cover-up resulted, in which he was portrayed as a hero; the Churchills probably never learned the shocking truth.

Jennie could not resist a handsome face and figure, and during Randolph's absence, or soon after he returned, she again met a man she had known before. John Delacour had been one of her two protectors against the Prince of Wales's wrath in the Aylesford–Blandford fracas, and she had been at parties with him, as the guest of, among others, their mutual friends Sir Arthur Sullivan and Fanny Ronalds.

Lean, willowy and slight, five-foot-nine Delacour was, like her other lovers, not massively built or overpowering; he was, like Kinsky, a fine horseman, though not in that class; he was independently wealthy, and kept a fine household at Cadogan Place. He had immense charm and unswerving loyalty to his friends and had the military bearing that came from regimental service and attracted Jennie always; she deplored round shoulders and slumping posture in a man.

Born in June 1841, Delacour was the illegitimate son of a former ambassador to Russia, Ulick John de Burgh, 14th Earl and 1st Marquess of Clanricarde, Baron Summerville of Kent, whose wife Harriet was the daughter and heiress of Earl Canning, of the illustrious political family.

Clanricarde's mistress (and John Delacour's mother) was the Galway temptress Josephine Kelly Handcock, known in that county for her promiscuity and dubbed, as if she were some wanton chambermaid, Pretty Kitty Kelly. Her husband, William Henry Handcock, owned several castles as well as the magnificent Carrantryla House at Dunmore, used as a summer residence by several viceroys of Ireland, including Jennie's father-in-law. Its notorious Black Chapel, with painted dragons and snakes and an evil monk looming over the altar, was thought to be used for worshipping the Devil.

The Handcocks had four daughters; Clanricarde had two boys and four daughters. In September 1840, Josephine Handcock became pregnant by Clanricarde who, faced with social ruin, made arrangements to hand over the child to his mother, a member of the prominent Galway family, the Burkes. His mother's brother, Sir Thomas Burke, raised the boy well; his name changed from John de Burgh, he was given the impression he was the adopted orphan of an Irish Huguenot family. The Delacours were well known as merchants and storekeepers in Dublin.

When Delacour was eleven, his natural mother died and John became heir to her estates. Three of her four daughters had passed away before she did, giving rise to tales of her having poisoned them to increase her illegitimate son's inheritance; actually, like the Brontë sisters, they died of tuberculosis. The dead woman's brother, John Stratford Handcock, sued her estate, charging that as a bastard, Delacour could have no legitimate claim; he wanted Moydrim Castle, Quaterstone House and Carrantryla, with 10,000 acres of land, for himself.

A furious and protracted litigation followed. Clanricarde eventually made a deal with John Handcock, pulling strings to legislate the matter through the House of Lords. Handcock would be allowed to keep the three residences in return for paying the boy £20,000 a year (worth about a million today) until he came of age. Thereafter, John would receive the full payment of the principal, which was a staggering £400,000 (£20 million).

Meanwhile, Sir Thomas Burke sent him to be educated in England, under the care of the Reverend George Link in Cheshire and at Melton Mowbray, the Churchills' favourite foxhunting centre. Gambling with cards and backing wrong horses forced Delacour to sell off his inheritance for a mere £4,500 before he was 21. But he would soon be rich through lucky streaks again. A dashing nineteen-year-old in 1860, Delacour joined the crack 11th Hussars; he was given his commission through the offices of Sir Thomas Burke, who had served in the 4th Hussars. Years later, the 4th would be Winston Churchill's regiment. Delacour was appointed as the officer who carried the colours into battle. The 11th were the famous Cherry Pickers or Cherubims, noted for their scarlet facings on blue uniforms and as Lord Cardigan's Bloodhounds in the Crimean War; many had died in the Charge of the Light Brigade. The Queen adored them because they accompanied her husband, Prince Albert, to London when he arrived from the Continent for their marriage. She dubbed them the Queen's Own Regiment.

After service in Ireland and India, Delacour sold his commission and in 1876 became a prominent social figure in London, aided by the Burke family, and doing his best to live down Lord Clanricarde's foul reputation. Lord Clanricarde was forbidden entry to the Privy Council; he was notoriously a vicious absentee Irish landlord, his business and private affairs a public scandal.

In 1885, the year that Jennie met Delacour again and fell in love with him after a two-year interval, he was co-founder with Blandford and Randolph of the Orleans Club, a spin-off of the Fourth Party with headquarters at 64 Kings Road, Brighton; this was convenient for the affair because not only would Jennie expect to attend meetings, but the location was close to Winston's school.

Other members were the homosexual millionaire Alfred de Rothschild, Jennie's brother-in-law John Leslie, the royal courtier Christopher Sykes, the socialite Tom Trafford, who had been with Randolph in India, and the popular author, George Augustus Sala.

At the same time as she was having an affair with Delacour, Jennie discovered Randolph was involved with the beautiful and brilliant society hostess and patroness of the arts Gladys de Grey, widow of the Earl of Lonsdale, who had died in 1882. Gladys had strongly supported opera and the careers of Gilbert and Sullivan as a friend of Fanny Ronalds; now she was about to remarry, and did so just after Randolph's return from India, on 7 May 1885. Her new husband was the heir to the Marquessate of Ripon; he was said to have bagged more partridges and pheasants in the course of a day's shooting than any man in England.

It was typical of those times that wives who had only just married embarked on sexual flings with other men, and betrayed family relationships to satisfy their lust; not only was de Grey betraying her husband but also her father-in-law, Lord Ripon; Randolph never ceased attacking Ripon as former viceroy of India, comparing him unfavourably to his successor, Lord Dufferin.

Jealous as she was of de Grey, Jennie attended Randolph's triumphant speech to the Primrose League, discussing his Indian adventure, and joined him in celebrating the imminent downfall of the Gladstone government, which was under pressure on many fronts: the Irish coercion issue, the proposed application of military force to suppress threatened rebellion; the betrayal of General Gordon, assassinated at Khartoum; and the awkward handling of a crisis in Afghanistan in May that almost caused war with Russia. Randolph seized the moment. He embarked on a policy of befriending, not to say seducing, the very man he had attacked for years: Lord Salisbury, leader of the Conservatives and the reluctant probability as next prime minister.

Salisbury would come before long to resemble a white-bearded Father Christmas, but in spirit, he was a burrowing mole. When met by chance on a train, he would refuse to say a word; at home, he tended to eschew the society his wife enjoyed at Hatfield House and make his way to a Blandford-like secret laboratory, conducting mysterious experiments far into the night. He fancied himself a British Thomas Alva Edison, rigging up a complicated electric light and heating system and a primitive telephone device that would replace the use of speaking tubes to summon up his staff.

This recessive personage did not approve of Randolph's style of flashy opportunism and overcoloured rhetoric, directed, as he saw it, treacherously against his own party; but now in the interests of solidarity, and certain of Randolph's potential in bringing Gladstone down, he must somehow find common ground. Their letters of the time have more to do with expediency than friendship, filled with the hollow sycophancy of a necessary alliance. In twisting his own quill, Salisbury even concealed his distaste for Randolph's newly formed Ginger Group, a radical conservative mosquito swarm aimed at assailing him whenever possible; Salisbury applied the reliable salve of self-protective hypocrisy.

In one attack Salisbury approved, Randolph, from his continuing seat below the Commons gangway, compared Gladstone, still on the Treasury bench, to the 'Turkish Terror', Rashid Pasha. He was reluctantly delighted when, shelving the idea of Irish coercion as a plank in his own platform, Randolph, with Jennie, had Charles Stuart Parnell to lunch at Connaught Place, and in return for a promise of cancelling his anti-coercion campaign, he secured Parnell's gift of the Irish Party vote.

*   *   *

During their visits to the Duchess of Marlborough at 50 Grosvenor Square, the Churchills met her next-door neighbour, the aforementioned and brilliant Sir Ernest Cassel, who soon would become a friend.

Cassel was chief financial adviser to Queen Victoria and the Prince of Wales. He was almost the prince's double: bearded, jovial, heavy in the stomach, bulging-eyed, endlessly puffing at cigars. Born in Cologne in 1852, he had arrived in London in 1869 with just one suit of clothes and a second-hand fiddle. Like Leonard Jerome, he invested in railroads, but with far greater success; with Jacob Schiff, head of the Kuhn Loeb bank, he invested royal moneys in railways from New York to California, always avoiding such questionable enterprises as Union Pacific. He plunged deeply into diamonds and gold in South Africa, and Cuban and South American sugar.

He took a hand in Randolph's and Jennie's finances and in due course in their sons' education; one day, he would give employment to her younger boy, Jack, and to her second husband, George Cornwallis-West.

At the same time, Jennie and Randolph found support in Natty Rothschild, Randolph's school chum, to whose family so many of the Marlborough properties had been sold. Natty had every reason to dislike them: he had been among those financiers who had involved Gladstone in Egypt, and Randolph had opposed British penetration there; like Cassel, he had had to put up with Randolph attacking 'Jewish usurers' who exploited countries for pernicious gain. But Natty was nothing if not shrewd: he knew that Gladstone was doomed, and he clearly saw Randolph in line as Secretary of State for India, a post that would insure protection (if he were made an ally and given financial support) for Rothschild cotton, railroads and mining interests in the subcontinent.

Above all, despite his onslaughts on the old fogeys of his party, Randolph, Rothschild knew, was an Empire man and above all things Rothschild was, too. He dreaded the idea of war with Russia or with Germany, when he had interests with the Czar and the Kaiser, and Randolph was in agreement with him there. His wife Emma was very friendly with Jennie, who helped her with a London Free School for children project.

Although the Rothschilds had no serious investments in Ireland, Natty supported Randolph's position on paternalism versus Home Rule, which he feared would result in his friends' properties being confiscated. In collaboration with the Churchills he used a spy in the Liberal camp – Cyril Flower, Lord Battersea – to find out their internal corruptions and intrigues.

As always, Jennie that spring was deeply involved in Randolph's political career. With the change of government in June, 1885 and his preparations for the post of India Secretary pressing, she became surrogate candidate for Woodstock. Blandford and other Marlboroughs took over the town before she arrived, and paid the local hansom cab and omnibus companies to fly the pink-and-white Marlborough colours; shopkeepers were bribed to put Tory slogans in their windows; villagers were armed with primroses and pinks; women were given free pink dresses; and the Bear Hotel was festooned with pink flags tied to Union Jacks, hung from windows and chimneys.

Every morning for weeks, Jennie started the day early at the Bear, then with Randolph's sister Georgiana she took off in an elegant carriage, drawn by spanking pink-ribboned horses, to conquer with irresistible charm all fourteen voting parishes; it was the most astonishing electoral campaign carried out by a woman in England in living memory. Many said she would make a better statesman than her husband; on 2 July the *New York Times* published a glowing report from its correspondent, citing an elderly Woodstockian who said, 'This Yankee wife of his will make him Prime Minister 'fore I die.' The inevitable sniping occurred; the Liberal candidate Corrie Grant accused Jennie of using 'improper practices' to influence a local mill owner. Whether that was true or not, she won the seat for Randolph.

Confirmed in his new post as Secretary for India, while retaining his seat at Woodstock, Randolph, before he moved into his London offices, had to present his credentials to the Queen. In view of the fact that he had only recently been forgiven for blackmailing her daughter-in-law, this could have been an awkward occasion. But Randolph turned on all his legendary charm and Victoria was captivated. He resembled her dead youngest son, Leopold, and that touched her; she had him and Jennie to dinner, where the conversation was, according to a royal custom Jennie found annoying, conducted entirely in whispers.

Twelve days later, Randolph sent her his first report from the India Office in the traditional dispatch box. Victoria opened it only to be assailed by the stench of cigarettes. Pulling out the sheets of paper covered in Randolph's near-illegible scrawl, she was horrified to find a litter of black Turkish stubs underneath. But when a nervous assistant secretary explained to her that Lord Randolph liked to smoke when working, she laughed loudly and long.

She would have been even more pleased if she had known that Randolph was in league with her supporter Natty Rothschild, who had substantial interests in railroads in the subcontinent; between 1881 and 1887 Natty and his brothers issued £6.4 m in Indian railway shares. As the Rothschild historian Niall Ferguson wrote: 'Churchill lost no time in establishing the kind of previous relationship with Natty and his brothers which he had earlier accused Gladstone's government of having . . . in relation to Egypt.' He told the viceroy of India, Lord Dufferin, that when the latest Indian railway loan was brought out he would fight a 'great battle' to place it in Rothschild hands, not in the government's, since their 'financial knowledge is as great as the Bank of England's and their clientele is enormous'. And indeed, Randolph saw to it that the shares were so issued.

In keeping with Leonard Jerome's boosting of railroad investments by articles in the *New York Times*, Randolph pushed Natty Rothschild's cause in every press statement the India Office released. And in return, he and Jennie to the end of his life received Rothschild financial help. Edward Hamilton, secretary to Gladstone, wrote in his diary that jingoism was popular, so long as it brought profit, and another commentator said that Randolph and Natty ran the business of Empire together. Salisbury's wife told the German Herbert von Bismarck that Randolph handed Natty state secrets and that people did not give great financial houses political news for nothing.

Randolph and Jennie were fortunate that they had the advice of the precise, dry Adolphus W Moore, perhaps the most informed man in England on Indian affairs, as his personal secretary. Randolph's power was absolute: with Moore behind him, and the approval of the Queen (though she differed with him when he disapproved of the Duke of Connaught as Bombay commander-in-chief), he was a force unto himself; he had the guaranteed ear of Lord Dufferin; he was paid not by Commons vote but out of Treasury funds; and he was backed personally by Salisbury, who doubled as foreign secretary, thus ensuring no interference with Indian colonial policy.

Although Randolph said that attending the council which ruled on India Office expenditure was like an Eton schoolboy addressing a masters' meeting, he soon had the members eating out of his hand, and they began supplying moneys he used for his own and the Rothschilds' benefit. When Natty Rothschild supplied him with a brilliant survey of the Indian railways, designed to show how they needed to expand, with the Rothschild Bank issuing more bonds, he presented the propositions in his budget.

Greed and overwork inevitably took their toll. Jennie nursed Randolph at home in August when he was ill, and she had him taking calumel, a palliative for his frazzled nerves. Later, she took him to Scotland, with treatments of digitalis, used for heart trouble, given in small doses every day.

It must have been a difficult break from Kinsky, who was in London that year, commuting to Paris on secret intelligence assignments, and from John Delacour, also in town; she remained jealous of Gladys de Grey.

Back at the India Office in London in late September, Randolph, with the enthusiastic approval of Jennie, the Queen, Lord Salisbury and the Rothschilds, embarked on the most corrupt adventure of his career: the annexation of Upper Burma for its rubies and cotton, its silk and its teak, and its slave army of men, women and children. Jennie was with him all the way; she was aware of how popular his action would be in Birmingham, whose seat he still coveted. The textile industry in that city would benefit from cheap Burmese cotton and a stream of delegates from that city, no doubt promising votes, appeared at Connaught Place; they were eager to have him as their representative in the Commons.

An exultant Lord Dufferin was delighted by the idea of annexation; later, he would become Lord Dufferin and Ava, adding the name of a Burmese province to his title.

Upper Burma was rich: its rubies were a Rothschild target and its Irrawaddy River the artery of fertile lands. While its jungles and mountains were spectacularly beautiful, the people were oppressed by successive royal tyrants. In 1824–26, Britain, greedy for spoils, had taken over the southern part of the kingdom; when the defeated rulers had proved rebellious, a second invasion in 1852–53 had conquered them.

Upper Burma retained a form of spurious independence, with British and French interests fighting for trade supremacy; successive agents of both countries were despicable in their treatment of the populace. In 1885, the tinpot King Thibaw reigned in Mandalay, the northern capital; he had slaughtered opposing relatives and former friends when he assumed power in 1878. His wife was a pocket-sized Marie Antoinette, squandering the national treasure in Worth and Paquin fashion houses, her rubies sifted by armies of female slaves from the dust of mines, set in magnificent necklaces and pendants in Paris and London.

Desperate for cash to satisfy his wife's latest demands, Thibaw in January 1885 made a deal with the French to hand over the nation's resources in return for millions of francs. Furious at the news, Gladstone supported an across-the-board deal in Britain's interests, calling for an equally large loan, the condition being that Thibaw sell all his teak to the Bombay-Burma Trading Company. That would give Britain a virtual monopoly in the then much prized source of furniture for the middle class.

The Bombay-Burma Company failed to meet its end of the bargain, not paying bills, terrorising natives into cutting down forests without reward, and smuggling consignments by freighter down the Irrawaddy at dead of night. Thibaw filed suit against it, which gave Randolph an ideal excuse for conquest. Unless Thibaw broke off secret arrangements with the French and let the Bombay-Burma Company off the hook, he would send an invasion force and topple the King from his throne.

Thibaw dared not lose face with his people, so he refused to comply. At once Randolph ordered Sir Henry Prendergast, a bristling Empire man and autocratic military commander, to bring Thibaw to heel; on 27 October Randolph sent Dufferin a telegram stating that Burma would be 'a most remunerative investment', and the Queen enthusiastically agreed.

Meanwhile, yet again taking a leaf out of Leonard Jerome's book, and probably with Jennie's approval, Randolph had his friends of the press point out the horrors of Thibaw's regime: an ideal excuse for conquest.

On 11 November 1885, the ultimatum to Thibaw expired and the invasion began. It was a walkover; the Upper Burmese people cared little who ruled them since they had no vote, but a few die-hard troops did put up some resistance. They hung on for seventeen days until, on 28 November, Prendergast marched into Mandalay.

There followed a comic-opera scene: Prendergast kept his shoes on, giving deep offence, as he arrested Thibaw and his queen in the royal palace; instead of placing them in a palanquin or even into rickshaws, his men bundled them into a bullock cart; tremblingly raising their multicoloured umbrellas against the sun, they were thrust aboard a steamer for Rangoon, and lifelong exile in India. The door was open for the Rothschilds to obtain their rubies; not to show their hand, they waited four years before floating a hugely successful ruby bond issue.

Randolph celebrated with Jennie at several parties in London; on 1 January 1886, he informed the Queen officially that Burma was hers. She couldn't have been more pleased: her collection of rubies, going back to the helmet gem of the Black Prince (actually an imitation), could always be enhanced.

Jennie had her reward. It is clear that Queen Victoria and Lord Salisbury knew she had influenced her husband in the annexation of Burma and the Indian railway issues, because she was given, most unusually for the wife of a secretary of state, the Order of the Crown of India on 3 December 1885, in a private ceremony at Windsor Castle; Randolph received no honour. And this was before Upper Burma had been officially declared a British colony; some pockets of resistance had to be mopped up in mountains and jungles.

The Queen fixed the Order on Jennie's breast only to pierce her accidentally with the pin. Apologising, the monarch pinned it a second time, and smoothed down Jennie's dress. Jennie was so flustered she almost forgot to leave facing the Queen; backs must never be turned in the royal presence. She left behind both the box and scroll that went with the Order, so the Marchioness of Ely, who doubled as lady in waiting and spiritualist medium, specialising in séance imitations of Prince Albert and the dead favourite John Brown, ran after her to hand her the items. Later, she wrote to Jennie: 'The Queen told me she thought you handsome and that it all had gone off so well.' In view of what she had done to achieve it, that reward was not its recipient's finest hour.

CHAPTER SEVEN

On 6 January 1886, Lewis ('Loulou') Harcourt, the best-informed society gossip in London, wrote in his diary that Jennie would shortly be suing Randolph for divorce and naming Lady de Grey as co-respondent, and that Randolph would in turn sue Jennie, naming John Delacour. He wrote that his source was a journalist who, reading between the lines, can only have been his chief parliamentary and royal court contact, Henry Labouchère. The reason for the proposed double divorce is clear: Jennie could not deal with Randolph's relationship with a woman who equalled her in looks and in social eminence and, furthermore, whose husband (the champion bagger of game and future Earl of Ripon) was a friend of hers.

While Randolph was able to tolerate the idea of an Austrian count sleeping with his wife, in what became popularly known in society as the Austrian Alliance, he could not endure the thought that she was in bed with the illegitimate son of a disgraced nobleman; but soon he would accept Delacour as well, chiefly because they were fellow members of the Orleans Club.

As it turned out, the Churchills didn't go ahead with their divorce: they didn't want the notoriety of a similar current case: their close friend, the eminent Sir Charles Dilke, MP, who for years had been in love with Jennie, was named as co-respondent in the divorce of Donald Crawford (another MP) from his wife Virginia.

Crawford created a stir in court when he stated that after receiving a series of anonymous letters charging that his wife had enjoyed intercourse with Dilke, he had asked her in the proper manner of a mid-Victorian melodrama, 'Is it true that you have defiled my bed?' She replied, daintily, 'It is perfectly true,' adding a description of Dilke's sexual performance that had the crowd in an uproar.

Crawford said he had told Virginia he would horsewhip Dilke, a promise he failed to fulfil; he found out that the anonymous notes were written by his mother-in-law, a revelation that caused waves of merriment in court. Giving evidence, Virginia Crawford was a riot. She said that if Sir Charles were to enter her bedroom now, she would do whatever he told her; informing the court that he had made her share his body with another woman, she added that – to more laughter – she 'would have stood on her head in the street' if Dilke had asked her to. She said he had taught her 'every French vice', and that because of him she knew more about sex than 'any other woman of thirty', which again brought the house down. The divorce was granted. Furious that his name had been taken in vain in the Divorce Court, Dilke filed suit against Donald and Virginia Crawford, charging them with acting in collusion to smear his name. It was a mistake: he lost and was ruined.

On 12 February, Jennie was awakened in the early hours by hysterical cries and the smashing of windows. In dense yellow sulphur fog, hundreds of demonstrators protesting at their unemployment in the Midlands poured off trains carrying flares to light up the murk, crossed bridges, invaded Mayfair and built a bonfire in Trafalgar Square before the police quelled them.

At the same time, the Churchills faced a painful situation: Winston, who always had a weak chest, and suffered from the chilly damp of the Brighton winter, collapsed at school and was diagnosed with double pneumonia.

Fortunately, a fine physician, Dr Robson Roose, was a member of the Orleans Club and lived nearby. Winston was too sick to be moved from the school; Randolph and Jennie arrived on 12 March. Randolph stayed only briefly before returning to London to attend to matters connected with the change of government – Gladstone was back in power on 12 February so Randolph lost his post at the India Office – but Jennie stayed on.

Roose's chief concern was to keep Elizabeth Everest, still not popular with anyone except Winston and Jack, away from the patient. Letters of concern poured in: from Salisbury, licking his wounds in Monte Carlo, where he was refused admission to the casino because he was mistaken in his shabby clothes for a tramp; from Sir Henry James; from the Prince of Wales; from Moreton Frewen; and from Jennie's sisters. Clarissa was in London with an ailing Leonard Jerome and could not come.

For days, the boy struggled with temperatures ranging from 100 to 104; the Duchess of Marlborough wrote from London saying she hoped Everest would be reasonable and not too gushing so as to excite the patient. The crisis brought Jennie and Randolph temporarily together again; Randolph wrote to her as 'My darling'. On 18 March Randolph returned to the sick bed, with his friend, Lord Castlereagh; Jennie was on nightly vigil. At last the fever broke, and Winston recovered.

On 6 May, the Churchills gave a dinner party at Connaught Place to which the Prince of Wales invited himself; embarrassingly, the basement dynamo gave out and the group was plunged in darkness.

Natty Rothschild was still around, paying the Churchills' bills; he foresaw the imminent downfall of the restored Liberal government as the ranks split and resignations followed on the Home Rule issue; and he also foresaw Randolph reassuming office. In June 1886 he wrote to Randolph saying, in effect, that he was pleased that the winds were changing; after the defeat of Gladstone's first Home Rule bill in July, he wrote, 'I hope you will have a go at the Grand Old Man on his own dunghill.' He called on Randolph, who met him at Connaught Place, to discuss a Conservative campaign in Scotland. It was typical of him that he should want Randolph to be chancellor of the exchequer when the Gladstone government fell on 20 July; what could be more convenient than having as a paid employee a man in charge of the nation's money?

The office was Randolph's; again he engaged Adolphus W Moore as his right-hand man. Simultaneously, there was bad news from Blenheim. Blandford had sold off, in three successive Christie's auctions, works by Rubens, Breughel, Van Dyck, Gainsborough, Holbein and Rembrandt, followed by Titians and Caravaggios. On this occasion, remembering no doubt the deceits of the jewellery auction, those in charge at Christie's were more cautious: the surviving catalogues show crossings out and marginal notations disclosing that items listed by Blandford as originals were, in fact, copies, or were falsely attributed to the masters.

On 20 March, Randolph had upset Jennie by staying at the Hotel Vendôme in Paris with Gladys de Grey. In September, Jennie's agony over Lady de Grey reached its peak. Her old friend Consuelo Mandeville was busy confirming her suspicions; her sister-in-law Lady Cornelia Guest didn't deny them; and now Jennie wrote to her mother-in-law, the duchess, which was a move both indiscreet and unwise; whatever she thought of her son, would she have anything damaging to say?

In response to Jennie's letter, which has not survived, Lady Marlborough showed sympathy for the de Grey crisis and urged Jennie to retrieve her marriage and to be careful in saying too much to Blandford ('He is indiscreet to say the least of it, and [he] does set people by the ears'). She urged Jennie to go down to Blenheim to be with the children and made veiled references to Delacour and Kinsky; Jennie must at once 'make sacrifices' and give up 'the racing, flirting and gossiping set'. Probably knowing that Delacour and Kinsky were regulars at the Newmarket races, she wrote on 26 September that she trusted 'for both your sakes nothing will be observed at Newmarket'. Gladys de Grey would certainly be there as well.

In the midst of this awkward correspondence, Jennie had lunch with her sister Leonie in London, talking in misery about Gladys de Grey; Leonie wrote to Clarita saying that although it was clear Randolph was in fact devoted to de Grey, she did not encourage Jennie to meet her and abuse her. She advised, she wrote, Jennie not to 'stir up' Randolph, 'as I think R has other loves, only Jennie had better not know this'.

That same month, Randolph, wayward and impetuous, irritating his own party again, committed an act of forgery. He was concerned with the British relationship with Bulgaria, a nation Russia was rapidly infiltrating, risking, as Britain saw it, the balance of power in Europe. When the foreign secretary, Sir Stafford Northcote, now Lord Iddesleigh, appointed the loud-mouthed and belligerent Alexander Condie Stephen ambassador to Bulgaria, seeking a Natty Rothschild loan of £400,000 to build up local anti-Russian resistance, Natty, who had investments in Czarist Russia, turned him down. Randolph joined in a conspiracy to remove Stephen, to back up Natty's Moscow investment: he sent a fake letter in diplomatic code, over Iddesleigh's forged signature, to the prime minister Lord Salisbury calling for Stephen's dismissal. The forgery worked and Stephen was fired.

When Salisbury found out what Randolph had done, he was furious, but in view of the need for party solidarity, he didn't press criminal charges. At the same time, Randolph found evidence in the chancellery files of colossal government corruption.

From 1882 on, there had been scandals on a scale unprecedented in English history. The rot had set in with defects in the administration of the commissariat department of the army in Egypt. Randolph saw proof of brittle swords, bending bayonets and jamming cartridges while the weapons makers were making substantial profits under government contracts. The Admiralty had spent one million pounds without the knowledge of the Treasury, skimming off personal profits while supplying, in the ships *Ajax*, *Agamemnon* and *Imperieuse*, virtually worthless sitting targets, equipped with guns that burst and caused injuries. In the present Salisbury administration, Randolph singled out for attack Lord George Hamilton, First Lord of the Admiralty, and WH Smith, Minister of War. In October, at meetings with the two men, he told them that unless there were a retrenchment of dubious spending and a full investigation, he would resign his position. He urged them to prepare proper estimates of army and navy spending to clean up the matter; later that month he wrote to Smith and Hamilton urging them to have estimates ready by Christmas.

He received no satisfactory response and continued his investigations; it is likely that Jennie occupied much of her time discussing the figures that he and Adolphus Moore brought home. Randolph found out that spending had increased abnormally from 1884 on; from an average of £25 m a year to £31 m, obtained from an excess of taxation: the entire sum of tea duty, two-thirds of tobacco duty, three-quarters of beer duty, and six-sevenths of death duties, plus three pence in the pound in income tax. He attributed the expenditure to corruption and inefficiency. The Queen got wind of the matter and advised the Prince of Wales not to associate with Randolph; the prince replied that he saw no reason to shun any public figure and reminded her that Randolph had given up five thousand pounds a year (in business) to become chancellor.

Randolph didn't stop there: he took a personal stand on reducing death duties (he had to consider his mother's ageing, though she didn't die until 1899). For obvious reasons, he wanted wine and corporation duties reduced, and he wanted to cancel tobacco tax, a serious consideration for a chain-smoker like himself.

To the Queen, for whom the idea of paying taxes of any sort was as remote as a study of the Madagascan water beetle, Randolph was at this stage – to echo Lady Caroline Lamb's description of Byron – simply mad, bad, and dangerous to know; to Salisbury, he was a breaker of the gentleman's code of silence on the malfeasance of one's superiors. Theoretically, he would be considered menacing even to his bread-and-butter suppliers the Rothschilds, but instead Natty kept up his income; the reason may be that if the government's profits in armaments and other military supplies were found to be irregular, the contracts for those supplies could turn up in Rothschild hands. And as for Sir Ernest Cassel, he had not yet become deeply involved in the financing of armaments that led to a killing, in more than one sense, in Vickers shells in future wars.

On 2 October 1886, Randolph delivered an inflammatory speech to a crowd of 14,000 at Oakland Park, Dartford: he brought cheers when he called for better conditions for agricultural labourers and for an alliance of Britain, Germany and Austria that would lead to future peace; he assured the excited throng that Britain would support Bismarck and the Austrian Emperor Francis Joseph in securing the freedom of the much-oppressed people of the Balkans. He gave a similar speech right after that at Bradford. Salisbury was upset, but Gladstone was delighted; and so, we can assume, was the ultimate financial peacemaker, Natty Rothschild. And now Randolph, with his old friend the society figure Thomas Trafford, set out for Europe.

It seems that just as his trip to India the previous year was designed to set himself up as future secretary of state for the subcontinent, so Randolph now had aspirations to become foreign secretary. Described at the time as a holiday undertaken for reasons of health, his was in fact a maverick political adventure, the details exposed in an elaborate rhymed lampoon by Henry Labouchère in *Truth*'s Christmas Day issue of 1886.

Labouchère referred to one of the trip's purposes as an avoidance of a divorce suit in which Randolph was

Above left A drawing of Jennie as a young woman (© Mary Evans Picture Library)
Above right Jerome Park racetrack was opened in 1866 and dedicated to Clarissa, Clarita and Jennie (© Hulton Archive/Getty Images)

Below left Royal financier Sir Ernest Cassel, a backer of Jennie and Randolph Churchill (© Hulton Archive/Getty Images)
Below right Natty Rothschild, also the Churchills' financial backer (© Hulton Archive/Getty Images)

Above An early photo of Jennie
(© Hulton Deutsche Collection/Corbis)

Above Lord Randolph Churchill
(© Mary Evans Picture Library)

Below Fanny, Duchess of Marlborough,
Jennie's mother-in-law (© Hulton Archive/
Getty Images)

Below The Duke of Marlborough,
Jennie's father-in-law (© Hulton Archive/
Getty Images)

Above left Jennie as the eleventh-century Empress Theodora of Byzantium (© Hulton Archive/Getty Images)

Above right A portrait of Jennie taken around 1880 (© Hulton Archive/Getty Images)

Left Jennie as a mature woman (© Mary Evans Picture Library)

Above Jennie with a young Winston and brother Jack (© Hulton Archive/Getty Images)

Above With Winston, shortly before he sailed to India with his regiment, and Jack (© topfoto)

Above With Jack on board the hospital ship *Maine* (Courtesy of the ILN Picture Library)

LORD RANDOLPH CHURCHILL.

THERE IS A MIDGE AT WESTMINSTER,
A GNATTY LITTLE THING,
IT BITES AT NIGHT
THIS MIGHTY MITE,
BUT NO ONE FEELS ITS STING.
ITS NOISE PERSISTENT, SHRILL,—SO SOME
SAY THERE'S NO STING, BUT 'TIS ALL "HUM."

Above Lord Randolph Churchill as a 'pesky insect' from *Punch* (© Mary Evans Picture Library)

Above Spy cartoon of Winston (© Mary Evans Picture Library)

Above Lord Salisbury (© Mary Evans Picture Library)

Right William Ewart Gladstone (© Mary Evans Picture Library)

Left King Edward VII
(© Bettmann/Corbis)

Below Prince Carl
Kinsky, Jennie's long-
term lover, on his hors
Zoedone on which he
won the Grand Nation
(Courtesy of Reg Green)

Left Jennie's second husband, George Cornwallis-West (© National Portrait Gallery)

Right Jennie's third marriage, to Montagu Porch, is announced in *Tatler* (Courtesy of the ILN Picture Library)

The TATLER

Vol. LXVIII. No. 884. London, June 5, 1918.

REGISTERED AT THE GENERAL POST OFFICE AS A NEWSPAPER

Price **One Shilling**

Hugh Cecil, Victoria Street

LADY RANDOLPH CHURCHILL MARRIES AGAIN
(INSET, MR. MONTAGU PORCH)

Above 4 July 1917, Jennie after a gathering in honour of America Day (© Hulton Archive/ Getty Images)

Left With Clementine, Winston's wife (© Hulton Archive/Getty Images)

not named as co-respondent; this could only mean that Randolph had decided, in view of his continuing affair with Gladys de Grey, not to risk social ruin by pursuing the case against Jennie and John Delacour. It is certain he had Rothschild support for the trip; like Natty, he was anxious to sustain a European peace that he correctly feared Salisbury, with his emphasis on increased armaments, was threatening. Above all, the Rothschilds dared not disrupt their spider's web of connections with potentially warring powers.

His purpose clearly was to reassure European heads of state that the increases in military and naval expenditures in England were not authorised by him, and that he was doing everything possible to reduce such warlike activity.

If he was also bent on proving to Salisbury that the government's fear of tensions leading to a possible war were unfounded, then he was mistaken. From the outset of 1886, Europe was as much of a powder keg as it had ever been. Throughout the first months of the year, Greece was in conflict with Turkey, leading to an international naval blockade which had forced the Greeks to disarm; on 20 August Prince Alexander of Battenberg was kidnapped and exiled after betraying the Russian cause in Eastern Roumelia in the Balkans, a situation that almost led to war; on 10 November there was a serious threat of Russia invading Bulgaria; and three days later Bismarck was struggling to avoid a confrontation between Russia and Austria.

Arriving in Berlin as 'Mr Spencer', Blandford's old pseudonym, Randolph was unable to obtain an audience with Bismarck; when Thomas Trafford complained, Bismarck laughed, saying to an aide, 'It's Tom Thumb trying to see a giant.'

Randolph received equally dusty answers in Vienna, Paris and Brussels, winding up finally as a desultory angler with Trafford in the Norwegian fjords. The diplomatic aspects of his trip had been an abject failure.

He was back in England on 9 November, when Jennie accompanied him to the Prince of Wales's birthday party at

Sandringham; painfully for her, Lady de Grey was present with her understanding *mari complaisant*; Salisbury was also there concealing annoyance with his customary hedge-hog recessiveness; Jennie enchanted the crowd by joining the Princess of Wales in duets of Brahms and Schumann at two pianos.

By mid-November, Randolph was again in full spate as a critic of his own government: Gladstone's aide, Edward Hamilton, wrote in his diary that his opinions 'exploded like a bombshell in the Conservative camp'.

His next ploy he kept, to her everlasting anger, a secret from Jennie: he would, in order to force reforms of expenditure and misappropriations of funds, offer Salisbury his resignation, whereupon he expected to be reinstated at once, and have his way. It was a plan that all too clearly reveals a combination of naivety, egotism and mis-calculation.

On 20 November Randolph wrote to the war secretary, WH Smith, that he was shocked by war office estimates of a staggering £560,000, which showed that all of his pleas for reduction had fallen on deaf ears. Much further correspondence followed, but Smith flatly refused to economise. On 15 December Randolph issued an ominous statement from the treasury: unless Smith did what he wanted, he would no longer be responsible for financing the war department. Lord George Hamilton had, as navy secretary, offered a partial compromise on figures; Smith had not. Smith replied the next day that he wouldn't budge and Salisbury supported him; Randolph again talked of resigning unless he got his way.

By 18 December he was in a fiercer mood than ever, writing to Smith of 'your frightful extravagance at the War Office'. On the same day he had Salisbury to dinner at Connaught Place, but little came of the conversation, mutual politeness barely disguising icy hostility. Four days later, Salisbury wrote to him, saying he was certain war was imminent in Europe; at this time, he added, there was no question of reducing army or navy requisitions. He mentioned the lamentable condition of defences at ports and the inadequacy of ship coaling stations; in the event of an invasion, Britain would be vulnerable.

More letters to Hamilton and Smith predictably received no response, and another meeting with Salisbury drew a blank. Randolph as chancellor of the exchequer had become annoyingly dispensable.

Randolph kept Natty informed at all times; anxious to keep him in office, Natty urged him not to press Salisbury too hard. But 20 December Randolph had run out of patience and Jennie could only wonder at his increasing state of tension. He still had given her no hint of his resignation plan.

He was summoned to see the Queen, but not with Jennie present. On the train journey to Windsor he by chance ran into his enemy Lord George Hamilton who, in the tradition of politics, put on a show of friendliness. Randolph told Hamilton he still intended to resign; nothing had been done to satisfy his requirements as chancellor beyond Hamilton's very minor concessions. Used to compromise as a way of life, Hamilton felt his attitude was extreme; surely something could be worked out. But the moment he arrived at Windsor Castle, Randolph, in Hamilton's presence, and without attention to his demurs – should he not consult with friends and with his mother the dowager duchess? – went ahead and scribbled the fatal letter to Salisbury. In order to reach the prime minister at Hatfield House that night, it must have been carried by messenger.

At dinner with the Queen, Randolph confined himself to a discussion of protocol at the next opening of parliament; he deliberately made no mention of the note he had sent. Jennie, busy that night preparing a reception at the Foreign Office, had no inkling of her husband's self-destructive move, perhaps because Randolph had an additional motive he didn't want to reveal. There had been sniping from the Liberal underbrush that he was in the pockets of the Rothschilds in urging peace abroad; and he resented the implication of bribery.

The next night, having had no reply from Salisbury, Jennie and Randolph were at the Strand Theatre in London at a performance of Sheridan's *The School for Scandal*. Randolph was nervous and fidgety; Jennie didn't know why, and much to her annoyance he left after the first act. He carried a copy of his resignation letter to *The Times* editor George Buckle. Buckle cleared the decks, locked the doors until 6 a.m. to prevent a leak, had the letter rushed to the print room, and it appeared the following morning.

Jennie was at breakfast alone when Adolphus W Moore ran in with the newspaper before she had a chance to read her copy. That loyal colleague was furiously upset, and cried out in agony, 'He has thrown himself from the top of the ladder and he will never reach it again.' Also furious, Jennie saw her world coming to an end. The Dowager Duchess of Marlborough was at Hatfield House with the Salisburys; Salisbury, who had received Randolph's note at a ball the night before, had kept it from her. She read *The Times* on her breakfast tray. Reduced to near hysterics, she ran to Lady Salisbury and cried, 'Why, oh why, are my sons not like other people?' Her maid packed her things and she left at once for London.

Talking to friends, Salisbury compared Randolph to the Mahdi, who pretended to be mad while Randolph pretended to be sane. Asked if he might decline the resignation and give Randolph what he wanted, he snapped, 'Did you ever know a man who, having a boil lanced on his neck, wanted another?' Angry that Randolph hadn't informed her, the Queen agreed; and Jennie, writing her memoirs many years later, described that Christmas as 'gall and wormwood'. Even his old Fourth Party colleague Sir John Gorst attacked Randolph in the Commons and Sir Henry Drummond Wolff and Arthur Balfour deeply deplored his action. Gladstone, of course, was pleased.

As always, the *New York Times*, not restricted by the same rules as the English press, was the only public source of the truth. Its editorial on 26 December read:

To refuse the usual grants to the Army and Navy at (a) time when war seemed merely a matter of months away, appeared to everyone to seem an incredibly indefensible error, but what Churchill did was refuse to heap fresh millions into two great spending departments unless given some guarantee they would not be wasted and stolen, as in the past . . . (Churchill) will make a raking exposure of stupidity and swindling of the British Army and Navy that will startle and scandalise the empire. *Whole millions have been paid for guns, stores and armaments not existing and for work never done.* (Emphasis added.)

Salisbury took the astonishing step of writing a two-column article in the London *Post* warning the Turkish government to remember following Randolph's resignation that England would not countenance its proposed submission to Russia, which Randolph had advocated. The prime minister told his British readers that Europe was in turmoil and that Russian, Austrian and German troops were being massed for war. But he was wrong; even as he wrote, Bismarck was drawing up the plan for peace that Randolph had envisaged. By 12 February, the German chancellor had engineered the First Mediterranean Agreement Randolph and the Rothschilds had dreamed of: Britain and Italy (and later Austria and Spain) agreed on a guaranteed status quo in the various regions of southern Europe; this consolidated Union would guarantee mutual protection and would assist British interests in the Middle East.

On 20 February 1887, again with Bismarck's support, the Triple Alliance of Europe's central powers was renewed for five years, assuring peace for many years to come. But the British armaments corruption continued unabated, without even the ghost of an excuse. When a political bookkeeper, George William Goschen, took over from Randolph in January, he had already been groomed for the post; 'I forgot Goschen,' became a famous Randolphian exclamation.

Randolph added insult to injury by breaking all tradition in not handing the Queen his seals of office; instead, he took off on a brief holiday without Jennie to Europe, and then returned to the Commons on 27 January to deliver the speech of a lifetime.

He drew attention to the robbery, deceit, corruption and extravagance in the army and navy; he mentioned the guns that did not discharge and the swords that were bent, causing loss of life. He exposed gross expenditures and villainous siphoning off of funds.

His mother never recovered from the shock of his resignation; her friend, the society hostess Lady Jeune, wrote in her memoirs that for the rest of her life the duchess was seen eating her heart out yet trying to keep a brave face before the world. On 28 December the Queen had seen Salisbury and told him she was sure Randolph had made 'a serious mistake, as he has no following'. But he did; the masses still loved him.

Gladstone was delighted with Randolph's speech; in a note to his secretary Edward Hamilton, he wrote that Randolph was 'a good Liberal'. In an earlier note in the Hamilton diary, the best available contemporary record, a game is given away: Randolph wrote to Edward Hamilton thanking him for all his help during the past six months. This can only mean help in terms of information, long garnered by Liberal spies, on the gross maladministration of forces funds.

History has not been forgiving, and even Winston, in a near-hagiography of his father written many years later, could not restrain his bitterness at the resignation. Yet the truth, overlooked by everyone, is that Randolph's was not an insane action, but though naive a decent one, morally superb in contrast with his acquisition of Burma. In taking on Lord George Hamilton he even took on a relative, albeit an unwelcome one; Hamilton was a brother of Albertha, Lady Blandford. And like so many noble and misunderstood exposés of evil in high places, Randolph's had no effect. In a prolonged period of peace that stretched over nine years until 1896, the wanton increase in armaments continued unchecked.

The New Year brought two deaths: Adolphus W Moore died from overwork and from the shock of Randolph's resignation; and Lord Iddesleigh died in despair after being pushed out of the cabinet, a genteel anachronism in a brutal political age. The dreaded Moreton Frewen lost one of his few authentic jobs; he was secretary to Goschen, and thus unacceptable in the enemy camp.

In the wake of the storm that followed Randolph's departure, Jennie calmed down; she and her husband found an unexpected ally in Blandford, who had proved support-ive throughout, despite his involvement in a famous divorce case that had begun in October. The *cause célèbre* had one good result: it made Randolph and Jennie, faced with even more of a scandal than a political one, finally call off plans for their own divorce. From then on Randolph would accept Jennie's lovers, and she would accept his, in the recognised manner of British high society they had fought against for so long.

Just before the resignation crisis, Blandford had told the Churchills that, following yet another rummage sale of masterpieces at Blenheim, and wearying of his present mistress, the tall and startlingly beautiful Vera Blood, Lady Colin Campbell, divorced from Albertha, since 1880 he had decided he must follow in Randolph's footsteps and wed an American heiress. Jennie wrote to her father in New York; he was to repeat the matchmaking skills he had used in securing the heir to the Dukedom of Manchester for her school friend Consuelo Yznaga. The new Duchess of Marlborough must be attractive, very wealthy and, most importantly, of child-bearing age. But unfortunately at that moment, Lord Colin, the son of the wealthy Duke of Argyll, filed for divorce, naming Blandford as co-respondent.

The Churchills came to the rescue. They engaged their old friend Sir George Lewis, still the most cunning and unscru-pulous solicitor in London, to look after Blandford; it was essential his name be cleared, or an American heiress might hesitate to marry him.

Just before the Campbell case began, Jennie introduced Vera Blood to artist James McNeil Whistler, who pictured her in a study named *Harmony in White and Ivory*; according to the Blenheim Palace historian Marian Fowler, he also painted her in the nude. Interrupted by the hearings, the first portrait was not completed; the second apparently was.

Lord Campbell was represented by a good friend of the Churchills, the brilliant Sir Charles Russell, who had worked with them to clear Parnell's name from charges that he had engineered the Phoenix Park murders; Blandford was represented by the attorney general, Sir Richard Webster.

The facts were shocking, even by London standards. Campbell had syphilis from the mid-1870s, causing a fistula (a rift between anus and scrotum), which made intercourse difficult.

Despite that fact, he had married Vera at the Savoy Chapel in London in July 1881; weakened by several operations, the unhappy husband could not perform his marital duties without risk and a nurse came on the honeymoon to make sure he didn't. Four months later Lord Colin did make love to his wife, but very seldom thereafter.

Lady Campbell contracted syphilis from her husband and lay bedridden at her London house in the care of a Dr Thomas Bird, whom Colin accused of making love to her and of aborting Bird's baby. He also charged Captain Eyre Shaw, the appropriately hot-headed chief of the Metropolitan Fire Brigade, with enjoying his wife's favours; finally, he accused Blandford.

In a court hearing, the details of which *The Times* amusingly described as 'utterly unfit for the pages of a national newspaper' it was revealed that in Paris when Vera was with her parents, Campbell had the police issue a warrant for her arrest on grounds of lewd behaviour and called for her imprisonment. Handed the warrant, she collapsed, and her parents rushed her to Belgium. Later, staying with her cousins Sir Philip and Lady Miles at Leigh

Court near Bristol, the warrant quashed (and anyway invalid in England), Vera found herself conveniently next door to Blandford's bedroom. A maid, advised that Blandford was ready to make love, walked into Vera's chamber with the prearranged code words, 'Cook wants you, my lady.'

Lady Miles had a lubricious nature: informed by Vera of the nightly couplings with Blandford, she kept a record of them with crosses under the Psalms in her daughter Violet's *Book of Common Prayer*; there was no quelling the courtroom crowd's hilarity at this revelation, or when a butler, asked how long Lady Campbell spent in Lord Blandford's bed or vice versa, replied that it was 'sometimes an hour, sometimes fifteen minutes ... depending'. 'Depending on what?' someone shouted, and the courtroom was engulfed in laughter.

Witnesses surpassed the figures in any comic opera. They described letters carried across London from Vera to Blandford, not pushed into mailboxes but delivered to the eager recipient by hand, following one very loud knock and instructions to staff not to answer. Replies were brought by cabmen, one of whom could barely be heard above the laughter when he described standing tremulously at the foot of Lady Campbell's bed, while she wrote a love letter to Blandford.

Staff talked of Vera dressing as a man as she made her way to her lover on foot, tucking his hat under her cloak as she returned, and at one stage almost losing her own headgear in the wind, which would have revealed the length of her hair.

Rose, her favourite Swiss maid, was the star of the hearings as she talked of finding her mistress's dress unbuttoned down the back after a nocturnal visit to Blandford's house; after satisfying his lust, he had turned her out in the rain. Keyholes peeped through, cushions in disarray, pets sent flying out of rooms, prearranged codes and curtains being drawn as signals – the melodramatic litany of adultery went on.

And after all, after the piles of letters and accounts of witnesses, the jury found the proposed divorce collusive and disallowed it as a conspiracy of opponents seeking freedom – so Lord and Lady Campbell stayed married for good and Blandford was free to wed an American. Jerome could now dig up anyone he wanted from the compost of New York society. As a challenge to any future partner, Blandford placed Lady Campbell's nude portrait over his bed at Blenheim.

The Campbell case, running coincidentally with the resignation crisis, ended in January 1887. Randolph took off to the Mediterranean with Harry Tyrwhitt-Wilson, a shrewd move since Wilson was equerry to the Prince of Wales. The prince was still, despite everything, a strong supporter of the Churchills; he had lunched with Jennie at Connaught Place during Randolph's resignation turmoil. Tyrwhitt had links to Kinsky and Bay Middleton; they used his family seat in Leicestershire for hunting and found him helpful as high sheriff of that county. In turn, they were helpful to Tyrwhitt with medical advice and doctors to treat his incipient tuberculosis, which everyone knew would doom him to an early death, and did.

Jennie received letters in which Randolph described his and Harry's adventures: fleeing a Sicilian cholera epidemic by fishing boat; running into the Churchills' friend, Lord Rosebery, in Rome (the future prime minister correctly described politics as 'a dunghill'); and various harum-scarum activities that brought out the schoolboy in Randolph, his most loveable feature.

Meanwhile Jennie made a significant addition to her staff: Rosa Ovendon, later to become famous as Rosa Lewis, the 'Duchess of Jermyn Street', and owner of the Cavendish Hotel. She turned out to be a superb cook, housekeeper and general help.

Once he returned, Randolph arranged with Blandford that Lady Campbell would move to a palazzo in Venice, where the sale of still more Blenheim treasures kept her in luxury, with flocks of servants.

And so far from abandoning his investigation into government finances, he set up, as continuing MP for South Paddington, since 1885 a Parliamentary Select Defence Committee, launching a stronger attack than ever on faulty shipbuilding, useless armaments and needless provocations of foreign powers to justify such wanton extravagances. Mindful of the Rothschilds' investments in Russia, he encouraged British friendship with the Czar.

And then came Queen Victoria's Golden Jubilee. The monarch swallowed her annoyance and included the Churchills in social events; this was due to the Prince of Wales's influence.

Meanwhile, as so often before, Winston, unlike the docile Jack, was behaving like some demoniacal changeling. He fought constantly with Rosa Ovendon, who resented his invasions of her sacred kitchen domain. He battered her with endless questions while she was trying to cook, thrusting his fingers into cakes and puddings and pies; she had to chase him out with a soup ladle, yelling that he was a 'chipperhead', in other words, a fool and a knave. She hated Mrs Everest for her mollycoddling, which she believed made him even worse.

Kinsky was away that summer, in Paris on spying assignments, and in Brussels, St Petersburg and Vienna. He had not recovered from a disappointment at the 1885 Grand National; he had started off in fine form, but soon his beloved Zoedone had haemorrhaged, and had to be withdrawn. It turned out that crooked bookmakers, fearful of heavy losses if the mare won, had poisoned her; the mare survived, but Kinsky never returned to the National, and Zoedone never ran again.

John Delacour drifted away from Jennie; he was involved now with the wealthy Theresa Harriet Towneley, of a prominent Lancashire coalmine and farming family, and three years later would marry her. Justice of the Peace in that county, he continued to be seen from time to time in Jennie's social set in London, and he was very friendly with Kinsky, and with Winston and Jack.

Randolph entered into a new love affair, this time in concert with Blandford, whose action in the matter was ill-advised while Jerome was wife-hunting for him in New York. But the gorgeous Frances Evelyn Maynard was a prize few men could resist.

She was known familiarly as Daisy: a daisy ready for the picking. She had inherited the sumptuous Easton Lodge in Essex, and the present day equivalent of a million pounds a year. At sixteen, she was coupled with the eminently desirable 23-year-old Francis Greville, Lord Brooke, and on 30 April 1881 they were married at Westminster Abbey.

While Randolph and Blandford shared her favours, she also enjoyed the attentions of the dashing naval commander Lord Charles Beresford, married son of the 4th Marquess of Waterford, he was a gallant cocksman who had fought with Kitchener at Khartoum and was famous for saying, when faced with possible death from a dervish spear, 'It is hard to die without knowing who won the Derby.' For a woman who had not known what to expect on her wedding night, Daisy had learned a thing or two.

Lord and Lady Beresford were frequent visitors to Easton Lodge, until one night Daisy dropped by Mina Beresford's room to inform her of the affair, and that she intended taking Charles away from her. Furious, Mina whisked Charles off to London; Daisy consoled herself with the brothers Churchill.

That spring of 1887, Randolph, with Jennie's enthusiastic support, began cheekily angling with Lord Salisbury for the post of Ambassador to France. Salisbury was opposed, because he saw that Randolph was in touch, against his instructions, with a political figure he disliked, the French national hero and minister of war General Georges Boulanger; the only motive one can adduce for this seemingly odd political liaison is that Boulanger had greatly reduced armaments as part of an intended entente cordiale with the other European powers and that Randolph wanted to use that example to effect similar changes in Whitehall.

At the time, Jennie found a new friend: Pearl Craigie, later famous as pseudonymous John Oliver Hobbes, novelist and playwright, who would one day name her son John Churchill, after Jack. Pearl was pretty, but sexually cold; there are indications in her letters to Jennie over the years that she was a frustrated lesbian. Impassioned beyond the normal degree of affection between society women in those days, bewailing their separations through travel, enraptured by Jennie's activities particularly in the field of music for which they shared a love, she had a serious crush on her.

Pearl had an eccentric father whose addiction to quack medicines and spiritualist mediums made him something of a laughing stock in London; she was married of all things to a Bank of England clerk. But Reginald Walpole Craigie had inherited a small fortune and apparently enjoyed his humble task. He was very good looking, which might explain the union, and a sadist, which constantly threatened it. Maddened by Pearl's frigidity, he would parade about their bedroom naked, in the hope that by seeing his well-arranged muscles she would long for his attentions, but the performance didn't work; in a fit of petulance, he threw her books in the fire and raped her. Later, he subjected her to what she would describe in court as 'filthy and disgusting practices' – presumably including cunnilingus and sodomy – but she did conceive a child. Jennie and Pearl were opposites: just as Jennie couldn't live without a healthy male making love to her, Craigie shuddered at the thought.

Kinsky returned to London, as special attaché to the Austro-Hungarian Embassy, and adjutant to the visiting Crown Prince Rudolph, son of the Emperor Francis Joseph. Mindful of his Viennese banking interests, Natty Rothschild took Rudolph under his wing, and so did Sir Ernest Cassel and the Prince of Wales. By now, Jennie's 'Austrian alliance' with Kinsky was accepted by Randolph and by society; at a party in the crown prince's honour at Buckingham Palace, the Queen showed her sympathy with Austria-Hungary by letting Rudolph take her arm as she entered the ballroom; Kinsky came next, with one of the Viennese court ladies, then, among others, Jennie and Randolph. Kinsky introduced the Churchills to visiting Austro-Hungarian society, undoubtedly to help secure relations between London and Vienna; it is clear that Natty Rothschild saw advantages in this, as his financial support of the Churchills continued unabated. A tripartite agreement between England, Austria-Hungary and Italy would be signed on 12 December of that year.

In the wake of the Austro-Hungarian visit, Randolph and Jennie decided to visit Russia. They kept their intention a secret until the last minute, pretending they were leaving for Spain. The trip's purpose has been speculated over, and further speculation will no doubt take place in future, but the only conclusion must be that it was engineered by Natty Rothschild, who had in mind that if Randolph made a good diplomatic fist of the excursion, he might in some future administration be foreign secretary, with all that meant of benefit to the Rothschild bank.

In addition, the Churchills' trip would be a peace mission and, of course, Natty wanted that more than anything. The conflict between England and Russia that had almost led to war over Afghanistan had to be settled down; and the presence of an attractive woman like Jennie could only be of help. For, after all, Russian politicians were men, and would succumb to the allure of one of the world's most hauntingly beautiful faces.

Kinsky arranged a temporary transfer to St Petersburg, obviously to make sure everything went smoothly, and quite probably to arrange for an accommodation where he and Jennie could make love. Salisbury, on learning of the trip, panicked; he issued a statement through the foreign office that the visit had no political purpose, although the French Ambassador to the Court of St James advised his government that it did.

The Churchills left at the end of October; with them in their party were Thomas Trafford and, Henri, Marquis de Breteuil, a friend of Natty and an investor in his South African companies; not only would Kinsky act as host but also Sir Robert Morier, the British ambassador, whose enthusiasm over the visit was occasioned by a passionate desire to secure an everlasting peace.

A ball at the St Petersburg Winter Palace, sleigh and troika rides, skating on ice rinks, the dazzle of domes and squares in Moscow; it was for Jennie an unforgettable visit and what Randolph hoped would be seen as a diplomatic triumph. He, adding to the proposals he had made to Bismarck's son Hugo the previous summer, made the Czar an offer: Russia would guarantee not to attack India, threatening the Rothschild railway interests along with British power in the subcontinent as a whole; in return, Russia would be given a free hand in Turkey. The bargain, emphatically unauthorised in Whitehall, could only have come from Natty, or have been inspired by Randolph's desire to maintain relations with him.

Russia had not been included in the Second Mediterranean Agreement of 12 December, drawn up when the Churchills were in Russia, between Britain, Austria and Italy, guaranteeing Turkey's protection and preventing other powers from encroaching on its sovereignty; the purpose of the agreement was to maintain a status quo in the Middle East. To indicate that Russia might be allowed to penetrate Turkey or worse, was in direct contradiction of the agreement; if Russia had acted on the suggestion, the aforementioned countries would have had to intervene. The irresponsibility of the idea did Randolph untold damage in Whitehall.

In Berlin, the Churchills suffered no snub from Bismarck, unlike the year before; Bismarck as peacemaker of Europe had much to discuss. But when the Churchills returned to Connaught Place, they received a slap in the face. Salisbury was furious, and so was the Queen, at so maverick a mission; Victoria wrote to the Prince of Wales on 3 January 1888, saying in reference to the trip that Randolph was devoid of all principle, and possessed of the most insular and dangerous doctrines on foreign affairs. But the mission helped secure peace with Russia for many years.

In the Churchills' absence, a novel had appeared which was calculated to bring them even more notoriety, and did. *Miss Bayle's Romance*, by 'Anonymous' (later confirmed as William Fraser Rae) was the story of Alma J Bayle, an American society arriviste described, to avoid a libel suit, as 'the chief rival to Lady Randolph Churchill', although every detail is pure Jennie. Alma admires Lady R, noting that as 'a fellow countrywoman' she has obtained much influence in British politics.

Alma, in her upward progress, captures a man of Randolphian stamp, Lord Plowden Eton (a sly reference to Randolph's school); he is described as 'a radical Tory' who admires Lord Randolph Churchill and the Primrose League. The picture of Yankee ambition is complete; in what amounts to a semi-fictionalised dual biography of the Churchills, Alma thrusts Lord Eton to the top, only to find opposition there.

Winston was still a headache at home; he had stayed with the Duchess of Marlborough at Grosvenor Square during his parents' Russian visit and had driven her almost beyond endurance with his antics; but she did adore the quiet and well-behaved Jack. Elizabeth Everest was definitely not to her taste, her affectionate nature in contrast with Lady Marlborough's increasing irritability and cantankerousness. When the ageing, redundant nanny came down with diphtheria, she found scant sympathy from Fanny.

Jennie was consoled by Winston's success at school and by his passing the entrance examination for Harrow. She had preferred its location to Eton's because Harrow stood on an elevation and was considered better for chronic bronchitis sufferers.

But Winston did not do well at Harrow. His headmaster Henry Davidson reported that he was forgetful, careless, unpunctual and 'irregular'; he lost books, wrote bad exam papers, and unless he improved his slovenliness would never be a success; his borrowing money from other boys was a disgrace. The Churchills were upset; they washed their hands of Winston and refused even to come to Speech Days.

All through that winter, Leonard Jerome was busy seeking a bride for Blandford; one whose family could afford the going price for British noblemen. He had moved to the Brunswick Hotel, suffering from arthritis, refusing any food except oysters washed down with champagne. But finally he sent Jennie welcome news. Leonard had found a mate for Blandford at last. Lily Hammersley was plump, had the shadow of a moustache, and was somewhat awkward; she was also very rich. A native of Troy, NY, she was known socially as 'Lily of Troy'. She had married in 1879 the homosexual multimillionaire Louis Carré Hammersley, who was conducting a sexual affair with his own father; even for sophisticated Manhattan, this was a bit much, and he was shunned by many. When he died, possibly a suicide, in 1883, he left the present-day equivalent of 160 million dollars, quite enough to buy a Marlborough with. When Leonard advised Jennie that Lily was willing and able, Jennie told Randolph and Blandford took off to New York.

A meeting was arranged in a box at the Metropolitan Opera; it worked, and Jerome wrote to Clarissa that he rather thought Blandford would marry Lily Hammersley. He primly disclaimed any role in the arrangement; he was still a king among liars. But he spoke the truth when he added that Lily had 'lots of tin'. And Blandford wasted no time in having his bankers find out just how much 'tin' – i.e. money – there was.

The matter was settled; Leonard sold Blandford on commission. On 29 June 1888, the Mayor of New York performed the wedding ceremony at City Hall. When an Episcopalian minister refused to conduct the religious service, as the widowed Lily had been married before, a Baptist parson stood in for him. On arrival at Blenheim, however, Lily was shocked to find the nude portrait of Lady Colin Campbell hanging over the marital bed and had it destroyed.

At the Goodwood races that season, Moreton Frewen gave a party in honour of a visiting Indian millionaire,

Nawab Sir Salah Jung, whom he hoped to interest in investments. At Frewen's Lavington Park house near the racetrack, Jennie, Randolph, Blandford's boy Sunny, John Delacour and Kinsky rejoiced in each others' company; Randolph showed no sign of discomfiture in the presence of his wife's past and present lovers. Kinsky entertained the group, performing with his Blue Hungarian Czardas band; another in the party was the New York tycoon W Butler Duncan, who had bought Miss Green's School for Girls and turned it into his home.

November 1888 saw the publication of a novel in which Randolph appeared in his own name as a principal character. The young James M Barrie, years before his fame as the author of *Peter Pan*, published at his own expense (since it was refused by every London house), a darkly brilliant novella entitled *Better Dead*, which he later tried unsuccessfully to disown. The work has intriguing parallels with Robert Louis Stevenson's *The Suicide Club*. Andrew Riach, a struggling young writer, arrives in London, where he joins the Secret Society of Doing Without, whose purpose is to eliminate those famous men who have obtained publicity in inverse proportion to their achievements. Each society member is assigned a certain quota of victims, for whose elimination he will be rewarded.

Riach is assigned Henry Labouchère, continuing as publisher of *Truth*. Ready to kill, the youth arrives at Labouchère's house; the potential victim is about to leave for church, a neat satirical touch, since Labouchère was an agnostic. Labouchère asks him in; Riach tells him that if he will agree to be killed he will achieve an immortality he might not obtain by any other means; as it is, the best that can happen to him, given his wealth, power and fame, is elevation to the House of Lords, which could damage his image as a Radical. Labouchère finds the idea unacceptable and has his butler show the young man the door.

Next on Riach's list is Lord Randolph Churchill. He first plans to shoot Randolph with an 'electric rifle' but decides a knife would be more effective – and quieter. From a window at Morley's Hotel he spies on Randolph strolling below, laughing at the discomfiture of pedestrians trying to cross the street in driving wind and rain.

Following Randolph step by step, he sees him making notes at shop windows. Riach finds that the objects of his interest are matchboxes with famous people's photographs printed on them; an echo of an infamous incident in which a magazine publisher and editor were put out of business by improperly using pictures of the Prince of Wales's mistresses Mrs Cornwallis-West and Lillie Langtry for financial gain. A step behind Randolph now, Riach prepares to draw his knife, but by chance Sir William Harcourt, a staunch Gladstonian and political enemy of the victim, steps between them, ironically saving Randolph's life. When Riach, desperate now, runs after his potential target, another political figure, Henry Chaplin, bumps into him and again the death thrust is prevented. Finally, in the lobby of the Grand Hotel, Riach loses Randolph in the crowd and has to make do with his dropped shoe; the end of the novel has Riach happily married, the souvenir footwear sitting on top of the sitting-room piano.

Instead of a writ for libel, Barrie received a warm note from Randolph, saying he found the novella amusing; the response reflected Randolph's mood, which was far from the dark, embittered depression recorded by historians all the way up to this century.

One of the reasons both he and Jennie were in a good mood was their joint and happy membership of the Beefsteak Club. This joyous coterie of theatre stars and lovers of the stage was situated in the former lumber room of Sir Henry Irving's Lyceum Theatre, where that reigning star of London joined his equally fabled partner Ellen Terry in performances of Shakespeare. From the memorable night in Dublin in January 1876 when Randolph had dared inform Irving that he had read no play by the Bard, the Churchills, when in England, seldom missed his productions; Randolph had acquired an encyclopedic knowledge of the canon, and could discuss all of the works with startling erudition, as Jennie could. At Beefsteak evenings the Prince and Princess of Wales were often present at learned if bibulous discussions in the grand, oak-lined room, flanked by portraits of the greatest stage performers.

One evening at the Beefsteak, when Irving and Terry were preparing a production of *Macbeth* (superstitiously referred to in discussion as the Scottish play), Jennie arrived at dinner in a rich, dark-green gown whose bodice was sewn with imitation beetles' wings. Terry was dazzled by it and asked if she could use it as Lady Macbeth; Jennie agreed at once, thus making the costume famous in theatre annals. John Singer Sargent painted Ellen Terry wearing it; the portrait was later given to London's Tate Gallery.

Four days after Christmas, Jennie was overjoyed to see the *Macbeth* opening, her gown bringing a ripple of applause. As a compliment, Sargent did a charcoal sketch of Jennie herself, which became almost as well known as the *Macbeth* costume.

The early months of 1889 were taken up with visits to Blenheim, where Lily Marlborough was proving to be Jennie's most extravagant relative and friend. With millions to spend, she installed electricity and central heating, banished the gaslight chandeliers and fixtures, replaced the roof, built a pipe organ in the library and splurged on society parties at which Jennie, Fanny Ronalds and Pearl Craigie played pianos and sang. Jennie adored her and so did Consuelo Mandeville; the three Americans were often happily together at a palace that had been transformed from a chilly, depressing pile to a far more comfortable home. Lily even managed to install a sufficient number of bathrooms, and chamber pots were banished; she gave Blandford an enlarged laboratory where he could conduct experiments to his heart's content.

There were indications that Lord Brooke's action against his wife Daisy, naming Blandford and Randolph as co-respondents, was in the wind, but it was not quite time for it yet. That summer, Jennie was to be fascinated by a major new court case.

CHAPTER EIGHT

O ne of Jennie's closest friends was Georgiana Charlotte, daughter of the 1st Earl Howe, and wife of the 8th Duke of Beaufort. One of her sons was Lord Arthur Somerset, equerry to the Prince of Wales; Jennie saw him with Georgiana often, at Badminton, the Beaufort family home, or at the races. His homosexuality was known to all society, including Jennie, who had no homophobic prejudices.

The *cause célèbre* that became known as the Cleveland Street Affair began in July of 1889, when a fifteen-year-old clerk in the London Central Post Office was found to have stolen fourteen shillings. Under questioning, he denied the theft but said he had been paid it by a client at a male brothel at 19 Cleveland Street off the Tottenham Court Road.

Another male prostitute was questioned, and named Lord Arthur Somerset as that paying customer; more evidence showed that the bordello's clients included the Duke of Clarence, eldest son of the Prince of Wales and potential heir to the throne (though in fact he was to pre-decease his father).

The brothel-keeper fled to France and thence to California and wasn't apprehended. As soon as royalty was mentioned, government department after department passed the matter from office to office; not a soul wanted to handle so inflammatory a matter. Police questioned Lord Arthur twice and told him to say nothing; Jennie, Randolph and their circle were required to remain silent. In order to disguise the truth, Lord Arthur, instead of being put under arrest, was allowed to leave the country; he even returned for some racing events to silence wagging tongues. He went on consorting for appearance's sake with the Prince of Wales, who refused to believe him capable of such vileness.

The hoodwinked prince invited Lord Arthur to join him at Bad Gastein to take the waters; meanwhile Henry Labouchère, provided with leaked information, took up the matter and called for Lord Arthur's arrest. It is clear that to protect Lord Arthur, Jennie arranged for Kinsky to help him in exile. There is no evidence he had even met Kinsky, and who else than Jennie would know where Kinsky was at the time, or would be in a position to ask for help for a homosexual on the run?

The two men met in Budapest, where Kinsky was staying briefly, between diplomatic assignments. Kinsky decently offered to buy horses from the Somerset stables in London to pay for Lord Arthur's exile, but Somerset said he dared not go to England to make the arrangements. Then Kinsky made a most generous suggestion: he would arrange for Lord Arthur to manage a cousin's magnificent estates in Austria, with free board and lodging and the command of a large staff; the appointment would run for twelve months, while the cousin was travelling abroad. With incredible folly, Lord Arthur turned him down, saying he had no idea how to run a large property. Somerset's sister was appalled, writing in her diary that she was sure Count Kinsky had behaved like the angel he was, and she berated Lord Arthur for his ingratitude.

Instead of managing thousands of acres of Austrian land, Lord Arthur went to Vienna, where he narrowly escaped arrest again when police put rent boys in his path; he had just enough sense to turn them down. In January 1890, at a trial of Cleveland Street prostitutes (with the Duke of Clarence's name excluded and Lord Arthur referred to as

'Mr Brown'), Somerset's lawyer, Arthur Newton, was dismissed from court and sent to prison for engineering the escape of his client the brothel-keeper, thereby obstructing justice. As H Montgomery Hyde revealed in his book *The Cleveland Street Affair*, the real reason for his going to jail was to silence him in the matter of the royal connection, which he was threatening to expose; worse would happen to him if he uttered a single word. Labouchère called in the House of Commons for a Select Parliamentary Committee of Enquiry, but understandably he failed and there the matter lay.

Randolph's friend Harry Tyrwhitt-Wilson played a role in the matter. On 21 December 1889, shortly before Lord Arthur left for Budapest and his meeting with Kinsky, Tyrwhitt sent him a forged note in imitation of the Prince of Wales's handwriting, and on the prince's personal stationery, which read, in direct reference to the danger of Lord Arthur exposing a member of the royal family:

Are you determined to add treason and shameful ingratitude to bestiality? For God's sake contradict the foul calumnies of your family.

The reference was to Lord Arthur's brother Harry who, to protect his own homosexuality from disclosure, had informed on Lord Arthur to the police.

Eighteen eighty-nine brought not only the tensions of the Cleveland Street Affair, but the shock of Randolph's failure to secure the Birmingham seat in parliament, following the death of his old enemy, John Bright. He rashly left the decision on whether he should run to a Liberal-Unionist clique that was headed by a treacherous false friend, Joseph Chamberlain. Jennie accused him of cowardice in the matter – she was furious with him over it – but the potential rift between the couple was rapidly healed by their much increased mutual interest in horse racing; their horse Abbesse de Jouarre won the Oaks that year.

In February 1890, Jennie was at Cannes, consoling herself with gains at the gambling tables for news of her ex-lover John Delacour's engagement to the Lancashire heiress Harriet Theresa Towneley; the couple were married later that year. Leonard was with her, still worse in health and very weak, and she sent a loving gift of oranges to Winston, who was suffering from the London damp. Back in England on 1 March, she could chuckle over a *Punch* caricature of Randolph of all people introducing a Temperance Bill in the Commons.

But it was a rotten summer: Winston was doing very badly at Harrow, so much so that Randolph gave up on him again and actually seemed to hate him. Jennie herself was bitter and she wrote of her unhappiness to her son at school.

There was some small compensation on 10 July 1890, when fifteen-year-old Winston was admitted to the Primrose League. Shortly before, Jennie and Randolph had taken a lease on a country home at Banstead, near the Newmarket racecourse.

In the severe winter of January 1891, breaking away from the problem of her father's failing health, Jennie went with Randolph to Wretham Hall in Norfolk to stay with the Austrian Baron Maurice de Hirsch, friend and financier of Kinsky and Crown Prince Rudolph. Present at a weekend party were Kinsky himself, Lord and Lady Brooke, Lord Hartington and Henry Chaplin; the Prince of Wales was guest of honour.

In the midst of the festivities, the prince shockingly announced that he was being sued by Jennie's former would-be lover Sir William Gordon-Cumming for libel after he and others had charged Sir Henry with cheating at cards at the Yorkshire estate of Tranby Croft.

Jennie, Randolph and other guests were aghast. However, when the case was heard the following June, predictably Sir William lost. It was the end of his social career, but he had millions and 40,000 acres of grouse moor to compensate him.

Jennie returned to London to receive very bad news. Her sisters were in Brighton, attending to their father, who was seriously ill. The old pirate was worn out; his long years of happy chicanery were behind him, along with the litter of broken lives of the shareholders he had ruined through his manipulations. Now he was reduced to living in a humble flat; his legs were swollen with phlebitis, pneumonia had set in, and now heart disease. On his customary diet of oysters and champagne, he passed quietly away. The funeral at Grosvenor Chapel in London was attended by Robert, son of Abraham Lincoln, who was minister now to the Court of St James. Moreton Frewen took the body across the Atlantic for burial; in a peculiar irony, Leonard wasn't buried at Woodlawn, where he had a financial interest from the old Bronx days, but by mistake at Greenwood, where he did not.

And now, at last, came the Darling Daisy affair: Lord Brooke's suit against his wife that would name Blandford and Randolph as co-respondents.

The facts were clear. Daisy, moving from Blandford's bed to Lord Charles Beresford's, was upset when Beresford returned to his wife; she was still more annoyed when Lady Beresford was found to be pregnant, sure proof of restored marital relations. Daisy sent Beresford a furious note, charging him with the mortal offence of fathering a child who was not hers; Lady Beresford, imitating a typical servants' practice of the time, steamed the letter open before her husband had a chance to read it.

Upset, she went to her own and the Churchills' solicitor Sir George Lewis, who said he would do what he could, and then improperly told Daisy her note had been intercepted. In panic in case it should be made public and cause an open scandal, Daisy on Lewis's advice went to see the Prince of Wales, who looked her over, saw her as a prospect for his pillows, and offered to help.

He asked Lewis to destroy the letter, but Lewis refused to do so unless Lady Beresford agreed. The prince paid a visit to Lady Beresford, who declined to oblige.

She then informed her husband, who was in the Mediterranean, conducting fleet manoeuvres; he returned to

London, stormed into the royal residence of Marlborough House, waved his fist in the prince's face and denounced him as a blackguard for trying to suppress the note. By now, Daisy was firmly installed in the royal bed.

No willing cuckold, Lord Brooke embarked with Sir George Lewis on plans for divorce, naming Randolph, Blandford and Beresford as co-respondents. But royal influence prevented the case from coming to court; installed as the Prince of Wales's mistress, Daisy would be a grave danger to the throne if she should speak to the press; it turned out that the Tranby Croft affair would never have become public if she had not spoken to society about it.

In the meantime, Randolph had gone to South Africa for the Rothschilds; others who invested in the trip were his in-laws Lord and Lady Wimborne. The Churchills had a stake in South African diamonds and gold through Natty and the plenipotentiary Cecil Rhodes, Prime Minister of the Cape Colony, whom they had met in London; in a move that would later be emulated by Winston, Randolph signed up to write a series of articles on his trip for the London *Graphic*.

On the face of it, he made a mistake in reporting to his readers that the Rothschild-backed British South African Company, which held gold deposits, and the famous DeBeers Diamond Company were in trouble, but there was a method in his madness. Taking a leaf out of Leonard Jerome's book, he waited until the stock fell and then bought it at bottom, making a killing; at first Natty Rothschild was furious with him, but benefited later by emulating him. Neither he nor his partners struck the Churchills off their list.

In Randolph's absence, Kinsky stayed handily in London at the home of Clarita and Moreton Frewen, where he and Jennie continued sleeping together; Winston, who admired Kinsky and regarded him as a foster father, found Jennie at breakfast with him when he called early one morning. Jennie had issued the invitation; she wanted him to know.

Kinsky was as devoted to the sixteen-year-old Winston as if he were his own son. He took him to theatres and to Lord's for the test matches, and when Wilhelm II, the German Kaiser, came to London he made sure that Winston attended the celebrations. He drove the boy to the Crystal Palace in his carriage where they saw 2,000 firemen parading in horse-drawn engines before the royal visitor; they attended the subsequent banquet and quaffed champagne.

When an official tried to stop them from using an aerial car, Kinsky almost broke the man's hand; leaving the exhibition, he and Winston beat all comers in a vehicle race back to the West End of London. In August, Kinsky was at Banstead, teaching Winston and Jack rifle shooting and setting up targets; he slept in the barn when the house was full of guests so that Jennie could make her way there at night.

Winston was influenced by Kinsky, who bought him a rifle, into planning a military career; there was talk of his going to Sandhurst. The boy was filled with imperial dreams; he loved the patriotic novels of H Rider Haggard, especially *King Solomon's Mines*, with its tale of high adventure in Africa, the erotically suggestive mountains named Sheba's Breasts sheltering the legendary treasure and the three adventurers threatened by native tribes.

Much of Jennie's year was taken up with Winston's misbehaviour: he was accused of stealing a tablecloth; he spent all his parents gave him, and money from Everest as well; with typical fussiness, the old nanny wrote that she would 'starve' if his demands kept up. In December, Jennie packed the boy off to Paris to study French under Baron de Hirsch's wing; Winston called de Hirsch 'a little brute', and complained hysterically about being sent away for Christmas. He cursed his fate, he groused and groaned; but Jennie (and his headmaster at Harrow) was adamant. At last he saw some of Jennie's friends, who, aware that he was a handful, delayed seeing him as long as possible. Among them were Thomas Trafford, the Marquis de Breteuil and, last but not least, Baron de Hirsch himself.

Without Randolph or Winston with her, Jennie faced a minor crisis at home. Elizabeth Everest almost drove the indispensable cook-housekeeper Rosa Ovendon into leaving; on Christmas Day she insisted on blowing tunes through a comb covered by a strip of paper, while the kitchen staff danced a jig. Rosa didn't stay long after that.

At last, Randolph returned from Africa. Jennie made a perilous journey with Jack through severe weather conditions to greet him off the ship at Portsmouth but missed all connections. When they finally found him he wasn't well; he was suffering from more symptoms of Raynaud's disease. He felt painful chills in his hands and feet as well as body spasms and a sense of deadness, numbness or tingling, relieved only by hot compresses or steaming baths. When circulation was restored, the parts became red, swollen and very tender and painful; heat applications improved the condition, but it recurred often, especially in cold weather. Randolph would suffer from Raynaud's for the rest of his life; he looked prematurely aged, bald, with a ragged, ill-tended beard, enough to give great concern to his family.

The shock at his reappearance in the House of Commons ran through the opposing parties; it seemed incredible that this powerful and dynamic orator should be seen with pale face and shaking hands in heavy gloves; rumours of syphilis recurred. Realising her husband's political career was running out and that she could do little to help him, Jennie took off to Monte Carlo in March, foolishly gambling away money that was needed for her sons' education; she announced her purse was stolen there – probably as an alibi.

Her losses – and Randolph's, at baccarat and roulette – forced the Churchills to give up 2 Connaught Place after ten years and move with Everest and the boys unhappily to 50 Grosvenor Square with the Dowager Duchess of Marlborough. At this time, Jennie found a new lover: the handsome, 28-year-old Frederic Carr Glynn, Baron

Wolverton, a Liberal whose father had been a mainstay of Gladstone. Lewis Harcourt noted in his diary (August 1892) that Jennie actually lived with Wolverton; Harcourt gave Randolph and Natty Rothschild as sources of the information. Randolph seemed not to care, though; he apparently was no longer having liaisons of his own, or sleeping with Jennie, staying many nights at the Carlton Club.

Wolverton was lord-in-waiting to the Prince of Wales and, like Randolph, a product of Eton and Oxford. He was engaged to Lady Edith Amelia Ward, daughter of Jennie's friends the Earl and Countess of Dudley, and he and Jennie spent a great deal of time in Scotland, where the Wolvertons had properties.

Jennie had much to do with her friend from schooldays Consuelo Yznaga that year. Following her father-in-law's death, Consuelo had become Duchess of Manchester. Her husband, Lord Mandeville, had been very short of money for some time; in his last year of life, Leonard Jerome had done his best to shore up the situation by brokering a marriage of Consuelo's brother Fernando to Jennie Vanderbilt, sister of the supremely wealthy William K Vanderbilt, but the marriage didn't last, and Vanderbilt support was withdrawn.

Consuelo's father was unable to help. Mandeville had squandered what was left of his money at prize fights and on the extravagances of his mistress, the male impersonator Bessie Bellwood who, dressed in top hat and dinner jacket and smoking a cigar, sang bawdy songs on the music-hall stage. When the old duke died, Consuelo and Mandeville inherited an almost bankrupt estate; Mandeville himself had declared bankruptcy in 1888. In a sensational court hearing, Bellwood sued Mandeville for deserting her and won.

In August 1892, Mandeville was dying and Consuelo was at his bedside in London, though her mother-in-law had no such sympathy. The appalling former German countess had for years been the mistress of Lord Hartington, now the Duke of Devonshire; typically abandoning her son on his deathbed, she married Devonshire at the age of sixty; two days later, Mandeville died.

While Jennie was living with Lord Wolverton, she suddenly fell ill. Brought to Grosvenor Square from Scotland, she was attended by Dr Robson Roose and Dr George Keith, a specialist in female complaints. She was diagnosed as suffering from pelvic peritonitis, a life-threatening condition that could have been of venereal origin, or caused by an abortion or appendicitis. Lucky to survive, she was bed-ridden for weeks.

She was unable to travel to a family gathering at Blenheim in November, when Blandford and Lily invited her and Randolph to join Clarita and Moreton Frewen, Leonie and Sir John Leslie, Consuelo Manchester, Albertha and several of Randolph's sisters and brothers-in-law. During that gathering, on the morning of 9 November, a valet found Blandford in his bedroom, exactly as his father had been, with what was described as 'a terrible expression' on his face. His heart had calcified, a condition usually found in much older men; Randolph and the rest of the family took the unusual step of ordering an inquest. The reason, since foul play could not have been suspected, was clearly for insurance purposes: suicide (and Blandford had remained depressive and hysterically self-destructive) could eliminate any payment to his widow. The verdict was death from natural medical causes; the insurance of one million pounds, the equivalent of at least fifty million today, was paid to Lily.

Jennie had no strength to come from London for the funeral, at which Albertha behaved as outrageously as ever. Not content with providing a vulgar and ostentatious wreath made of flowers that Blandford detested, including gladioli and marigolds, she announced in the middle of the service that she had found a new lover: Lord William Beresford, who would in 1895 marry Lily and actually had no interest in Albertha. Charles Richard John, her 21-year-old son, would now be Duke of Marlborough, but nobody was excited by the prospect. Sunny, as he was known, was an insignificant weakling; but at least, unlike his father, he was spirited, cheerful and didn't take drugs.

It emerged that Blandford had left the present-day equivalent of one million pounds to Lady Colin Campbell, who had dared to appear at Blenheim Palace several times during the marriage, making a nuisance of herself to Lily and easily eclipsing her in looks; on one occasion she had suggested Lily have her 'beard' removed by an expert barber. Now she could live on in her magnificent palazzo in Venice with her flock of servants indefinitely.

Lily ransacked cupboards that Blandford had forbidden her to unlock, found scores of pictures of Lady Colin, and cut them to pieces. Then she took off to London to persuade the editor of the *Pall Mall Gazette* to drop an article Blandford had written just before his death, naming all his lovers in chronological order. The editor was a gentleman, and she succeeded in her purpose.

Lily gave up the hated Blenheim Palace and moved permanently to Brighton, where Jennie often came to stay with her at 8 Brunswick Terrace. She soon became the adored friend and helper of Winston and Jack, known to them always as 'Duchess Lily'.

Jennie heard the sad news, after the funeral rites at Blenheim, of the demise of her father's Jerome Park racetrack; a syndicate had bought it from Leonard's executor William A Duer, pulled down the clubhouse, torn up the track, and broken up the property. The land was sold later to the Bronx Council for a reservoir.

Central Avenue in New York had long since been renamed Jerome Avenue. The Council, and influenced by the new owners, tried to restore its original name, but Lawrence Jerome's widow Kate objected furiously and rode the length of the thoroughfare on horseback, breaking off the hastily erected wooden signs. The authorities, unable to resist her headlong resolution, kept the name Jerome.

It was not until January 1893 that Jennie, after five months of illness, was fully recovered. But then she suffered a shock when she was staying at Randolph's sister-in-law Lady Wimborne's house at Bournemouth on 10 January. Winston, pursued by Jack, took off on a wild chase through a forest. Trapped on a footbridge, he jumped on a branch to escape; he started to slide down the trunk but lost his grip and fell some 28 feet; his fall was broken by branches or he might have been killed.

Jack ran to the house and told Jennie what had happened; she rushed to the spot, cradled Winston in her arms and gave him a tot of brandy, then sent for Dr Roose. Randolph came over from Ireland. Apart from multiple bruises, Winston had also injured his neck: X-rays throughout his life continued to show the damage, and he had recurrent pain for many years. He did not, as he claimed in his memoirs, have a ruptured kidney.

His accident was the butt of London jokes; one much quoted (and unattributed) exchange went as follows:

FIRST CLUBMAN: I hear Lord Randolph's son has met with a serious accident.

SECOND CLUBMAN: Yes, playing a game of Follow My Leader.

FIRST CLUBMAN: Well, Randolph isn't likely to come to grief that way.

A few weeks later, Fanny, Dowager Duchess of Marlborough, to Winston's lasting fury, dismissed Elizabeth Everest from her service. Playing a pocket-comb concerto in the kitchen would have been reason enough, but the warm-hearted old nanny was definitely redundant in what was a chilly household. Everest had spoiled the now eighteen-year-old Winston constantly, something Jennie and Randolph had tried to avoid; he remained spoiled throughout his long and matchless political career. Everest, supported by a small pension and a job or two from Randolph, Winston and Jennie, died in 1895, with a little over two hundred pounds in her estate; her beloved boys visited her whenever they could.

In April 1893, Jennie was in Paris, her old self again at 39 as she rode, skated, gambled at the racetrack and danced up a storm at society balls. Randolph was back in the thick of politics; his pocket borough of Woodstock abolished by parliament under electoral reform, he was busy representing South Paddington, London, and running (unsuccessfully) for Bradford; he was more of a Whiggish Tory than ever, ever more overtly a supporter of the now aged Gladstone instead of Lord Salisbury. That summer, Winston finally entered Sandhurst; Randolph wasn't impressed, writing as a once-caring but now disappointed father that he should have been admitted to the infantry, which was considerably superior to the cavalry. He warned him that he was destined to be 'a social wastrel, one of the hundreds of the public school failures ... you will degenerate into a shabby, unhappy and futile existence'. The letter burned into Winston's memory for the rest of his life.

The Churchills left with their sons on a walking tour of Switzerland; at Kissingen, a favourite town of Jennie and Randolph's in earlier years, Otto von Bismarck, out of office as German chancellor, paid a visit to Randolph while Jennie was away with friends; forgetfully, Randolph, in a letter to his mother describing the meeting with Bismarck, showed he had not recalled the previous visit to Bad Gastein when the chancellor was his host.

Back in London, with Winston settling into Sandhurst, Randolph at last softened in his attitude to his errant son, sending him cigars, going with him to plays during school breaks, and to the racetrack; part of the reason may have been that he was in failing health, and knew instinctively that he had little time left.

Dr John H Mather, as Churchill medical historian, has obtained records that show Randolph suffering, throughout much of 1893, from continuing Raynaud's disease – dizziness, palpitations, and numbness of the hands and feet – not, as most have said, from tertiary syphilitic blindness, deafness and incipient madness. His continuing love of Jennie expressed in letters written to her when she was in

Paris in April of that year show no sign of disordered thought, and there were no indications of syphilitic dementia in his appearances in the Commons. On 28 May, he exchanged quips with Herbert Asquith in the Commons on the pressing subject of 'furious bicycle riding'. Rawson Shaw, member for Halifax, had raised the issue of adherents of the bicycle craze causing accidents; Asquith stated that the police were ready for any contingencies. Randolph enquired: 'Has the attention of the Right Honourable gentleman been drawn to the case of the pneumatic-tyred cycles, which come silently and stealthily upon one?' Asquith replied jocularly: 'My experience is not that of the noble Lord. I hear them continually ringing bells.' The House burst into laughter.

By the autumn Randolph was showing signs of severe neurosis. He had difficulty speaking both on provincial hustings and in the House of Commons. When he accidentally shot a dachshund belonging to Lady Curzon on a country weekend shoot he sent it stuffed to its owner, and at a party given by the society doctor Henry Thomsen, he shrieked that a plate of game he had been handed was badly cut; he demanded another serving and when it arrived, wolfed it down like an animal. He suffered from headaches so severe that he could barely function.

Dr Mather has reached, from reports by Randolph's physician Dr Ralph Buzzard, the determination that the sufferer by now had, as well as nervous illness and Raynaud's disease, a tumour of the left side of the brain, perhaps brought on by a lifetime of chain-smoking forty cigarettes a day. He was placed on the classic Victorian remedies of laudanum as a painkiller, and belladonna and digitalis for his heart condition. Jennie had to face the prospect of watching her beloved husband die. Randolph again visted Bad Gastein for the waters, but it had no effect. In consultation with Roose and Buzzard he said he would undertake a world tour, which they rightly considered out of the question. Randolph nourished the forlorn hope that the journey would be restorative; his courage and folly were as much in evidence as they had ever been.

On 8 June 1894, he wrote to his mother that he had agreed with Jennie to give up political life for a year, that 'New Court' (Natty Rothschild) had made all the arrangements for the world trip and that his doctors' caution was absurd. Though his journey to the Continent had done him no good, he admitted, he was sure that this one would; he was not afraid of Manhattan heat after India, South Africa and Egypt. Roose and Buzzard begged Jennie to stop the insane plan, but she knew from long experience it would be hopeless.

With a maid, two valets, and Roose's associate, Dr George Keith (an odd choice, since he was a gynaecologist), plus a coffin, just in case, the Churchills left on the first lap of their world voyage on 28 June 1894. When they reached New York, they ran into a devastating heat wave and a railway strike that paralysed the city, so the political leader Chauncey M Depew chartered a special train to take them to Bar Harbor, Maine, where Lord Wolverton – unhappily for Jennie he was still engaged to Lady Edith Amelia Ward, daughter of the Earl of Dudley – was present.

While Jennie and Randolph continued their trip, Randolph suffering intermittently from Raynaud's and brain cancer, then going through periods of remission, Kinsky remained Winston and Jack's surrogate father. In August, he took the boys to the Grand Exposition in Brussels where he was attaché to the embassy, and made sure they had a very good time. To Jennie's distress, Randolph was ill again in Banff, Alberta; his speech was irregular and blurred and he had to be given sleeping drafts at night. In California, though, he was coherent again, writing a sharp note to Winston opposing his idea of enlisting in a cavalry regiment. In Japan in September he was full of joy, out of control and refusing medicines; in October, while still there, he haemorrhaged, a typical symptom of a brain tumour.

He had violent changes of mood, making Jennie's life almost unendurable; he fired one of his valets and threatened an attack on a tour guide. He wrote to his mother that he had to soak his hands and feet in hot water to restore feeling, that he suffered from cold in his fingers and toes, and had had to buy fur slippers and gloves. He pretended his Raynaud's condition was improved, and attacked Dr Keith for not seeing that, but his handwriting can have brought no consolation to his mother: it was a hopeless, almost illegible scrawl.

By the end of October, he was suffering delusions, and his alternative states of violence and apathy again must have dragged Jennie through hell. In London, Roose, who all along had wrongly diagnosed syphilis, had Winston to his office to convey the incorrect news in secret; Winston was shocked beyond imagining. By mid-November in Singapore, Randolph was losing weight, his lips and chin paralysed, his gait staggering and uncertain; he insisted on going on tram rides in Hong Kong, and to parties and a Maharajah's luncheon in India; and then he insisted on going on to Burma, to see the fruits of his 1886 triumph.

He longed to visit the Royal Lakes and the Schwei Dagon Pagoda; when the Churchills arrived in Mandalay the exiled King Thibaw's relatives were forced to welcome the couple who had destroyed their beloved leader. Ironically, it was there, at the scene of her husband's questionable triumph, that Jennie experienced her greatest personal defeat.

Kinsky, disappointed she had not promised him marriage when he had defied his much-opposed aristocratic family in order to ask her, cabled her to say that he was engaged to the wealthy and beautiful Countess Elizabeth Wolff-Metternich, whose brother would later be ambassador to the Court of St James; it was a devastating blow, and she decided that they must come home. Soon after that, she received word that Wolverton would also be married soon.

She suffered severely through a seven-week voyage home. She wrote to her sister Leonie from aboard ship saying that Kinsky was the only man she could have made a fresh start with, but that his abandonment of her was deserved by her since she had treated him badly and refused to marry him. She blamed Wolverton for asking her to give Kinsky up. She fantasised that Kinsky would, once she saw him, give

Metternich up and that Metternich would not object once she knew the situation. She pleaded with Leonie to reason with Kinsky, telling him that she was 'suited to him' and that her troubles had sobered her and she would be 'all that he desired' again. There is something disturbing about the scene the letter conjures up: Jennie in the cabin in the heat of the voyage, scribbling away in telegraphese, urging her sister to clear the way to her marrying her lover while her husband was racked with pain and delirium.

Returned to London, she met Kinsky and, deciding to be a sport, made no further demands; they would remain friends. She wrote to Leonie saying she should no longer waste sympathy or pity on her and that she was not a meek person (not that Leonie could ever have thought it). She added that Kinsky had not behaved well and she could not find much to admire in him, but she had given up: the subject was closed.

Wolverton's marriage took place on 7 January 1895 and Kinsky's, also in London, two days later, most cruelly on Jennie's 41st birthday. After rallying briefly at Christmas, Randolph had declined again and his headaches made him scream with pain. He imagined he was aboard ship and talked of arriving soon at Monte Carlo, though in a moment of lucidity he asked Winston about his Sandhurst exams.

Jennie was a devoted nurse; she kept vigil round the clock until it was feared she would collapse. She suffered from neuralgic headaches and her mother had to force her to take even two hours of rest, while her sister-in-law Georgiana insisted on taking her for carriage rides in the park. The house in Grosvenor Square became a spectacle of pain and grief; the duchess was beside herself as relatives paraded through the sick room, giving no solace and not a little annoyance. Then, in a state of advanced pain and mania, Randolph sank into his final and merciful sleep on 24 January 1895.

The will was, like all the Marlborough wills, unsatisfactory. It had been drawn up on 1 July 1883, in London, and made Jennie, Blandford and George Curzon joint executors and trustees. Just as Marlborough and Blandford had left their spouses mere hundreds of pounds, so did Randolph; Jennie would receive five hundred and his 'consumable household stores and provisions', namely, the food. Then, almost as an afterthought, she would get horses, carriages, plates, linen, china, glass, books, pictures, furniture and other household effects. All this was meaningless, since she had no home by 1895 and very little, if any, of the items listed at Banstead Manor; nothing at 50 Grosvenor Square or Blenheim was hers, as Fanny Marlborough would no doubt take pleasure in reminding her.

The rest of the estate, which included, significantly, Rothschild Indian railway stock, was to be held in trust: Jennie would enjoy the income and, after her death, the principal would be divided between her sons and heirs.

A codicil was added to the original document. Randolph's private papers – correspondence and notes on political matters included – were to be divided between Louis Jennings, a treacherous hack journalist who had spread the false rumour that Randolph had syphilis, and pretended to be Randolph's friend, and (again) Lord Curzon. Fortunately, Jennings, who would have leaked the letters' secrets, had recently died himself; Curzon could be relied upon to lock everything up.

One wish of Randolph's was denied: Winston entered the cavalry. Jennie's choice was the 4th Hussars, the regiment of Sir Thomas Burke, John Delacour's adoptive father. Though not the equivalent of the Cherry Pickers, the 4th had a very fine record.

On 18 February 1895, Jennie sent Randolph's backgammon board to his closest Irish friend and frequent host at Christmas, Gerald Fitzgibbon, blaming, in an accompanying note, Lord Salisbury for Randolph's political downfall; she named jealousy as Salisbury's reason, an irrationally sustained belief. In a similar vein, Fanny Marlborough had written to her friend Lady Salisbury, describing Randolph as brooding and eating his heart out and saying that the

Tory party that he had saved had abused him and he was never the same afterwards. Then she added plaintively, contradicting her previous outcry with all it implied of Salisbury's guilt, that she sorrowfully admitted he was wrong; he had suffered for it and her heart was broken. 'My darling has come Home to die and oh it seems such bitter mockery that now it is too late he seems to be understood and appreciated.' She was referring to the politicians' encomiums that inevitably accompany the deaths of public figures they hate.

Soon after Randolph's death, yet another work of fiction was published with Jennie as a character. George Moore, the famous Irish novelist, a long-time and unsuccessful pursuer of Pearl Craigie, brought out a novella, *Mildred Lawson*, based on her life. Just as James Barrie had named Randolph as a character in his work, so did Moore specifically name Delacour, now happily married, as the target of Jennie's (Mildred's) affections.

In this peculiarly suggestive work, Delacour, portrayed correctly as Catholic, and less accurately as an aristocrat (a sly reference to his position as illegitimate son of the Earl of Clanricarde), is married and living in Paris, where in fact John and his wife Theresa kept a house. 'Mildred' moves in with the couple and threatens their happiness – Jennie was in Paris when the book came out – and the complications start from there.

On 2 May Winston, calling him 'Sir John', wrote to his mother saying that he had run into Delacour at Newmarket races, along with her other ex-lover Lord Wolverton and Natty Rothschild, all three with their wives. And Jennie's other love was present in Winston's life; he bought, for the princely sum of one guinea, Kinsky's portrait from Jack, transferring it from Jack's study at Harrow to his own at Sandhurst.

Jennie had to face the fact that of Randolph's estate, about £72,000 (well over three million today), was owed to Natty Rothschild. Much of it consisted of loans for remaining shares, not listed in the will. The company of which

Randolph was a partner had been floated in 1893 and immediately the Rothschilds had snapped up 27,000 of the initial stock issue; thus they controlled a considerable share of South African gold and diamonds. There was every advantage to them in this, despite the window-dressing of their attacking Randolph for making adverse statements that lowered the value of the shares; in no time they had snapped up far more, sending the value soaring. When Randolph died, Jennie's holdings were considerable in value, and the statement that she owed £72,000 was in fact meaningless; Natty wiped out the debt by simply buying back the appreciated shares from her, transferring money from one pocket to another, then generously gave her some more.

In London, Lady de Grey, whom Jennie had finally forgiven for her prolonged affair with Randolph, gave a lunch party at which Oscar Wilde was a guest (he had dedicated *A Woman of No Importance* to her). Thomas Lister, 4th Baron Ribblesdale, whose son was a friend of Winston, was also present. Wilde, enjoying the wine, tipsily announced that he could discuss any subject that might be presented to him, so Ribblesdale mentioned the Queen. 'The Queen is not a subject,' Wilde answered, and the room dissolved in laughter. Jennie made a bet with several friends on the accuracy of a quotation from *The Importance of Being Earnest*; she wrote to Wilde seeking confirmation, which he provided, and she had the nerve to quote his response in her memoirs:

How dull men are! They should listen to brilliant women and look at beautiful ones – and when, as in the present case, a woman is both brilliant and beautiful, they might have the ordinary common sense to admit she is verbally inspired. I trust your bet will be promptly paid as I want to begin writing my new comedy and I have no pen!

Soon after that, Wilde was destroyed by his ill-advised libel suit against the homophobe Marquess of Queensberry.

April brought news of Jennie's mother's death after a stay of several years at Tunbridge Wells; as austere and morally correct as ever, she had stripped herself of every comfort to pay off Jerome's debts when his fellow crooks outsmarted him and damaged him. She left nothing to Jennie, writing in her will that she had already advanced sums to her, and so her meagre estate was divided between Clarita and Leonie.

No arrangement had been made by any of the three daughters for their mother Clarissa's burial; a funeral was held, but the body was left in a cold-storage vault while they made up their minds what to do with her. Jennie made a perfunctory appearance at Tunbridge Wells for the ill-attended funeral, then returned by the next boat to France.

That spring, Jennie met the New York political operator William Bourke Cockran, who was in Paris recuperating from the shock of his second wife Rhoda's death in New York; the two bereaved had much to talk about. More than one biographer has recklessly elevated a mutually sympathetic relationship into a love affair, but there is no evidence for this. Quite apart from her emotionally drained condition, Jennie would never have found Cockran attractive: he wasn't her type. Tall, well into middle age, ugly, daunting and overweight, with a shock of black hair, he was a woolly mammoth in the Theodore Roosevelt mould.

Born in Ireland, he had risen through the corrupt Democratic party political machine, run in New York by the notorious 'Boss' Tweed, supplying voters who had been threatened, cajoled, or dragged from sick beds at elections, along with providing names of the dead or those resident abroad, and hiring actors in various disguises to vote again and again. It was a poisonous and well-paid raffle of body and souls. When Tweed deservedly went to prison, Cockran didn't stop; he backed the equally infamous 'Boss' Croker, whipping up gangsters to ensure that contemptible Irish Democrat the position of 'King of Manhattan', with graft, payoffs, and a murder or two along the way.

By the time he came to Paris, Cockran had decided life was too dangerous as he lived it. Abandoning Croker, he had embarked on a policy of reform, defying his former friends to kill him. He even switched to the Republicans, and he later revealed to the Cincinnati *Enquirer* (28 September 1895) the names of those he betrayed. Cockran took in the Paris sights with Jennie and his stentorian voice and ample rhetoric, famous in America, impressed her; she decided that Winston should emulate him in oratory if he should go into politics, and that is in fact what happened – with major improvement.

In July, Cockran took Clarissa's body back to New York, with Clarita and Leonie accompanying him; he buried that unhappy woman next to her husband at Greenwood Cemetery; in the fullest sense, she had never really lived.

Jennie was in London at the time, attending the two-day Divorce Court hearing at which Pearl Craigie charged her husband with a multitude of new sins: once again, *The Times* primly announced that the details were 'too filthy' to be published in the pages of a newspaper. She charged Reginald with having sex with several women, despite his having syphilis; wilfully infecting her with the disease by raping her when she had her period; threatening her life with a pistol; stripping off her bodice and trampling on it; hurling off her bedclothes, and trying to strangle her. After her recitation of these sins, the offending Bank of England swain withdrew his defence and Craigie was free.

The same day the divorce was granted in July, Jennie learned of Elizabeth Everest's death. Winston had rushed to the dying woman's bedside when Dr Roose contacted him at Sandhurst; Jack, for some reason, wasn't informed at Harrow. Everest's last hours of suffering from peritonitis following an appendectomy were lightened by Winston's loving attentions; the moment she was gone, he rushed to Harrow to convey the news to his brother. Jennie did not attend the funeral – she had never been fond of the old nanny – but she paid for the burial and gravestone and sent a wreath from Paris.

She spent the summer in Switzerland and Scotland, where she stayed with Lord and Lady Tweedmouth, and where she received word that Winston was planning to go to New York, and to Cuba for adventure: there was a rebellion against the Spanish government and he would be involved, he hoped, in battle. She sent him a characteristically sharp note on 11 October, saying that instead of announcing he was going, he might have asked her first, adding that New York was very expensive (true) and that most men found it boring (false). But she had given birth to a whirlwind, and had no chance of stopping it.

Meantime, an earlier matchmaking plan, embarked on by Jerome shortly before his death, came to spectacular fruition when it was too late for him to benefit from it. He had long since made his peace with his old enemies the Vanderbilts, and he had in mind that William Vanderbilt, the late commodore's son, would marry off his daughter Consuelo to Sunny Marlborough, now that the boy was of age. Vanderbilt money added to Lily's Hammersley millions would ensure Blenheim's upkeep for years to come, and Sunny, in his early twenties, could presumably sire an heir, despite uncertain health.

When Consuelo's mother Alva divorced William, there was still plenty of cash; the equivalent today of a million pounds a year filed in the settlement, as well as fifty million pounds of principal. Breaking off Consuelo's love affair with the sportsman William Rutherfurd, Alva (through Jerome and Jennie) met Sunny at a ball at the Duke of Sutherland's in London. Smelling huge profits, and up for sale, Sunny invited mother and daughter to Blenheim. Consuelo was not attracted to Sunny's weak-chinned, fragile appearance – she wanted a powerful man's man like Rutherfurd – but her mother's will was absolute.

The wedding took place at St Thomas's Church, New York, on 8 November 1895. Jennie sent a set of china but a more interesting gift came from the Duchess of Marlborough: rubies, the loot of Burma, set in bracelets, a solid gold belt, a brooch and a tiara, fit for an empress, as well as a diamond-encrusted dagger and ruby sleeve clasps. With bad timing, Winston, arriving in New York as a guest of Bourke Cockran, missed the wedding of the decade by two days.

Winston and Bourke Cockran became fast friends: Cockran's windy rhetoric (hiding his duplicitous politics – he would support Williams Jennings Bryan for president when he had promised support to William McKinley) left him inexplicably impressed. Jennie was anxious when, in Cuba, Winston had his first skirmish with the rebels, enjoying the danger thoroughly, a sure mark of his future character. He correctly foresaw the future Spanish-American War and carried a bullet in his pocket back to London.

CHAPTER NINE

On 11 February 1896, Alan Cameron Bruce-Pryce, a Welsh barrister of some repute, but an eccentric homophobe in the Marquess of Queensberry tradition, wrote to Ian Graham Hogg, a recently appointed 4th Hussar, charging Winston with 'acts of gross immorality of the Oscar Wilde type' with another officer, who had been flogged publicly for the offence.

Hogg showed Winston the letter. Winston at once went to Jennie's continuing solicitor, Sir George Lewis, and on 21 February filed suit against Bruce-Pryce for libel, calling for £20,000 in damages. Colonel John P Brabazon of the 4th Hussars stood firmly with Jennie and her son against the charge; but he advised against a Wildean libel suit. The matter was settled after Lewis delivered a threat, and Bruce-Pryce apologised on 12 March.

There the matter should have lain, but Henry Labouchère, betraying his friendship with the Churchills from the days of the Fourth Party, and eager for improved circulation, couldn't resist mentioning the matter in his magazine *Truth*; and he exposed more than one alleged scandal in the process.

In the issue of 19 March 1896, he charged Winston and his fellow subalterns with acting improperly at the 4th

Hussars' Challenge Cup Race in March 1895, by entering a substitute horse under the name of Surefoot, challenger to the favourite Lady Margaret, an illegal act. When 'Surefoot' won, and the deception was discovered, the winner's cup was withdrawn. In addition, Labouchère charged that Winston's clique, known as the Nimrod Club, had acted viciously against Bruce-Pryce's son, known as Alan Bruce, who had made the homosexual charge to his father. At a Nimrod Club dinner, Labouchère wrote, Winston told Alan that he wasn't wanted in the regiment, that he had not enough money to pay for his keep, and that the Club had already banished Lieutenant George C Hodge for insufficient funds and Alan would suffer the same fate. Furious, Alan said he would on no account leave the regiment. He was a superb athlete, horseman, fencer and shot, and a model soldier in looks, dedication, physique and deportment.

Alan reported the matter to a superior officer, who did nothing; and nor did Winston, for the time being. However, on Boxing Day, 1895 the matter blew up again.

Alan went to the sergeants' mess that night to meet a veteran of the Crimean War; he drank the man's health. According to Labouchère, Winston reported him for that; visits to the mess were not permitted to lieutenants on the principle of military rank. Three days later, the regiment's Colonel Brabazon arrested Alan and he was charged with 'improperly associating with non-commissioned officers'. He was forced to resign his commission and his military career was ended.

Not content with exposing the matter that had led Alan Bruce-Pryce to charges of homosexuality against Winston, Labouchère struck again. He accused Winston and his friends of dragging Lieutenant Hodge from his bed, hurling him downstairs and tossing him into a horse trough, and then returning him bleeding to his room and tearing his night attire to shreds. At a debate on 19 June in the House of Commons, Labouchère stated that the Nimrod Club's chief objections to Hogg were that he couldn't afford hounds and horses.

More came to light: Winston and his fellows had threatened Hogg with death by throwing him from a window; they had burned his clothes and broken open and rifled his locker. The War Office buried the matter, and no more was heard of it after that summer. Labouchère constantly attacked in the pages of his *Truth* – and was not sued for it – the race fixing, bullying and ruination of two young men's careers by Winston and his Club.

On 16 March 1896, Jennie was at Victoria Station with Lily and Beresford, Fanny Marlborough, Albertha and her daughters Lillian and Norah, to greet Consuelo and Sunny after their miserable and loveless four-month honeymoon marked by all the quarrels of an arranged match in the capitals of Europe. Sunny was his usual pallid and insignificant self but Consuelo was glamorous in a sable hat and coat, bought during an all-out shopping spree in Paris.

Jennie found in her the rare combination of wealth, beauty and intellect that her brilliant memoir, *The Glitter and the Gold*, would many years later disclose; they at once became friends.

Next night, Albertha and Fanny Marlborough gave a welcome dinner party that, even by their depressed standards, was a fiasco. At one stage, Albertha asked Consuelo, 'I suppose all you Americans live on plantations with Negro slaves and Red Indians are there to scalp you as soon as you round a corner?' Since Jennie was widely believed to be of Iroquois descent, this was more than a random insult. When Consuelo asked her why she hadn't come to the wedding, Albertha replied that Sunny had refused to pay for her passage; could anyone blame him?

In her memoirs, Consuelo Marlborough wrote (not without an affectionate cattiness) that Jennie was 'the mistress of many hearts'; she meant, of course, men. And she added, meaningfully, 'The Prince of Wales was known to delight in her company.' Was Jennie in fact sleeping with the prince?

It is true he had dropped Daisy, Countess of Warwick, his most recent bedmate, in 1894, since she had dared to dress up as Marie Antoinette at a costume ball at Warwick Castle and was attacked in the press for matching that monarch's extravagance when many in England were starving.

When he became King Edward VII in 1901, he included Jennie in the so-called 'Loose Box' at his coronation in Westminster Abbey; it was said to be restricted to women whose favours he had enjoyed. There is another clue: in late 1896, he stayed at Blenheim Palace for a week and he had asked that the only person present apart from the Marlboroughs would be Jennie; he had used that device to secure mistresses before, and it is possible he did so in Jennie's case.

During much of 1896, Jennie was involved with the multimillionaire William Waldorf Astor; how they met is unknown, and whether they had a physical relationship can not be established, but tall, sturdy, pipe-smoking, middle aged and broad of beam, he was not her physical type. He had been a friend of Jerome, who may well have mentioned Jennie as a possible future bride, and of James Gordon Bennett and Pierre Lorillard. By 1896 he was a widower with two sons, one of them at Eton. He owned the *Pall Mall Gazette*, and he had appointed as its editor Harry Cust, one of her admirers, and some have said, without evidence, her lover.

Wryly humorous, Astor was a famous practical joker: on 11 July 1892, he had instructed his office in London to announce his death to the press; only James Gordon Bennett was told the truth. Headlines announced his demise, which, like Mark Twain's, was greatly exaggerated; he read the obituaries, made a note of who liked him and who did not, and acted accordingly. When Bennett announced in the *New York Herald* that the reports were false, that newspaper's circulation doubled.

Swept off to Astor's English homes – Cliveden in the country, a house on the Thames embankment and another at Carlton House Terrace – Jennie was captivated by his wealth, but premature announcements that they were happily engaged ruined the relationship. Fearful of committing to a second marriage, Astor backed out, and Jennie, who could have been supremely rich, also retreated. It's doubtful anyway if she would have married a man she didn't desire physically.

Her visits to Blenheim were miserable that summer. Sunny and Consuelo could not communicate, so mealtimes were silent ordeals. Sunny developed an unpleasant habit, later copied in Patrick Hamilton's famous play *Angel Street*, of hiding pictures and ornaments, then complaining they had been stolen. There was a foul smell in the Blenheim Chapel when the coffins of dead Marlboroughs had exploded and hurled their distinguished occupants through the air.

On 11 September 1896, Winston left with the 4th Hussars for service in India; from the day he sailed to his final return, Jennie received from him a stream of lively and informative letters that show the great affection existing between mother and son. She had her hands full in London: while Sir Ernest Cassel, no doubt on the Prince of Wales's instructions, was doing his best for her, despite her gambling losses at Monte Carlo and her reckless extravagance with dresses, jewellery and furs, she embarked on a speculation that proved to be ill-fated.

She met through Randolph's friend Lord Cadogan a swindler named James Henry Irving Cruikshank, who specialised in fleecing the unsuspecting by having them invest money in an imaginary railroad syndicate in America. Cassel had made fortunes for his clients in United States railroad stock, and Jennie must have remembered her father's successful railroad speculations. So it is incomprehensible that she would have accepted all that Cruikshank told her without checking him out at the highest level. But he had great charm and considerable skill in conversation, and she placed a good deal of her available capital in his hands, all of which she lost. Through her old friend, the solicitor Sir George Lewis, she managed to have Cruikshank brought to justice, but at the trial on 25 November 1897 it turned out the man was bankrupt, and had spent most of her investments on fast living and fine horses and houses.

She had moved from Grosvenor Square and the constant enmity of Fanny Marlborough to a handsome house at Great Cumberland Place, a sure sign she was enjoying royal privilege and the near certainty that she was the Prince of Wales's mistress. The prince also cast a warm eye on Jack's progress and shared Jennie's and Cassel's hope that he would eventually become a stockbroker.

There was good news in November, when Jennie learned from Winston that he had found an attractive girlfriend, Pamela Plowden, daughter of a government official in India; a previous romantic involvement had been broken when the young woman left him for a son of the Marquess of Queensberry. Most of his correspondence with Jennie involved his need for money; he wanted to send a pony to England for sale, which she opposed. He also gave advice from Bangalore on how to get out of the Cruikshank situation and sue for fraud. She approved of his expressed desire to run for a seat in parliament when he returned – the expected thrill of Indian service had already dissolved in heat and boredom. And he shared, he told her, his late father's fury at reckless government expenditure on the army in time of prolonged peace.

During the move from Lord Londonderry's estate at Wynyard Park, where she'd been spending some time, to Blenheim for Christmas, Jennie was determined that Winston would find an appointment in Egypt. Disregarding the fact that the sirdar (head of the army of Egypt) Lord Kitchener had never been a fan of Randolph's, and would surely remember Fred Burnaby's disgrace during the Sudanese campaign, she besieged him with requests, but no answer was forthcoming.

Christmas at Blenheim was unpleasant for Jennie; Fanny Marlborough, blowing hot and cold, was distinctly hostile to her, and they didn't speak through the holidays. Sunny and Consuelo had reached the point of an armed truce.

Back in London, Jennie found that Winston had over-drawn his account at Cox's Bank, had issued a cheque knowing it would bounce and had squandered his allowance. She was forced to cover for him to avoid his being prosecuted. Her former disappointment in him returned; she was bitter and felt he should be supporting her as many men of 22 did their mothers, not the other way around. On 5 March 1897, she wrote to him explaining her financial situation: she had an income of £2,700 a year (about £80,000 today), out of which £800 was paid to Winston and Jack, and £410 for house and stable rental. Of the rest, £1,500 went on taxes, servants, food, dress and travelling. But she couldn't have run Great Cumberland Place on those sums; she was obviously concealing income continuing after Randolph's death from Natty Rothschild, Sir Ernest Cassel and the Prince of Wales.

Queen Victoria's Diamond Jubilee that summer kept Jennie in a spin of social activities; she attended the celebrations at St Paul's Cathedral with seemingly all of society. Yet another embarrassing incident occurred in the long list of royal mishaps. So great was the crowd at a Buckingham Palace reception she attended that the Office of Works erected a marquee in the grounds; Jennie's friend, Reginald Brett, later Lord Esher, was in charge, and he soon found he had made a very serious mistake. He hadn't provided relief from the heat in the form of fans or open areas and several women, in the heavy clothes of the time, were in a fainting condition. He called frantically for an attendant to cut holes at each end of the marquee but nobody responded. Then, to general amusement and applause, he took the ceremonial sword he was wearing and slashed away at the canvas. In doing so, he accidentally pricked a prying housemaid, who screamed and ran, paid back for spying on her superiors. In the shredded marquee, the party went on.

On leave in London for the celebrations, Winston after patching up their differences over money joined Jennie, at the Duchess of Devonshire's fancy-dress ball on 2 July 1897, the biggest social event of the season. As mother of the Duke of Manchester, the ghastly German Countess Louise von Alten, who had so ruthlessly married Devonshire while her son was on his deathbed, the duchess was scarcely Jennie's favourite. But how could she miss the biggest social occasion in years?

Jennie, with Winston dressed in a military uniform of no known period, arrived as the eleventh-century Empress Theodora of Byzantium, in an elaborate, embroidered dress copied from a traditional likeness.

The Duke of Devonshire appeared as the Holy Roman Emperor Charles V, the duchess as the Syrian Queen Zenobia; the Prince of Wales was dressed as a Grand Prior of the Order of St John of Jerusalem, and Princess Alexandra as Marguerite de Valois, wife of Henry of Bourbon (an odd choice, since de Valois was no friend of the British). Fanny Ronalds, as the Spirit of Music, wore a headdress of electric light bulbs that threatened to set fire to her hair.

One guest through his odd behaviour stole the show. Daisy, Princess of Pless, daughter of the Prince of Wales's mistress Patsy Cornwallis-West, arrived as Cleopatra with, among her slaves, her brother George, an extremely handsome youth, fair and slight and made for Jennie's bed, his chiselled muscles ready for anyone who could afford him. Black-faced, swathed in blue, hating his make-up and costume, he was visibly restless and impatient; finally, to general amusement, upset by mocking laughter, he fled the ballroom, making a stir in the newspapers that otherwise would have ignored him. Jennie had seen him before, at the Princess of Pless's society wedding in 1892. And soon she would see a good deal more of him.

Christmas for once was fun: she and Consuelo Marlborough prepared a comic masquerade to raise money for restoring St Mary's Church in Woodstock. In a series of *tableaux vivants* reminiscent of Jerome and August Belmont's in the Civil War, she appeared with Consuelo, Sunny, George Curzon, and Albertha Blandford as a waddling Sancho Panza to Lord Chesterfield's Don Quixote.

Jennie appeared in a musical satire as Jubilee June, a reporter in the Labouchère mould, singing an evil ditty ('No subject's too private for me').

In the wake of this happy event, at which she satirically settled a number of scores against old enemies in song and dance, Jennie faced more naggings for money from Winston, who had returned to India. He served bravely on the Northwest Frontier with the Malakand Field Force; he wrote of his experiences in the *Daily Telegraph* and turned them into a book, published the following year.

By early 1898, Jennie's need for money led her to borrow £17,000 on her life insurance, and Winston and Jack had to sign off part of their expected inheritances to make that possible; in return, Jennie signed a document guaranteeing her sons a life income under Randolph's trust.

During the wrangling over terms, and dealing with Winston's nervousness over losing his inheritances, Jennie found a new lover: Caryl John Ramsden, known as 'Beauty' for his slight but sinewy physique and classically handsome face. A 27-year-old Scot, he was a brevet major in the famous Seaforth Highlanders Regiment, noted for their bravery and for spectacularly good-looking men. Back in England after an uncomfortable stint in Malta and Crete, Ramsden was, like Winston, eager for action with Kitchener in Egypt and the Sudan. Now Jennie had a new motive to get Winston into Kitchener's force; she could join Ramsden there.

Jennie had a long-term friend in Mary, Lady Jeune, the society hostess who had entertained the Fourth Party; her husband was the judge who treated Pearl Craigie fairly at the divorce hearing. Jennie pulled strings with the Jeunes and also with such military figures as Sir Evelyn Wood and Sir Ian Hamilton, both of whom she knew through Randolph. It helped that, despite an atrocious editing job by the ever-disastrous Moreton Frewen, Winston's book-length account of the Malakand Field Force, published by Longmans, was very well received, and many felt he could do a similarly fine job on Egypt.

Early in 1898, Jennie decided she couldn't wait for Winston to be appointed by Kitchener, and she took off to join Ramsden in Cairo; while there she pressed Kitchener on the matter of her son; he proved insincerely sympathetic; and untrustworthy. She and Ramsden slept together at Cairo's Continental Hotel and then embarked on a romantic voyage up the Nile; when Ramsden received orders to return to the Sudan, she went to Port Said to catch a ship for England only to learn that her ship had engine trouble and would be in dry dock for several days. She at once left for Cairo, where she had discovered Ramsden was staying before his move.

Jennie found out he was back at the Continental Hotel and burst excitedly into his room only to find him in bed with the wife of Kitchener's aide, Major Robert Pacey Maxwell. She returned, furious, to Port Said.

With his armies of spies, the Prince of Wales learned of the matter quickly. In a term he used often for his mistresses he wrote to her from Cannes as 'Ma Chère Amie', telling her she should have stuck to her 'old friends', namely himself, rather than going on her expedition up the Nile. Jennie replied from London that she was grateful for his sympathy and that, of course, he would have known exactly how she felt since Georgiana, Lady Dudley had just jilted him. Detecting acidity in her tone, the prince responded that he was sorry if his letter of sympathy had proved hurtful and that he had no idea her feelings for Ramsden had been so serious.

Back in London in July, Winston was as anxious to get to Egypt as ever. Jennie swallowed her pride and pleaded with Lord Salisbury, still prime minister, who at last made the longed-for arrangements. Her charm had worked its customary magic. By the end of July, Winston was in the Sudan, replacing a young officer who had died; in this, the prime minister overruled Kitchener, who had not approved the appointment.

In September, Winston was involved in a famous charge against the dervishes in which over 10,000 were said to have been killed. 'It must have been a good massacre,' Jack wrote at the time. Winston gloried in the battle of Omdurman, the flight of the rebel Pasha Abbas Hilmi and the reconquest of Khartoum that had London crowds cheering in the streets. But he received no praise from Kitchener who blamed him for not capturing Hilmi. Winston wrote to Jennie that he couldn't fight back; he commented that he 'might as well throw stones against the rising sun', as oppose that formidable commander.

The Prince of Wales got wind of the setback and wrote to Winston that he was sorry indeed and recommended a life of politics and books. But Winston wasn't ready yet to follow that well-intentioned advice; the thrill of the bugle call, the uniform that flattered his figure, the challenge in taking on swarms of dervishes – he was living the life AEW Mason would portray in 1902 in his immortal *The Four Feathers*; not to be a man of action was to show the white feather of cowardice.

And now, Jennie was involved with the ravishing George Cornwallis-West, first seen at the Devonshires' costume party. He was believed to be the illegitimate son of the Prince of Wales himself.

George's background was as richly colourful and questionable as Jennie could have asked for. William, his father, owned the crumbling but romantic Ruthin Castle in Wales; Lord Lieutenant of Denbighsire, William was the grandson of the Earl de la Warr.

On 8 October 1879, in an act of envy of the upper crust, three society gossips, Adolphus Rosenberg, William Wilfred Head, and Henry Robert Mark, had published in their *Town Talk: A Journal for Society at Large*, that William allowed his wife Patsy ('The bone of his bone and the flesh of his flesh') to exhibit her picture in various degrees of undress next to photographs of naked Zulus and music-hall stars in shop windows for sale, on the theory that Patsy, as mistress of the Prince of Wales, would be worth souveniring. The authors claimed that William had photographed Patsy in a studio hidden behind a house in Eaton Square, where pets were given appropriate names: the collie dog was Collodion, an element in photography, the cat Iodide of Potassium, and the parrot, Camera Polly. On one occasion when her husband was out, Patsy had a youth take her pictures in bed.

William Cornwallis-West sued *Town Talk* for libel and won; the three tattletales served eighteen months in jail.

Soon after that, the Cornwallis-Wests sold off their two daughters: one, as we know, to the Prince of Pless, the other, much later, to the Duke of Westminster, who owned most of London. At their home of Newlands Manor at Lymington in the New Forest, the family had a staff of fifteen, from the butler, Sim, down to the scullery maids, nannies and kitchen hands.

George was a disappointment to his parents; despite his spectacular looks, and the fact that his presumed parent the Prince of Wales acted as his godfather and showered him with gifts, he was clearly not going to amount to very much. The only hope was he might be sold to a rich American. 'I am dross,' he wrote of himself many years later, and looking forward to his final suicide, it was true: he was petulant, spoiled, a gambler and profligate; the Prince of Wales's erstwhile mistress, Daisy, Countess of Warwick, did Jennie no favour when she introduced them at a party.

He was definitely a manic depressive: despite his physique he was not good at games, and at preparatory school he was stretched on a hastily improvised wooden rack and made to eat flies; he tried to kill himself at the age of twelve by swallowing a bottle of ink. He did better at Eton but a heart murmur kept him off the cricket field and he developed a profound homophobia when a fellow student tried to give him a biology lesson through sexual stimulation.

But George was eminently consumable, especially since like Ramsden he served in the army, always, for Jennie, a sexual lure: he was a lieutenant in the 1st Battalion of Scots Guards. Stories of his adventures scarcely proved a dampener: he invaded a maid's bedroom at a hotel claiming he had lost his way; he fell off his horse in a bog; he excelled at the hunt, and would in due course be master of Natty Rothschild's staghounds.

He resembled Kinsky in many ways: he had considerable charm and skill in writing love letters, and he had the colourful job of guarding the Crown jewels in the Tower of London; he also helped guard the Queen when she attended a service at St Paul's Cathedral. Although he was almost exactly Winston's age, and thus young enough to be Jennie's son, he genuinely found her attractive, and at over forty, she was still strikingly beautiful. But neither his parents nor his sisters approved of the relationship; their chief objection was that Jennie was past child-bearing age, so that there would be no direct Cornwallis-West heir, and that, although she was American, she wasn't really rich.

CHAPTER TEN

It was early in 1899, with a new century looming and no real sense of what role she might play in it, that a seriously adrift Jennie decided to start a magazine. She would engage as collaborator Pearl Craigie, who in July of the previous year had appeared with her and the virtuoso Maria Janotha at the Queen's Hall in a performance of Bach's *Concerto in D Minor for Three Pianos* and who shared with her many visits to concerts arranged by Lady de Grey. George Curzon was supportive as always, remaining Randolph's skilled executor and never less than anxious to help; she approached Lord Rosebery, who had been prime minister for a short period in the 1890s, the poet Algernon Swinburne and Cecil Rhodes for their approval, and they gave it.

John Lane of the Bodley Head, who had enjoyed a great success with the notorious magazine *The Yellow Book*, agreed to publish and Lionel Cust of the National Portrait Gallery would supply paintings and comments. The magazine would be quarterly, and Jennie and Pearl would underwrite the first issues against loss. It would combine literature, art and politics in equal measure and would avoid sensationalism – not a strong recipe for sales. It would be up against *Truth*, the *Pall Mall* and the *Strand*, all of which supplied more or less newsy material and a certain amount of gossip, disguised or not.

The name had to be settled: the *Area* and the *International Quarterly* were mentioned as possibilities. Jennie decided on the *Anglo-Saxon*, an extremely ill-advised choice.

A magazine of that name had already started to appear, to favourable attention, after years of planning and heart-breaking struggle by its publisher, the accomplished James Mortimer; its first issue contained pieces by Randolph's old friend Lord Dufferin and Ava; Jennie's friend and fellow clubman-actor Henry Irving; Algernon Swinburne and Joseph Chamberlain. It carried the slogan 'Blood is thicker than water' on the front page and its agenda was identical to Jennie's.

As soon as Jennie learned of it – and all London was talking about it – she should have abandoned her own title and format and sought another approach. Instead, she announced with her customary rashness that she was going right ahead anyway.

Sir George Lewis advised her not to, and Mortimer's lawyers filed suit against her. She pressed on though, using the name the *Anglo-Saxon Review*, thereby assuring the magazine's doom, not to mention its questionable legality, and even announced that 'Blood is thicker than water' would be her motto until forced by threats to abandon it. She dropped the motto and the lawsuit was also dropped.

Her first number appeared on 1 June 1899, from her house at Great Cumberland Place, with contributions by Rosebery, Henry James, Gilbert Parker and Pearl Craigie, writing as John Oliver Hobbes.

Soon after Winston returned from India in April, Fanny Marlborough died suddenly at Grosvenor Square. It cannot be said that Jennie was grief-stricken, and nor were many others. As if she were not irritating enough, the duchess had taken in recent years to travelling by train from London with a cage full of canaries that made passengers' lives a misery. Consuelo Marlborough in particular couldn't stand her and the feeling was mutual.

Winston, who with Jennie's blessing had taken army leave for politics, headed for Oldham to run for the local seat where a member had died, leaving a vacancy. Using his father's notorious oxymoron, he called himself a Tory Democrat, bent, he said in speeches, on improved conditions for the working class and the aged poor. As if she didn't have enough on her hands, Jennie took off in June to support him and appeared with him on the hustings. He lost, but would win in 1900.

Engaged on a romance of his own (with Pamela Plowden), Winston was uneasy about George Cornwallis-West and rendered more so by letters George's father sent him opposing the match with Jennie. Jennie was under a strain, but after the second issue of the *Anglo-Saxon Review*, contributed to by Sir John Gorst, she was in a better mood.

In October, after much preliminary skirmishing, war broke out with the Boers in South Africa. It was a war based, like the Burmese campaign, on greed. Paul Kruger, the Boer leader, surrounded in the Transvaal by British forces, furious that his Dutch farmers might be dispossessed, and protective of his mining and agricultural interests, decided to strike out. Mutual suspicion was at work: Kruger was certain the British, eager for gold and diamonds, wanted to drive him out of the Transvaal, while the British suspected that Kruger wanted to drive them out of South Africa for the same reason. Both were probably right; war came on 12 October.

England had only 25,000 men stationed there, while Kruger had far more – plus the support of Germany in the form of Krupp artillery, and Cruesot guns the French had sent him.

England's youth was spoiling for adventure: war fever gripped London and cheering crowds filled the streets as troops marched off to battle. Winston, as correspondent of the London *Morning Post*, kept Jennie informed of his preparations; George Cornwallis-West reported catching a glimpse of Winston in the street, looking like a dissenting parson, his badly brushed hat worn on the back of his head, his coat and tie awful. With Jennie's blessing, Winston obtained letters of introduction and credit for Cape Town from Alfred Beit, Natty Rothschild's associate in South African gold and diamonds, and his investment partner Friederich Epstein; they gave him the benefit of investment in the Corner House Group, which had made Cecil Rhodes rich.

As Cornwallis-West and Jack, both of whom Jennie wanted to keep at home, joined the colours, the news from South Africa was devastating. Sir Redvers Buller lost battle after battle: Laings Neck, Mafeking, Kimberley – the names rang like death knells in a gloom-filled London. In the midst of the crisis, the *Anglo-Saxon Review* seemed decidedly superfluous; articles on the reasons for Kruger's actions were needed, but instead there was a superficial piece entitled, 'Is South Africa to be English or Dutch?' which stirred no comment, and deserved none. Depressed, with the magazine failing, Jennie had to do something for the war effort, and she did; she adopted several friends' suggestions that she bring a hospital ship to South Africa. With the thought of joining George, Winston and Jack, she was fired up at once.

She turned to America for money. But blinded by egotism and a degree of naivety, she overlooked the fact that America was in support of the Boers and that President McKinley saw the war as an expression of the oppressed against the British Empire. After being turned down by Theodore Roosevelt and Chauncey M Depew among others, she at last found support in Bernard Noel Baker, head of the Atlantic Transport Company of Maryland, who handed her a beaten-up cattle boat named the *Maine*, after the famous ship that had sunk in Havana harbour on 15 February 1898, sparking off the Spanish-American War.

She enlisted friends to raise money: the two Consuelos, Fanny Ronalds, Clarita, Leonie, Lily, and several of Randolph's sisters. William Waldorf Astor refused to help, and Bourke Cockran, assailed by New York friends, could do little. Queen Victoria summoned Jennie to Windsor Castle to give her approval, but then came upsetting news:

Winston, in a gallant exhibition of daring, had been captured by Boers. Soon his escape from a schoolhouse prison would make him world famous, but Jennie would not learn of it until she reached South Africa, which led to a worrying time for her.

Word of support came from Kinsky in St Petersburg, and love letters from George at the battlefront were very cheering. Working with furious energy, Jennie supervised the conversion of the *Maine*, and daringly flew the Stars and Stripes from the masthead when President McKinley had forbidden her to do so, adding the Red Cross flag and the Union Jack for good measure. Then George wrote to her that, evacuated because of sunstroke, he would be coming in the opposite direction; their ships would pass in the night. This must have been a great disappointment to Jennie.

Embarked from London's West India dock on 23 December, 1899, the *Maine* soon ran into fog, and the rest of the voyage was for Jennie something of an ordeal. A relentless six-day gale had her confined to her cabin; furniture, cutlery, plates, glasses, surgical instruments and medicine cupboards crashed onto the decks. When Jennie gave a piano recital at the birth of the 1900s, her stool ran away with her and the piano fell. She didn't arrive in Cape Town until 22 January, where a trim and handsomely uniformed Jack was there to greet her, with news of Winston's escape and recent military success.

Instead of giving aid to the wounded, the *Maine* team was dispatched by the medical authorities to Durban, battered by hurricane and hailstorm. Winston was there to greet his mother and brother, and Jennie and her team of nurses and volunteers worked long hours taking care of the wounded.

Jack was injured and evacuated to the *Maine* shortly afterwards. He had served gallantly with the South African Light Horse and was disappointed he would have to withdraw from combat, at least for a time. But soon he was back in action.

Jennie had an opportunity to see at first hand the wisdom of Randolph's (and now Winston's) attacks in political speeches on the wastefulness and corruption of the British army leaders; the uniforms which were supposed to justify the outrageously increased budgets whipped up irresponsibly (or worse) in Whitehall were a disgrace. The khaki was of the cheapest fabric: coarse wool or cotton, stitched so badly that it tore at the slightest touch, and for her many stricken patients there were no supplies of new clothing, no reserves prepared in Durban. After weeks of battle, the men were depressed, transferred meaninglessly from one field hospital to another, sometimes trouserless or shirtless; if it hadn't been for Jennie's organising skills, there would have been insufficient bandages and splints.

She battled red tape day and night; if a man was ill and needed a special diet, a medical officer had to sign a notice of approval, which could involve a fatal delay; at last, exhausted from the strain, she left the shipboard wards and clinics in her capable team's hands and took off to visit the war front.

With a handful of others, she went by train to Chieveley Camp; disturbingly, two spies were arrested in her carriage and dragged off in handcuffs in the middle of the night.

At Chieveley, she heard guns in the distance; she saw the ragged procession of soldiers and canvas-covered horses through a swarm of flies that invaded her clothes and hair. So far from being nervous, she was characteristically enthralled ('It was a grand and thrilling sight', she wrote in her memoirs). But she wasn't thrilled by the condition of the horses, always her favourite animals; at a farm she saw some 2,000 of them waiting to go to the front line after six weeks crammed in the holds of ships; they were thrust into open trucks in the dusty heat and driven to certain slaughter at the front.

Back in Durban, she joined the excited crowds in celebrating the Boers' defeat and the relief of Ladysmith and she obtained a pass and went with Winston to the reoccupied city. What she saw was appalling: the train was filled with the wounded, the town stank with dead men and horses, and great heaps of spent bullets and shells littered the broken streets. She would never forget the blinding clouds of dust, the flies, the ferocious sun.

Riding on a mule cart she returned to the *Maine* with mementoes: a shell casing from the '4–7' cannon named Lady Randolph Churchill, which had killed many Boers, soft-nosed bullets, bandoliers and a chocolate box stolen from a dead man.

On the voyage home after many weeks away, Jennie went ashore at St Helena to see Napoleon's grave and reflect on the passing of former glories. She returned to London, to find that the newspapers had leaked every detail of British troop movements and that Boer sympathisers had telegraphed word of them to the enemy.

She resumed work on the *Anglo-Saxon Review*, persuading the author Stephen Crane, in letters that survive today, to contribute a short story; she also enlisted the support of George Bernard Shaw and the famous writers Max Beerbohm, Maurice Maeterlinck, Edmund Gosse and George Gissing. In conversation and correspondence she could hold her own with them all. She found time to keep up the activities of the Primrose League, while enjoying her renewed relationship with George Cornwallis-West, who was on injury leave. Winston continued to impress her and everyone with his adventures and dispatches, and she was pleased to note that Jack also served well and bravely. Winston sailed home in good spirits on 3 July 1900, his book *London to Ladysmith* selling well in England and America; Sir Ernest Cassel's investments for him and for Jennie were paying off.

Jennie was not as happy; she suffered from society's opposition to George and especially the idea of his marrying her. The double standard – in which women were allowed to marry men old enough to be their father but should not marry men young enough to be their son – operated against her in full and brutal force. The Prince of Wales's opposition had all the earmarks of jealousy. During Jennie's absence, he had harassed George in interviews.

Leonie, who had kept an eye on George for Jennie's benefit, was assailed with vicious notes from William

Cornwallis-West, talking of an insane infatuation, as Jennie was older than George's mother. That angry parent, in a fit of fury occasioned by his annoyance that Jennie wasn't rich, invented a proposal of marriage George was supposed to have made to another woman.

Jennie swept off her enemies, like wasps from a breakfast table. She wrote to Winston on 24 May that she was moved by George's devotion, and she was practical enough to add that he might be able to help with money in the future. The opposition was unrelenting; when she decided she would visit the Countess of Warwick with George, the Prince of Wales rushed her off alone to Sandringham to be in his house party; the prince was greatly annoyed at her fractious insistence she would marry George. But there was no stopping her: encouraged by Consuelo Manchester, always a wonderful friend, she announced the engagement at last, only for what can only have been a royal intervention to almost upset her plans.

George was informed by his commanding officer Colonel Ian Hamilton that if he married Jennie he would be cashiered out of the regiment. There was no possible cause for such a threat in army regulations; only the prince could have pulled that particular string. Jennie was furious and George went to see Sir Evelyn Wood, adjutant-general of the army, who intervened, but Hamilton was adamant: George must, if he followed his desires, accept dismissal.

Jennie must have known what royal figure was opposing her. She dashed off a letter to Lord Landsdowne, Secretary of War, demanding an explanation. Landsdowne gave her his reassurances, and first Jennie and then George went to see the Prince of Wales at Marlborough House, to plead their cause.

The prince was less than helpful. He suggested George should take six months' leave at half pay – then look for some other job. He did not intervene on George's behalf with the army leaders, but he did finally crumble – he was very much in love now with his mistress Alice Keppel – and at last reluctantly let the marriage go through unopposed.

Late in July, Jennie was back at Oldham with Winston, helping him in his impassioned Conservative campaign ahead of the coming general election in October. She was thrilled when 10,000 people greeted him there with flags flying and drums beating; they returned to London for her wedding to George at St Paul's Church, Knightsbridge, on 28 July 1900.

It was a gala occasion, with George at his handsomest, and Winston smiling gamely (though privately irritated and disapproving, and eager to get back to campaigning in Oldham); Jack was still in South Africa. Jennie's sisters and their husbands were in good spirits; Sunny (who gave the bride away), Georgiana Curzon, the Tweedmouths, Fanny Ronalds, Lady de Grey, Lady Jeune and Albertha were there.

Clarita and Moreton Frewen gave the reception afterwards, where Jennie opened a huge pile of gifts. One gave her pause: it was a Fabergé egg from Kinsky in St Petersburg, accompanied by a black-bordered card as if it were a funeral announcement, with the tactless inscription, 'Always in mourning'. He was still in love with her and always would be. Still angry, the Cornwallis-West parents stayed away.

Her honeymoon with the best-looking man in England took place variously at Lord Saye and Seal's Broughton Castle, at Daisy's palace of Pless in Germany, and at the Tweedmouths' in Scotland. Always a workaholic, Jennie took with her a pile of manuscripts, proofs, budgets and bills for the *Anglo-Saxon Review*, strewing them over beds where she and her husband made love. She never stopped supporting Winston at Oldham, or Jack in South Africa, with words of loving encouragement. Jennie was back in England in time to help Winston win his seat; Lord Salisbury was among the first to congratulate him.

She also returned to very sad news. Jennie's old friend, Sir Arthur Sullivan, whose first nights she had almost never missed when in England, was fatally ill and Fanny Ronalds, still his devoted lover, was devastated. The newlyweds visited the dying man at his flat at Queen's Mansions, and messages came from the royal family. On 21 November, seeing that he was losing his fight for life, Sir Thomas Barlow, the royal physician, summoned Fanny Ronalds in a rainstorm; she was unable to find a hansom cab and when she arrived on 22 November, she was too late.

With Jennie's blessing, Winston now embarked on an American lecture tour in December, marred by quarrels with his manager, Major James B Pond. At Christmas, she received a sly note from George Curzon, Viceroy of India, who wrote to her as 'My Dear Lady' ('I cannot identify you as Mrs West – Dear Mrs West, no, that will never do'). And he blamed her cancellation of a planned Indian visit on a 'too luxurious husband', another underhand dig. In addition, he sent her a silver Burmese bowl – a reminder of the inglorious matter in her past.

Winston wrote from Toronto in a mood of equal spite, though it was not directed at his mother. On New Year's Day, he spoke of George's parents netting the unfortunate but wealthy Duke of Westminster, trapping him into marrying their daughter, George's younger sister ('He doesn't love her, really').

On 16 January, Winston wrote to George. For Winston, military service remained, and would always remain, thrilling; but Jennie clearly had changed his mind about George's army career and she didn't want George risking his life in arms abroad; Winston sent a mendacious series of comments on army life that utterly contradicted his actual feelings. Perhaps under Jennie's influence, he said that military service was sheer drudgery, a waste of time, the rewards barren unless killing was considered a reward, and that George should forget all about his plans and instead become a civil engineer. The letter seemed to be fatal in its effect. Life in uniform would have been the perfect future for George; he could have risen through the ranks to a high position and he wouldn't have suffered from the sense of inferiority, reduced as he was to insignificant jobs in industry, that undermined the rest of his life and finally caused him to end it.

When Queen Victoria died in January 1901, the entire Marlborough clan accompanied Jennie and George for a ceremony of mourning at Blenheim; everyone was in black, the ladies in heavy veils, as they took the train to Windsor for services at St George's Chapel.

Few who attended the occasion would forget the array of crowned heads, the ranks of aristocrats, the thunder of guns, the funerary music, and the temporary alliances of mortal enemies. Even Albertha Blandford managed to get through the ceremony without saying anything stupid, but Sunny Marlborough was at his worst. Noticing the number of famous men, including royal figures, who cast a lustful glance at his wife, he snapped, 'When I die, you won't be a widow for very long!' The chorus of hushes can easily be imagined.

For Jennie and all those she knew, six months of mourning were required; when she wore a pair of white gloves on one occasion, her hostess sternly handed her a black pair. She escaped more than once to Paris, where she could wear any clothes she wanted, but when she visited George's Ruthin Castle in Wales (his parents were conspicuous by their absence), she found the household in black from housekeeper to kitchen hands.

At least she could ride there; the stables were excellent and the family was known locally as the Wild West Show. Indoors, matters were less pleasing: a tour of the ancient torture chamber and dungeon, or exploring the musty, cobwebbed wine cellar, entirely lacked appeal.

In London, Jennie approvingly attended Winston's maiden speech as member for Oldham in the House of Commons, and then took off with George on the usual freeloading rounds of country houses, as always useful in saving money.

She especially enjoyed Alfred de Rothschild's house at Halton. It offered flamboyant delights, redolent of Alfred's homosexual tastes: Sir Algernon West wrote of 'an exaggerated nightmare of gorgeousness' and Gladstone's secretary Edward Hamilton added his own comment: 'sadly overdone . . . all gilt and gold'.

Hundreds of paintings, sixty Sèvres vases, an Indian pavilion full of hangings, rich carpets and incense from braziers, all made an unforgettable picture of reckless self-indulgence. Rothschild conducted his own orchestra in the ballroom, in his own compositions, originally written for piano. He offered a private circus, with horses, dogs, hens and cockerels prancing to his whip around a sawdust ring as he strutted about in midnight-blue coat and breeches, with pale lavender gloves. When somebody suggested all he lacked was a golf course in the grounds, he installed one. When George Cornwallis-West said he enjoyed a cigar, 300 arrived in a humidor.

Sir Ernest Cassel could easily have arranged for George a meaningless directorship in the City of London, with pay for doing nothing; he was descended from aristocracy and such positions were commonplace if one had influence. Instead, Cassel condescendingly fixed up the unhappy young man with a dim position in Scotland, as a kind of 'unpaid plumber' (George's description) in overalls. He was a semi-glorified clerk with the Potteries Electric Traction Company, which kept him in Glasgow all week, followed by a long train journey to spend the weekends with Jennie. By contrast, Cassel set up Jack, who had left the army, with a post at a London stockbrokers, learning the business from the ground up; but at least he was paid a decent salary. The contrast was cruel and vicious.

Jennie was struggling with the *Anglo-Saxon Review*; John Lane of the Bodley Head had withdrawn his support and she had to publish it on her own; this put a strain on her finances and Winston and Jack had to forego their allowances for a time.

And now, there was the matter of the Prince of Wales's elevation to the throne. The coronation was delayed by his serious illness and did not occur until August 1902, at Westminster Abbey in record heat, with a spectacular throng led by the greatest figures of England; the Duke of Norfolk was in charge.

Vulgarly humorous, the new King played a practical joke on the world. He placed in the royal box (known thereafter as the Loose Box) all of the women who were, or were understood to be, his past and present mistresses. Jennie found herself placed with Patsy Cornwallis-West, still her arch-enemy, and with Alice Keppel, Daisy Warwick, Lillie Langtry, Lady Dudley, Hortense Schneider, the Princesse de Sagan and the Duchesse de Mouchy.

Jennie stole the show by wearing a simple white dress with almost no jewellery while her Loose Box companions were festooned like Christmas trees. In the body of the audience, the most dazzling woman present was Consuelo Manchester, with necklace and bracelets of Burmese rubies, South African diamonds and Brazilian emeralds.

The Archbishop of Canterbury was enfeebled and almost blind from old age; he forgot half the words of the Prayer of Atonement and in trying to read it, lost his glasses; he almost dropped the Coronation ring; he trembled so violently as he tried to fix it on the royal finger the monarch had to put it on himself. He fainted and had to be helped to his chair of office; a second time the King lifted him bodily and planted him in his place. He recovered, then almost put the crown on back to front; the monarch fixed it correctly, only to stumble as the lights went out. Somebody yelled out to put them on and titters were heard. Then the electric system flooded the nave so brightly that many put their hands to their faces.

After the King's speech, the archbishop almost collapsed again; supported by bishops, he managed to get through the Communion. There was a commotion outside: arriving very late, Lord Pelham Clinton's coach collided with another and there was a mêlée of spilled passengers and rearing horses; as the crowd left, it was noted that Lady Stafford's coronet sat sideways on her head. Informed of this, she laughed and continued on her way.

Even with Cassel's support, the new King's gambling and gifts to mistresses had left him in very bad financial straits. A dampener followed: several of the Crown jewels at the

Tower of London were sold by Carrington's of Regent Street, and paste substitutes were put in their place; an attempt was made to sell Osborne House, Victoria's favourite residence, to the government; the government refused it and it had to be given as a bequest to the nation.

That autumn, Sir Ernest Cassel, continuing the British financial and political ownership of Egypt, the dominance that Randolph had fought against for so long, completed his personally financed Aswan Dam, designed to bring fertility to the Nile valley and, through increase in cotton production, prosperity to the North of England and Midlands textile industry that owed so much to Winston's representations. Winston was at the opening of the Aswan Dam late that year, a gala occasion to which neither Jennie nor George was invited.

Cassel issued new Egyptian bonds, and so did Natty Rothschild and while there is no record of Jennie benefiting from them, she probably did. George was frustrated every day: he managed to persuade his boss, who had engaged him to help in the building of the Glasgow Municipal Power Station, to let him at least have an honorary place on the board of directors. But the post meant nothing, and paid him no more than a pittance. Sadly, he made up stories which have found their way into various books, the most absurd of which was that, transferred to the company's offices at Stoke-on-Trent, he was at one stage late for work; unable to find transportation, he chartered a special train to get him to town. No such incident has been documented. He was sadly mendacious and adrift: a lost male beauty in distress.

On the political front, 1903 saw Jennie increasingly concerned that Winston was in conflict, as Randolph had been, with the Conservatives, who he felt were worthless. Like his late father he was at heart a Liberal, fighting for free trade with Europe.

And he constantly hammered away at military and naval extravagance and in support of free food for the poor.

Jennie agreed with his views, but she can only have been concerned that they would imperil, or even destroy, his political career as they had Randolph's.

Prime Minister Arthur Balfour, in office since July 1902 when Salisbury had resigned, had not been her favourite since his skittish relationship with the Fourth Party; and his presidency of the Society of Psychical Research can only have struck her – still a convinced agnostic – as harebrained. Weak, vacillating and over-civilised, he was definitely not her idea of a great man; yet surely, to sustain his career, Winston must give him support. But Winston never ceased to carry on his father's onslaught on fogeydom, the grey-haired ghost battalion of the older Conservatives.

On 24 October 1903, Winston put his cards on the table, writing to his friend Lord Hugh Cecil, 'I am an English Liberal. I hate the Tory party, their men, their words, their deeds.' It was as if Randolph had spoken; yet he still made the mistake his father had, a mistake it seems that Jennie shared: he wanted to fight the party from the inside, not from across the House of Commons. It was a futile pursuit at best.

In April 1904, Jennie sought relief from her son's political conflicts in music: her former rival Lady de Grey had launched, with the impresario Henry Higgins, a series of Wagner performances at Covent Garden, including a full-scale Ring Cycle. Much as she enjoyed the composer's work, Jennie found the experience difficult: she had to arrive at the theatre in the early afternoon, sit through hours of performance, then take a break for dinner and start all over again. When Jennie published her book *Small Talks on Big Subjects* some years later, she described the discomfort in those terms.

Pearl Craigie was very much in her life, writing from India in a gush that seemed to go beyond normal friendship. One note reads, 'I have wished for you every moment since I came out'; another, 'I missed you every second'. She had been busy writing a novel, *The Vineyard*, published in 1904, filled with repressed desire for the heroine, Jennie Sussex, whose beauty and charm she dwells on in every page.

Sussex is radiant with health and love of life; she plays the piano and sings; she enjoys the works of Swinburne, Keats, Ruskin and Thackeray. What could be more accurate a description of the real Jennie than this?

> The music burning in her heart like wine was inaudible; the wonder at the world, the desire for love, the passionate fear of disillusion, the reluctance to hear all that could be heard lest she should hear too much – these were her own secrets, never to be told.

Gerald Federan, with whom Jennie Sussex falls in love, is a combination of George and Kinsky in equal parts: gorgeous, he 'filled incomparably the romantic ideal'. Gerald, like Kinsky, wins steeplechases, with Jennie in the audience; he is 'the best rider in the country'. Like George, he has served in the army in South Africa. In one scene there is an exact parallel with Jennie's reckless ride at Blenheim when nine months pregnant. ('Drive on! Drive on! Don't let these people pass us!')

Like the original Jennie, Sussex carries a tiny mirror on a belt's gold chain, consulting it rather too often; her swinging walk, reckless curiosity, feathered hats and dangerously high-heeled shoes complete an accurate word picture.

The author shows her heroine as utterly dependent on a young and muscular male body as the very basis of life. Sussex's hunger for Gerald Federan overcomes her disappointment at his failed business ventures (à la George):

> The woman without human love sees no happiness for herself in heaven and no agony to fear in hell ... she belongs to the suffering, incomprehensible sex who are eternally distracted between the loneliness of the body and the loneliness of soul ...

Nothing could better illustrate Jennie's passion for George than this:

> It was Federan's love of pleasure that had been the cause of all his troubles and her own: because she had loved pleasure herself, and with pleasure all that was beautiful, rare, moving and, subtle and luxurious, she had been drawn to him irresistibly.

The words might equally have applied to her desire for Kinsky, and for Delacour, Ramsden, Wolverton and Randolph.

Throughout this extraordinary and forgotten biographical novel, there is an unmistakable undercurrent of love for the heroine, and a painful unease in drawing the men who love her. In dwelling on passion to the degree that she does, Craigie reveals her own; her disguise as 'John Oliver Hobbes' doesn't work; and this was long past the age when a woman writer had to pretend to be a man.

As well as dealing with inflammatory fiction, Jennie had to face the long-expected crisis in Winston's political career. On 29 March 1904, furious at the concealment of secrets from the public, he called in the Commons for the people's 'right to know', his most American – and therefore Jennie-inspired statement – to date.

Furious, Balfour and his cabinet walked out, followed by all except twelve Conservative members; Winston boldly continued his speech, and the Liberals cheered him to the echo. On 31 May he crossed the House and, to Jennie's approval and an ecstatic response from those same Liberal members, he became one of them. His long Randolphian campaign against the irregularities in armed forces' procurements worked; the Committee of Imperial Defence condemned unsparingly all War Office methods in the Boer War. He and Jennie rejoiced in the fact that Balfour's pro-tariff policy reduced support for the government, while free trade with France, following an entente cordiale, was very much approved. By 1905, Arthur Balfour was forced to resign.

That same year, Jennie decided to sell her long lease on Great Cumberland Place and move to the country. She and

George, who had resigned his Scottish job and was beginning to speculate in the city, picked up an attractive house,
Salisbury Hall, near St Albans, a medium-sized Stuart
manor with a moat and drawbridge. No sooner had they
moved in and Jennie had decorated the rooms with her
customary skill, than George announced he had seen the
ghost of Nell Gwyn, mistress of Charles II, who had once
lived there, standing on the stairs; he brought in a spiritualist medium to confirm that Gwynn haunted the house.

Jennie had no time for such foolishness, nor for George's
frequent séances, though at one of them the table rapped
out the name of a future Derby winner and proved by
chance to be correct.

When the couple visited Versailles, George, no doubt
influenced by the famous turn of the century story of two
schoolteachers who claimed they had been transported back
to the time of Marie Antoinette at Fontainebleau, told
Jennie he recognised a path and statue from his previous
incarnation as Antoinette's courtier.

In addition to such nonsense, Jennie had to put up with
George's Kinsky-like practical jokes. When they visited
Ireland, he stole his host's dress clothes on that same man's
wedding day; on a visit to Ruthin Castle, he posed as a
Montana tycoon, offering his parents' guests a business deal
in a disguise of black wig, moustache and monocle so
perfect they didn't recognise him.

Jennie's marriage was going sour; she wearied not just of
the spiritualism, but of endless rounds of weekend parties,
golf, lawn tennis, the marriage market – and George's
business ineptitudes. She barely struggled through visits to
her sister-in-law the Princess of Pless's Castle Fürstenstein in
Germany, with paper chases in the woods, spins in automo-
biles, fancy-dress balls, partridge shoots, fishing trips, golf
and croquet. She was over fifty, and growing bored and
heavy.

Needing money, she embarked on a memoir, which she
rudely called *Reminiscences of Lady Randolph Churchill*,
not the least because it would sell better, but perhaps as a

deliberate slight to George. It is a very strange book, published successfully by Edward Arnold, and well received by critics. Virtually ignoring her sons, it hides all the pain of the final days of Randolph, the description of that last, ill-fated world tour more suitable for a bland book of travel than the record of a hellish experience. She invents a childhood spent in Trieste – she never visited it and was born after her father had ended his diplomatic period there. She omits any record of human feelings, her marriages, and her political convictions. The only passages in which the book comes alive are in those that deal with her activities in the Boer War, with vivid descriptions of her experiences in South Africa.

Following the death from cancer of Randolph's sister Fanny, Jennie had befriended the bereaved widower Lord Tweedmouth more than ever; she visited him at his Scottish estate, always her favourite retreat when Randolph was alive, as often as possible. *The Times* started a campaign against Tweedmouth in his role as First Lord of the Admiralty and on 1 April 1908 it accused him of treason: of sharing without authorisation classified information on the fleet with the ever-threatening German Emperor Wilhelm II, who already had plans for the conquest of Europe.

In one letter, Tweedmouth wrote that Lord Esher, King Edward's trusted friend and comptroller of the royal household, who had taken exception to certain of Tweedmouth's actions, 'would be better occupied with the drainpipes at Windsor Castle than with meddling in Naval policy'. The letter was published in the press on 1 April (the same day as *The Times*' damaging accusation); dismissed by some as an April Fool's joke, it was in fact the ruin of Tweedmouth's career. Forced to resign, he became insane from the stress and there was nothing Jennie or anyone else could do to help him.

He did, however, introduce Jack, who was doing very well in the city with both Cassel and Rothschild in stock and bond trading (much of it à la Jerome in American railroads), to the pretty young Gwendeline Theresa Mary, daughter of the 8th Earl of Abingdon; she was John Delacour's cousin by marriage and the niece of Lord Bertie of Thame, the pretentious ambassador to France, that same Bertie who had introduced Jennie to Randolph at Cowes in 1873. Goonie, as everyone called Gwendeline, adored Jennie, and the feeling was mutual; she was enchanting, sweet and pretty, but she had a very peculiar family for Jennie to get used to.

Her father the earl changed houses with alarming frequency, making it almost impossible to know where he could be found at any given time; determined to leave no money to his family, he embarked on a futile attempt to spend all he had. He would make his house guests stand all through breakfast, eating porridge with salt instead of sugar while looking, on his instructions, out of the window. His wife was a manic collector, cramming every inch of her successive houses with bric-a-brac from India, and forever planting rose gardens, stripping the flowers and strewing the petals all over the houses in bronze bowls. She hated to spill or lose even a drop of milk; when the milk bottles were almost empty she saved the last drops and combined them to make cheese in bags, hung from the kitchen ceiling.

Jack embarked, no doubt to Jennie's delight, on a courtship of Goonie straight out of the pages of Sir Walter Scott. When the Abingdons were briefly in residence at Whytham Abbey, seven miles from Blenheim, he rode on horseback like a knight on a charger to see her every day. Sunny, the Duke of Marlborough, did not approve of the match, nor did his mother Albertha or his aunts and uncles. As for the Abingdons, they were upset; of ancient heritage, they considered the Churchills beneath them socially, and they harped on the Marlborough family motto, 'Faithful But Unfortunate', as a harbinger of doom.

If the Earl of Abingdon presented a threat for the future, then so did Sir Henry Hozier, 'father' of Winston's new romantic interest Clementine, daughter of Jennie's friend Blanche. He had met her socially on several occasions, most notably at Salisbury Hall, where Jennie introduced them formally for the first time. It was bad enough that Clementine, enchantingly beautiful and intelligent, was illegitimate (Jennie was one of the handful who knew she was Bay Middleton's daughter). But it was worse that Sir Henry might in a loose moment reveal to the press that she wasn't his child. He had struck an ominous note by omitting any mention of her or his wife in his personally corrected entry in *Who's Who*; and perhaps some gossip columnist would notice that. But Jennie, anxious to see both her sons married, and as bold as ever in defying every risk, strongly encouraged the match. Clementine didn't object to Winston's Randolphian attacks on the stuffed shirts of the Conservatives: a Liberal at heart, she already had a strong desire for the cut and thrust of politics.

Jack was married first, to Goonie, at St Aloysius Church, Oxford on 5 August 1908, with Winston as best man. Very few society figures came; Jack carried no weight in social circles.

Sunny Marlborough, separated from Consuelo following the collapse of their marriage, was there, making it impossible for Consuelo to come. The Marlborough clan also turned up, and others present with Jennie and George were Lady de Grey, Lewis Harcourt and Lady Jeune, now Lady St Helier, Sir Ernest Cassel and the Natty Rothschilds. Of all the gifts, Jennie's and George's was the most extravagant: a sapphire and diamond tiara. By contrast, the bride's mother sent a lace dressing bag and Sunny a Worcestershire tea service he hadn't bought but had extracted from the Blenheim china storeroom. Moreton and Clarita Frewen excelled everyone in stinginess: they sent a toast rack, a lampshade and an umbrella handle.

Jennie and George left after the ceremony for Salisbury Hall, but Winston and his private secretary Edward Marsh stayed with Jennie's cousins Frederick and Henry Guest at Burley-on-the-Hill near Oakham. At one o'clock in the morning of 6 August, a maid was lighting up a stove in the kitchen when the flue, with its long accretion of animal grease, caught fire, and within minutes the house was ablaze.

Winston was in his element. He immediately took charge, pushing his hosts aside, as he telephoned the local fire brigade, grabbed two marble busts, one under each arm, stuffed his Board of Trade dispatch box into Edward Marsh's hands, ordered him to pick up every official document in the room, and raced downstairs just seconds before the roof fell in. Then he berated Marsh for dropping the Board papers.

The moment the fire brigade arrived, Winston became their resented leader, ordering the placement and use of hoses, overriding the appropriate chief. His efforts were useless, though; the house was lost. Glowing with excitement, he scarcely cared about that or noticed the annoyance he had caused; his hosts were devastated, as priceless paintings, sculptures and the letters of Oliver Cromwell were destroyed in the blaze. On that same night, Henry Labouchère's home at Horsham was also destroyed by fire.

On 11 August, in a garden temple at Blenheim, Winston proposed marriage to Clementine Hozier and was accepted. The ceremony at St Margaret's Church in London on 12 September 1908 was spectacular; Winston, like his mother, was world famous, and the streets were choked with traffic. Thousands stood for hours to catch a glimpse of the groom and his mother; in a typical touch, Jennie engaged the famous Pearly Kings and Queens, the costermongers in their shiny rows of mother-of-pearl buttons, to sing and dance to keep the crowd in the very best of moods.

She worked for endless hours to fill the church with her favourite white lilies and chrysanthemums, and she even had palm trees, brought from Cornwall and Torquay, framing the nave; smilax and maidenhair decorated the choir stalls and the pews and, with the aid of Lady de Grey and the impresario Henry Higgins, she had a band play the overture from Wagner's *Tannhäuser* she had first heard at the de Grey/Richter concerts at the Queen's Hall.

Sunny stayed home so that Consuelo could come and Lily was also there; also, unavoidably, Albertha. The guest list dazzled: Sir Ernest Cassel, Natty Rothschild, Lady St

Helier, Fanny Ronalds, Chancellor of the Exchequer David Lloyd George, the German Ambassador (and Kinsky's brother-in-law) Count Wolff-Metternich, and the American Ambassador, Whitelaw Reid. The best man was Winston's friend Lord Hugh Cecil, while Sir Henry Hozier smilingly gave his 'daughter' away.

The press coverage was considerable. The magazine *Current Literature* lied gallantly that Jennie looked two years younger than the bride. The reception afterwards was at Lady St Helier's; Jennie left early to supervise work on Winston's house in Bolton Street to make sure it was spick and span for the couple's return from their honeymoon.

The wedding gifts, opened at Lady St Helier's, were parsimonious: the Prince of Wales, future King George V, sent a walking stick; Jennie had to club in with friends to come up with another tiara; Prime Minister Herbert Asquith sent a set of Jane Austen's works; there were far too many inkstands for the author husband, dozens of pairs of cufflinks, and silver spoons. But Winston splurged on a necklace of Burmese rubies for his bride.

In April 1909, it was announced in the press that Kinsky's wife had died in Vienna. Jennie at once sent a note of sympathy, and despite a deluge of equally warm letters he, still in love, responded with his usual lack of tact: he referred to the 'peace and pluck' Jennie had left him as 'the last gift of love'.

Deprived as she saw it of her two sons, unhappy in her marriage to a fading Adonis who gambled his money away on bad business and at the card table, not satisfied with writing articles on dress codes and society manners for popular magazines, such as the *Century* (her own magazine was now defunct), Jennie decided to become a playwright.

And she made another decision: she would have one of the reigning stars of the London stage appear in her play, the man-eating Mrs Patrick Campbell, for whom she would write the principal role of Fabia Sumner.

Ellen Terry's only serious rival as a West End diva, Mrs Pat was tempestuous, sharp-witted and nobody's fool; too frank and outspokenly honest for her own good, she had never learned the devious craft of flattery. She was in appearance very much like Jennie herself: dark, gypsyish, full-blown in a style that today would be considered overweight. Indeed in 1909 she, like Jennie, was beginning to billow alarmingly. Her strange relationship with George Bernard Shaw was the talk of London; it was presumed that his failure to consummate their romantic involvement was due to impotence, as his wife Charlotte and he had never had intercourse. Like the novelist Henry James, Shaw was a brilliant eunuch in the brothel that was London society.

His Borrowed Plumes, the society melodrama Jennie wrote as a vehicle for Mrs Pat, was the story of the glamorous Fabia, a novelist who marries the Delacour-like Major Percival Sumner. Angela Cranfield, an unscrupulous rival for the major's affections, steals Fabia's new play and gives it to him as her own; he then reveals at the first night that it had been stolen.

The nonsense at least provided her a starring part and at early rehearsals Mrs Pat made a meal of it. And it gave Jennie an opportunity to get rid of George; by making him the dramaturge, she could hurl him in real life into Mrs Pat's bed.

It can only have been with her blessing that George, now boring to her, his charms used up (he was as tired of her as well), spent night after night at Mrs Pat's house, allegedly working on matters of dramatic construction, dialogue, exits, entrances and blockings, about which he knew nothing. Seeing before her a pale-copper Apollo, Mrs Pat, always voracious for the male body, wasted no time in unveiling her new prize. For years she would call him her Golden Boy.

As for George, he had to deal with a rival: George Bernard Shaw, who offered Mrs Pat stage vehicles, brilliant conversation and highly literary love letters – scarcely competition for a bedroom bombshell who made her feel ten years younger.

As a disembodied intellectual, Shaw could hardly call George out for fisticuffs or an (illegal) duel at dawn; he pleaded his cause with all his matchless eloquence, but what could he do against a male beauty on the make?

His Borrowed Plumes opened at Hicks Theatre (later, the Globe) on Shaftesbury Avenue on 6 July 1909, for a 'limited run', caused by poor advance sales. Jennie had spent far too much on costumes and sets, and far too little time on necessary rewrites and hiring a good director; in the end she and Mrs Pat essentially directed the play. She insisted foolishly that every woman in the audience wore a hat; they would have worn one anyway in 1909. As a result, several offended ladies wore hats so enormous that no one could see around them.

Friends came loyally to the opening night: Lady de Grey, Fanny Ronalds, and all the others, including the brilliant Margot Asquith, wife of the prime minister, and her daughter-in-law Cynthia. It didn't help; the play was a disaster. But it achieved one of its aims: to rid Jennie of her husband. In July 1910 she would write to his mother Patsy, 'George can have his freedom if he wants it – to marry Mrs Patrick Campbell or anyone else he thinks would make him happy.'

He didn't make Mrs Pat happy. Additionally, on a trip to New York, he seduced her daughter, and he took Mrs Pat's money and squandered it; she soon would have cause to regret her gilded plaything. But for the moment she was happy from sexual satisfaction and blinded to the possibilities of the future.

And so Jennie was alone again; she had written in a premonitory mood in *His Borrowed Plumes*:

What is love without passion? A garden without flowers, a hat without feathers, tobogganing without snow.

On 31 May 1909 Jack and Gwendeline Churchill had a boy, John Junior, and on 9 August Winston and Clementine had a girl, Diana.

Jennie had little rapport with Jack now that he was grown. The one thing mother and son had in common was a love of Wagner. Jack had no interest in literature; his only reading was AEW Mason's *The Four Feathers* and *The Times*. He was, however, in touch with Jennie on financial matters, as her broker; he invested for her when he could, and he was witty and charming, as his memoirs would one day show.

The forces of social change were fierce. Winston and David Lloyd George were among those Liberals who saw in the future a more democratic approach to working-class problems, so evident in Randolph's attempts to introduce reform on a Conservative ticket, but far more operable on a Liberal agenda. Jennie can't have failed to notice the ironical contrast between Winston's proselytising for the underprivileged and his lavish weekends at Blenheim, not to mention his and Jack's dependence on the capitalists Rothschild and Cassel. As always, friends in the House of Lords crushed the more serious efforts at reform; when Lloyd George tried to increase income tax to over a shilling in the pound (more than 5 per cent), to introduce new inheritance taxes, and to tax land and acquisitions, the Marlboroughs and her other relatives neared hysteria.

On 19 November 1909, Jennie's dear friend Consuelo, Dowager Duchess of Manchester, died of a heart attack following a year of agonising cancer. In deep mourning, Jennie attended the funeral service at the Manchester family house at Huntingdonshire, Kimbolton, and the memorial service later that night at the Chapel Royal, St James's Place, London, in the company of the Prince and Princess of Wales. There can be no calculating Jennie's grief for a wonderful fellow American whom she had known since her schooldays.

On 30 November the House of Lords rejected Lloyd George's 'People's Budget' and a national crisis blew up: fearing for the safety of the throne, the King intervened and asked the former premier Lord Rosebery to support the Budget in the House of Lords, but it was too late. Prime Minister Asquith, with Winston's support, declared the Lords' action unconstitutional, saying that only the

Commons could decide on legislation and on finances. When Winston, backed by Jennie, denounced the Lords' action, he was snubbed socially. Accompanied by acid throwings, stormy public meetings and upheavals all over the country, the Liberals were returned at the next election, but with a reduced majority; for Jennie, Winston and all their family, 1909 had been a stormy, exhausting year.

And then, Winston took up the most controversial cabinet post available. To Jennie's delight, he became home secretary, with (among other things) powers of life and death over condemned criminals. While maintaining his reformist attitude to the working classes, he took a strong line against insurrections in the form of mass meetings and strikes.

Jennie hadn't forgotten her experiences at Dublin Castle, seeing the conditions of prisoners there and she was deeply interested in prison reform. On 21 February 1910, she was at the first night of John Galsworthy's play *Justice* at the Duke of York's Theatre; concerned that Winston should use his new post to improve jails in England, she watched the drama with very intense interest.

The first act opens in a lawyer's office in London; a young clerk, Felder, is accused of embezzling funds, money he needed to send an unhappily married woman he knows abroad.

Felder is found guilty and goes to prison. Galsworthy attacks religion when he has a parson tell the accused that his 'peculiar eyes' prove he is not Church of England. In a powerful scene, played daringly without dialogue, Felder is shown in solitary confinement; making buttonholes in shirts, he starts at the slightest sound. Then, in a shocking effect, the dimly lit cell explodes in a sudden blaze of electric light and it is clear that sleep will be impossible.

In the final scene Felder, free now, is a shadow of himself: after two years in solitary confinement he is pale, skeletal, defeated. His firm is prepared to take him back, but a police sergeant arrests him because he has failed to report to his parole officer. He throws himself from the window to his death.

In an era of teacup-and-tinsel comedies and purple society melodramas, *Justice* was a considerable shock. When the final curtain came down, the stunned audience was silent for several minutes before the cheering began; Galsworthy had fled the theatre, certain the play was a flop. Jennie saw it for what it was: written at white heat in six weeks, on trains all over England, it was the author's heartfelt plea against long terms of solitary confinement; it was a nervous, jarring masterpiece. She joined the crowd in cheering until midnight.

Wasting no time, she telephoned Winston that night, telling him to see the play at once; he did, and was impressed. Not content with that, she gave a dinner party for the Galsworthys and invited Winston to it, to make sure her wishes were carried out. Galsworthy was grateful to her for the rest of his life; it was one of her finest hours. Winston in the Commons demanded better conditions for forgers and embezzlers and shorter periods of solitary confinement; on Jennie's advice, he called for lectures and musical performances in prisons. Although he was out of office before legislation could go through, under Jennie's influence, Winston set the path for reforms that continued for over half a century.

In May 1910, Jennie shared the grief of millions at news of the death of her beloved Edward VII. Whether or not she had been his mistress as Prince of Wales, she was deeply fond of him, and may well have believed he was in love with her, so intense was his jealousy and anger when she married George Cornwallis-West; certainly, though, there is no evidence to support the much-published theory that he was George's father.

Through Cassel, he had done his best to sustain Jennie financially, and he had been an impassioned and loyal friend to Randolph after their initial disagreements leading to Churchill's exile; he was, with all his vulgarity, his promiscuity, his gourmandism, and his love of luxury and splendour, the most human and accessible of monarchs, the very essence of life itself. Even if he failed to understand homosexuality, he had protected his son the Duke of Clarence, and Lord Arthur Somerset; and when he was sued for libel, he, unlike any other royal figure, didn't seek royal privilege and actually appeared in court like an ordinary mortal. If she wasn't in love with him, and she may have been, Jennie certainly adored this man; she would have no such feeling for his son and dull, correct successor King George V, or he for her.

With her lifelong interest in crime, Jennie was fascinated by the famous Hawley Harvey Crippen case of 1910–11. My grandmother, Amy LePlastrier Webb, told me she saw Jennie at the trial day after day, eyes moving fascinatedly between judge, jury and the accused.

Crippen, an American doctor, had killed his wife, the former music-hall singer Belle Elmore, with an overdose of hyoscine, a sexual suppressant, when her bedroom demands had become excessive; he had cut up her body and placed it in his cellar. He fled to America with his mistress, Ethel le Neve, disguised as his son; passengers noted the 'boy' had wide hips, a moustache that blew off in the wind, and that father and son were locked in a passionate embrace when they thought nobody was looking.

Arrested on arrival, the pair were brought back to London; the trial became the sensation of the hour, and Winston was informed of all the evidence. Le Neve was acquitted; Crippen was found guilty and sentenced to be hanged.

The public was outraged. Thousands believed that Crippen had killed his wife by accident, and that at worst he was guilty of manslaughter. It would be in character for Jennie if she had sought mercy for the prisoner, and it is likely that she did; few were left untouched by Crippen's deep love for le Neve, and his concern throughout the trial that she would be found not guilty. Thirty thousand people signed a request for a reprieve; Winston's desk at the Home Office was flooded, and his telephone rang day and night.

It was a painful matter for a man of 35 with no legal background and he had to spend long hours weighing the evidence. In the end, he had no alternative but to uphold the jury's verdict: Crippen's hanging would take place.

He was unpopular as a result, and on 22 November, while the scaffold was being erected, and Crippen was handing over a suit of clothes to a representative of Madame Tussaud's Wax Museum, an angry crowd besieged Winston's house. This was, though, unrelated to the case: the rioters were not Crippen's supporters, but suffragettes, furious at Winston's fight against votes for women; they broke his windows with bottles and stones.

If police hadn't arrived in time, they would have invaded the house; they had already struck the prime minister over the head as he entered the House of Commons, and they had assailed Lewis Harcourt, Secretary of State for the Colonies. The leader of the gang, Emmeline Pankhurst, and her cohorts were thrown into jail. Winston celebrated his escape, and showed his pleasure at his decision on Crippen, by throwing a dinner party for friends the following night.

Another trial took place at the beginning of 1911, shortly before she left for a long stay with Cornwallis-West's sister, the Princess of Pless, in the South of France. On New Year's Day, 1911, a Russian communist agitator named Leon Beron was found battered and knifed to death on Clapham Common. The letter S was carved on his forehead and left cheek. His best friend, Steinie Morrison, was arrested for the crime.

Despite a skilled defence, Morrison was found guilty of murder; when the judge passed sentence of death saying, 'May God have mercy on your soul,' the accused snapped back, 'I decline such mercy. I do not believe there is a God in Heaven.'

Winston commuted the prisoner's sentence to life imprisonment, but Morrison was angry, and demanded the hangman's rope; he wanted to die a martyr. It emerged later that Beron's death was an act of ritual murder by a revolutionary group he had betrayed as an informant; it was led by Yakov Khristoforovich Peters, known as Peter the Painter, who figured in another matter that occupied

Winston at the time; it turned out that the S stood for *Spiccan*, a Russian word for spy, and not for Steinie.

In early January, Jennie was told that Winston had been summoned from his bathtub to bring troops to Whitechapel, the slum scene of the Jack the Ripper murders and a hotbed of anarchism and terrorism since Joseph Stalin had lived there in 1907. Police had found members of Peter the Painter's gang at 100 Sidney Street, and three officers had been shot dead. Reflecting Jennie's American aggressiveness, Winston ordered up a detachment of George Cornwallis-West's old regiment, the Scots Guards, still on duty at the Tower of London, and made his way to Sidney Street himself, relishing the storm of bullets around him. As at the fire that followed Jack's wedding, he enthusiastically led the fire brigade when the terrorists' boarding house went up in flames; it was an inappropriate role for a home secretary, but utterly characteristic of him and his inherited traits from Jennie. He was pleased to see the building reduced to ashes, and two anarchists dead inside. He was again unpopular with the public because of these deaths.

When newsreels showed him conducting the operations that led to 'burning' anarchists without trial he was booed and hissed in cinemas. Peter the Painter's escape from England was attributed to his carelessness and, indeed, it was a blunder that he was not caught. That astonishing individual turned up in the 1920s as head of the GPU, the Moscow police Special Branch, where, as described by the international journalist George Seldes in his *Witness to a Century*, he presided over a basement prison where he enjoyed the sight of men being beheaded night after night.

Winston was no more popular when he used 50,000 troops to crush a railway strike. Charged with bloodthirstiness, diabolical tactics and arrant medievalism, he was demonised totally when troops at his command occupied Manchester's Central Railway Station. It is hard to believe Jennie approved of such actions.

While George commuted between Jennie's house and Mrs Patrick Campbell's, Mrs Pat starred in a flaring melodrama,

Bella Donna, written by Robert Hichens, a former lover of Consuelo Manchester. Set in Egypt, it was the purple tale of a poisoner who disposed of her lover when she could not bring herself to join him in the killing of her husband. For appearance's sake, though few in society were fooled, Jennie was at the first night with George.

She had long wanted a National Theatre in London, a dream not realised until 1963, more than forty years after her death. She gave at the Royal Albert Hall a fundraiser for the venture: a Shakespeare Memorial National Theatre Ball in which the edifice was transformed into an Elizabethan court, with the virgin queen and courtiers on the stage and an orchestra playing dulcimers and lutes. And now she would cap that event with 'Shakespeare's England', an evocation of the Tudor world, the most ambitious exhibition and masquerade in London in more than half a century.

She settled on Earls Court, a seedy district then which few society figures visited, as the venue; she raised money from anyone who would help, even sending her feckless husband to influence his part-time mistress, the wealthy American Nancy Leeds, in Paris. Winston was enlisted to help, and Jack, with Natty Rothschild and Ernest Cassel, was instructed to whip up funds in the City. She invited everyone from the King down; top of her list was Kinsky, a recent widower, together with George's sisters, the Princess of Pless and the Duchess of Westminster, who were also milked for funds.

With the architect-designer Sir Edwin Lutyens, Jennie set out to create nothing less than a microcosm of sixteenth-century England. She began with a replica of the Globe Theatre, with gallants on the stage and groundlings in the pit; she added the Fortune Playhouse, also built to scale and based on ancient charts; there would be concerts of sixteenth-century music day and night, and displays of morris dancing.

She would stage a replica of St Bartholomew's Fair and a club was converted into the Mermaid Tavern. She put a strain on her staff by insisting they learn Elizabethan forms of speech, and talk in no other; even Queen Victoria might have hesitated to issue so unwelcome a command. Female guests were required to wear only those flowers to be found in Shakespeare's plays; after a long rummage through his works she came up with a list that included the lily, the marigold and the larkspur. She supplied Elizabethan coconut shies; prizes correctly in period could be won by shattering the largest number of china cups and plates. She told the *New York Times* that married couples were expected to win as they would 'enjoy what they normally do at home'.

Her round-the-clock activity was interrupted on 4 March when a disaffected shareholder tried to shoot Natty Rothschild's brother Leopold in the dark streets outside his offices at New Court. And then, on 14 April 1912, an event threatened to unseat the entire Elizabethan project at a blow.

The sinking of the *Titanic*, after colliding with an iceberg, cast a black shadow over London life, and parties were cancelled. Work had to stop at Earls Court for days as workmen and society members were shocked and in some cases bereaved. But not even so major a tragedy could stop Jennie for long. She was back whipping up her team of hundreds within two weeks.

At last, on 12 June, the exhibition was ready: the houses were built, the greensward laid down, the shops stocked with Elizabethan goods, and the restaurants serving period food. The famous theatrical impresario Charles B Cochran, in charge of the entertainment, was run to the point of exhaustion. Jennie threw an introductory dinner at the Mermaid Tavern for guests who had supplied funds, including Leopold Rothschild, the Marquis de Soveral, US Ambassador Whitelaw Reid and the Duke of Rutland. Lord Lytton proposed the toast, calling Jennie a 'grand organiser'. Oddly, she didn't respond with a speech of her own; she said with a laugh that she hadn't had time to prepare one and that she had hardly had time to have her hair done. As a result she was the subject of a humorous article in the editorial columns of the *New York Times*.

In an interview in the same newspaper on 14 June, Charles Cochran, who was about to open his quasi-religious spectacle *The Miracle* with Lady Diana Manners at Olympia, said that Jennie surpassed Phineas T Barnum and Max Reinhardt as a theatrical producer: '[She is] the greatest lady hustler that ever came out of Hustlerville. She is as full of ideas as a cake is of plums . . . a real showman is born not made. Mrs Cornwallis-West has found her sphere in life at last.'

Attendance was disappointing from the start. The constant rain kept people from the outdoor events and the open-air Globe was usually deserted. But the biggest disaster came on 12 July 1912, when the much-advertised medieval tourney of noble knights attracted only a small audience; clearly the public realised that nobody of the aristocracy would really be hurt, and all the grisly appeal of the original spectacle would be lost. If nobody lost an eye from a spear piercing a visor, and nobody was sent crashing to the ground in a full suit of real armour, what would be the attraction?

Those who did attend were greeted by a sorry spectacle of England's manhood in disarray. The initial bout was between Sunny Marlborough and Lord Crichton; as soon as the two horsemen entered the arena, Crichton, a compulsive smoker, begged leave to take puffs through his helmet, causing much mocking laughter; when Sunny took out a large pocket handkerchief, raised his visor and wiped his brow, the audience roared.

The contestants were unable to make their horses budge; they kicked them vigorously, but nothing happened. Finally the reluctant steeds began to trot forwards, but the two men missed each other and their lances splintered against the audience stand, making many of the spectators run out in fear. Frustrated, Sunny galloped off and sulked in his dressing room until Jennie persuaded him to return and joust with the Earl of Craven; when he broke his lance against Craven's breastplate, he left the arena to general amusement and refused to continue. The rest of the tourney was called off and the audience given its money back.

King George and Queen Mary, after many broken promises, at last condescended to appear on 20 July, but it was too late to save 'Shakespeare's England'. Winston's appearance, also very late, was under armed guard, because of threats against him by the suffragettes. Then, on 30 July, came the worst blow of all: the Japanese Emperor died and the King ordered mourning for all society; the show closed.

In an article headed FIASCO AT EARLS COURT published on 3 August 1912, the *New York Times* said that there was another reason for the disaster; that Jennie had behaved erratically throughout, alienating many society figures by arranging fundraising dinners and then cancelling them without warning at the last minute. No reason was given for this, but she did not deny it.

Amazingly, until late 1912, George was still living with Jennie while spending his nights with Mrs Patrick Campbell. Jennie had given up Salisbury Hall and had taken a lease on a house in Norfolk Street. It was not until just before Christmas that she finally threw George out and he moved in with Mrs Pat. Then, characteristically, she sent him a note wishing him well.

She filed for divorce on 20 January 1913. In order to achieve it, the grounds had to be invented: by law she had to swear that she had begged George for restoration of conjugal sexual rights and he had refused; a convenient lie accepted by the courts at the time. She even had to write notes making the demand. On 3 March, dressed dramatically in black furs as if in mourning for her marriage, strikingly handsome and looking more like Mrs Pat than ever, she appeared before a judge, told one lie after another with considerable tearful flair (she had a cold), and was told it would be a year before the decree would make her completely free.

George Bernard Shaw was on his mettle now. Fearful that Mrs Pat would marry George Cornwallis-West, he threw his genius into writing *Pygmalion* for her; he would flatteringly cast her in a role suitable for a woman of her daughter's age: Eliza Doolittle. When she finally appeared in the part, he was miserable; at her delivery of the famous 'Bloody' line, the laughter was so prolonged he was certain it ruined the play.

After her separation, in January 1914, Jennie badly needed a new lover; and soon, improbably, she found one.

CHAPTER ELEVEN

Jennie was in Rome in January 1914 for her sixtieth birthday and the wedding of Clarita's son Hugh Frewen to Maria, daughter of the Duke di Magnano. Jennie stayed with an old friend, the Duchess di Sermonetta, at her magnificent sixteenth-century palazzo with its gardens designed by a papal architect. Following the wedding on the Via Appia, the reception was held at the Grand Hotel; and one of the guests immediately caught her eye.

Montagu Phippen Porch was exactly and classically her type: five feet seven and slight, but hard and muscular, he had dark blue eyes and a passionate, intensely sexy look; like Kinsky, Delacour, Ramsden, Wolverton and Cornwallis-West, he was a figure from a kitchen maid's romantic novelette.

Born on 15 March 1877, he was at 36 almost 24 years younger than she was and younger than her son Winston. Like George he had served in the army in the Boer War; the ship taking him to Cape Town in 1900 had crossed hers going north on her return.

A native of the ancient town of Glastonbury in Somerset, he was raised there and in Weston-super-Mare; his father, a colonial government official in India, died when he was a child, and his mother, an Australian, married the Mayor of Glastonbury; she brought in her dowry much money in land

and sheep holdings at Geelong, in the Australian state of Victoria, and money from investments in Melbourne.

Montagu Porch cut a dash at Bath College and at Magdalen College, Oxford; on 5 February 1900 he enlisted with the Imperial Yeomanry for service in the Boer War. It was a great honour, as the volunteer soldiers were fine equestrians, sons of rich landowners, clubmen and leading lights of the City of London; they supplied their own horses, uniforms, saddles, swords and guns. They paid their own fares to Cape Town and were famous for their high standards of fitness and skill with rifles.

Desperate for a scrap, Porch joined his noisy and boisterous companions on a voyage marked by stormy weather and stormier temperaments aboard. No sooner were they arrived at the war front than they tasted the salt of disillusionment. In the first engagements Porch saw many of his friends slaughtered or dead from disease; he hated burning Boer farms and killing civilians – even children died as villages were set on fire. Prematurely aged – Porch's hair was white on his return – the troops came back sick, exhausted and bitter.

Porch returned to Magdalen with the Distinguished Service Order and Queen's medal for gallantry to complete a Pass Degree; he then worked as an archaeologist in Sinai before the lust for military action returned. In July 1906, Winston, as Secretary of State for the Colonies, approved him joining the Nigerian Political Service as district officer in a Nigerian area known along with the Gold Coast as the White Man's Grave.

It was a grim and thankless assignment. He had to act as liaison between the British High Command and the local emirs or chieftains who often resented controls; rebels threatened the colonial government and Porch had to hand out rough justice to thieves and murderers in the form of hasty imprisonments and hangings. Surviving official reports on his behaviour show that he was tense, high-strung, nervous and undisciplined; he was also sexually deprived, as white women were forbidden in the area, and he and his fellows could do little but work off their tensions by kicking footballs in the yard or thrashing recalcitrant natives. Conversation was the test match at Lord's, women left at home and whether someone had cheated at poker.

He was posted to the remote railway whistle stop of Zaria, on the way to the country's highlands, a jumble of huts plagued with flies and disease. When he met Jennie in Rome he was on a much-needed long leave and was desperate to find a woman, even though she would never be able to accompany him back to Nigeria.

Like George, he was that rare type of young man attracted to women old enough to be his mother. When he asked her to dance at the Grand Hotel reception she reversed the technique used by Randolph and Winston on their first encounters with their future brides and said that Porch could surely find a better dancing partner. The two men had originally said that to her and Clemmy.

They talked instead, in a tête-à-tête that exactly resembled her first conversation with Randolph at Cowes. When he returned to Nigeria, Jennie received a love note from him, saying he was disappointed she hadn't sent him a promised photograph as a keepsake that could live in his letter case. He was already in love and so was she. Winston and Jack had to deal once again with a man of their own age having an affair with their mother.

During the time she was in Italy and then back in London, Jennie was in secrecy preparing a lawsuit against her own sons, with FE Smith (later famous as Lord Birkenhead) as her counsel. Through influence, Smith was able to have the case entered at the Court of Chancery in June 1914 without her name or those of the defendants entered in the record; not a word of the matter appeared in the English press. It took a vigilant *New York Times* correspondent to publish an account of it, and no word of it has appeared in any book since that time. She even added to the list of defendants, Winston's children Diana and Randolph, and Jack's, John Junior and Harry.

The cause of her action was Lord Randolph's will dated 1 July 1883, which named her as joint trustee. It stated that after the second marriage of Jennie and another party – or her decease, whichever happened first – half of the children's and grandchildren's expected capital share should be advanced to them on their request. Evidently the problem lay in the word 'after'; this should have been 'following'. As it was, Winston and Jack took it to mean after the second marriage took place; they didn't see it as meaning when her marriage to Cornwallis-West would be concluded. They wanted the money immediately, but there was no provision for such distribution.

This very tough and unfilial move infuriated her; she was benefiting from her income on the boys' share and for them to acquire it would seriously affect her financial situation. With both Winston and Jack absent, and the case heard in camera behind locked doors, the judge directed that since the terms of the will made her joint trustee, her consent in writing to such an agreement must be required, and since she would not issue such consent to any distribution of funds, then the boys could not get their money. It says much for Winston and Jack that after this defeat they made no more of the matter.

Also in July, Jennie was told by her solicitors that if she wanted to marry Porch, who was still in Nigeria, there was an impediment: her decree of divorce from George had still not gone through and there were a hundred cases ahead of it. She pulled a string through Winston (now at the Admiralty), and the case was put at the head of the list; it was even omitted from the official Register of Actions.

But the matter slipped out, if only in America: the *New York Times* wrote on 15 July, 'In legal circles the whole proceeding is considered a scandal [showing] what as the First Lord of the Admiralty Winston Churchill can do in his capacity as a Cabinet Minister in defeating the public court rules and procedures.'

Jennie went with Jack to the Divorce Court for the issuing of the decree. Her collusion with George was absolute: he had spent, by arrangement with her, the nights of 28–31 March at the Great Western Hotel at Paddington with a professional co-respondent, and the divorce was granted; two hours later, George married Mrs Pat. Jennie went to Glasgow to christen a battleship; having been told she would not have to give a speech she found she had to, so she improvised desperately and to laughter and applause admitted as much to the guests at the banquet that followed. She was her old self – and more so.

In July 1914, Jennie and her family assembled at the pleasant seaside town of Overstrand in Norfolk for the summer holidays. Winston was in charge of everything: passers-by were greeted by the spectacle of the First Lord of the Admiralty issuing instructions to his family in building a giant sandcastle, with turrets and a drawbridge made of wooden planks, strong enough to resist the incoming tide. Unfortunately, the structure collapsed under the weight of waves, and everyone laughed.

It was the last joyful time before the outbreak of war in August. The assassination of Kinsky's friend the Archduke Francis Ferdinand of Austria-Hungary on 28 June had caused anger in Vienna; it was felt that the murders had been instigated by the Black Hand, a Serbian secret society, on orders from the just-appointed regent, Prince Alexander. There was immediate talk of war. Russia demanded its puppet regency not be attacked, but Austria-Hungary ignored the threat and declared war on Serbia. The Russians, after a brief delay, mobilised for action in support of Serbia; Germany, certain that France would support Austria, had long been looking for an excuse to over-whelm Western Europe through its so-called Schlieffen Plan, so declared war on the French on 3 August and invaded Belgium, always a longed-for target. Britain had guaranteed to protect Belgium in the event of an invasion, and Asquith, with some opposition, decided to honour it. On 4 August, Britain declared war on Germany and Austria-Hungary, with France and Russia as allies. The British motive was to protect the balance of power on the

Continent; but, in the end, it was a war that everyone would lose.

Jennie's concern over Kinsky must have been deep. He was now an enemy of her adopted country and she must try and remember that, while still being in love with him; and he must also keep that in mind, although he loved her.

He was instructed by his government to poison his beloved horses in English stables, in case they should be used by the cavalry; he refused, risking court martial for disobedience, and in fact several of his prize mounts were ridden by generals during the war.

He also refused to fight against the British troops in France or Belgium, an act of outright mutiny; but his family's immense influence in Austria protected him from the firing squad. He was sent to the Russian front, where in anguish he had to kill men whose compatriots he had loved during his many stays in St Petersburg. Desperately unhappy, he had no more wish to live and, with the war over and all chance of returning to England and Jennie gone (as he would now be regarded as a former enemy alien), he died of what was widely described as a broken heart in December 1919.

Another whose fate would be little known to Jennie during the war was her close friend Daisy, Princess of Pless; forced also to be part of a conflict in which her own brother George Cornwallis-West and sister the Duchess of Westminster were on the opposite side, she was condemned to hand over, with her husband, Castle Pless as the headquarters of the German High Command.

Jennie was able to receive word from Montagu Porch, but his letters were cause for anxiety. Appointed an intelligence scout, fighting the German colonial army in the Cameroons, he had to crawl through swamps, ford snake-infested rivers with backpack and camera, and stalk through miles of six-foot-high elephant grass at night so the sun would not flash on his field glasses. His worst job was rifling dead enemy soldiers' pockets for telltale documents, the bones picked dry by vultures.

Nor were things better for Jennie at home. She was battered by criticism of Winston as First Lord of the Admiralty, and by the fact that Jack, as a stockbroker (he planned to enlist), suffered from losses in the market. Natty Rothschild and Sir Ernest Cassel, Jennie's continuing backers, were severely damaged by the war; these wizards of finance had bet too heavily on the peace they fought for until the last minute, and then they were attacked for war profiteering.

The most deep-seated fear for Jennie and her friends – though this never happened – was that Ireland would join Germany against Britain and bring about a revolutionary war; and provide a basis for a German invasion across the Irish Sea.

But above all there was the war fever that infected young men; after years of peace, there was a lust for dangerous action on both enemy sides, a collective frenzy that spread through every nation like an uncontrollable disease.

Jennie plunged into the war effort, her energies unabated, her anger at the Germans intense. She raised money for the troops through American friends, most notably from Bourke Cockran; she gave recitals for medical supplies with a friend of Boer War days, Lady Warrender; and then she embarked on the most ambitious programme of all.

With troops returning wounded and dying from the front, hospitals were needed badly. She talked Paris Singer, heir to the Singer sewing-machine fortune and sometime lover of the American dancer Isadora Duncan, into buying up an old, early-Victorian house at Paignton, near Torquay in Devon, and turning it almost overnight into a handsome medical facility. The American Red Cross came up with much of the money and Jennie raised the rest. It became known as the American Women's Hospital, and it was the subject of many articles in the press.

Through her relentless advocacy, architects and builders turned what had been a dark Victorian pile into a sparkling, ultra-modern new structure rather like an American movie house, filled with brilliant electric light; the atmosphere was greatly cheering to the wounded. She was a tough boss, dismissing staff when they didn't meet her high standards, and jarring awake any night watchman who fell asleep on duty, while neglecting no man in his suffering. When the soldiers wanted music, she arranged for five gramophones to play jazz at the same time in the communal ward; if a man showed her a souvenir of shrapnel taken from his back, she managed great excitement and interest.

Working day and night at this hospital, at another American Red Cross facility at Lancaster Gate in London, and at Lady Limerick's war canteen at London Bridge Station, Jennie had meanwhile to endure increasing attacks on Winston. The navy he had so painstakingly built up was outmanoeuvred frequently by the Germans; in one humiliating disaster, for which the press excoriated him, two vessels were sunk and some 1,600 men drowned at the Battle of Coronel off the coast of Chile. Not even the birth of his daughter Sarah on 8 October could relieve his deepening gloom.

Few forgave him for leaving Clementine during her labour and taking off for Antwerp in Belgium, a strategic target of the Germans; and few admired him for arriving at the best hotel by Rolls-Royce when men were marching miserably on foot, or equipping himself with fine food and wine. The Scots regiment he inspected included Lieutenant Colonel George Cornwallis-West, who was, to Jennie's distress and his own, later charged falsely with being a deserter and a spy.

Winston was back in London for Sarah's arrival, but he was savaged again by the press, this time for failing to save Antwerp; its occupation and defeat were also sore points in Whitehall. Among his defences were that he had managed to delay the German attack and had persuaded King Leopold of Belgium to act loyally to his country, but his arrogance infuriated many reporters along with his inability to apologise, a sure sign of future greatness. Jennie was unhappy with his quixotic misadventure; when she accompanied him to Aberdeen for his investiture as Lord Rector of the University, there were catcalls from the audience. It was not until 1 December that a report by Sir John French, Commander in Chief of the British Expeditionary Force, absolved him of all blame for the Antwerp disaster. But many remained unconvinced. And now came his Turkish imbroglio.

Within two weeks of the war's beginning, Winston had been convinced that Turkey would join the central powers of Germany and Austria-Hungary; after seizing two Turkish vessels on Merseyside, he proposed that Greece should attack the Gallipoli peninsula in order to admit the British fleet to the Sea of Marmora to support the Russians. General Charles Callwell, director of War Office military operations, said that such an attack was beyond Greek capacity as it would take an army of 60,000 to overcome the Turkish defences. Winston was certain the attack was feasible and would result in revolution in Constantinople. But the plan rapidly dissolved when King Constantine I of Greece declined to co-operate.

Lord Kitchener, Churchill's old nemesis, was approached to assist as Secretary of State for War. But concerned with maintaining the forces protecting British financial interests in Egypt, including the Suez Canal and Sir Ernest Cassel's Aswan Dam, he would not co-operate, even when a joint military and naval mission seemed improbable, with most other British troops committed to the northern European theatre of war. Winston, with some ambiguous support from Lord Fisher as First Sea Lord, decided to launch a sea attack only, at least at first; he was handicapped by the unwillingness of French commanders to send their men to the Middle East. Amid much waffling, nobody in the war council, Winston included, decided to investigate other troop availability (from India for example); neither Fisher nor the naval adviser Sir Arthur Wilson was asked to present an argument whether a naval attack alone was feasible. Behind Winston's back, Kitchener's right-hand man Colonel Fitzgerald arranged it so that no transports would be available; when finally in February

1916 Kitchener agreed to the 29th Division (of which Jack Churchill was a member) being sent to Turkey, weeks more were lost in meaningless prevarication and delays.

Winston's dislike of Turkey was not only based on its alliance with Germany; his mentor, Sir Ernest Cassel, had long dreamed of establishing in Constantinople a British-controlled National Bank and, in 1909, with Foreign Office approval, that bank was set up and shares issued to British interests; tobacco for Turkish cigarettes – Randolph's famous weakness – was a much-traded item. The French played on British investors' resistance to buying Turkish bonds by opposing the National Bank with their own aggressive Ottoman Bank, but in 1911 Cassel placed Turkish bills on the London market, and triumphed. Now his entire operation had collapsed – and must be regained.

Jennie was burdened more and more by word from Montagu Porch in Nigeria: he was still crawling through elephant grass, swimming across rivers, suffering severe heat and fighting off swarms of jigger insects that burrowed into his skin. He went through what his fellow soldier the novelist Joyce Carey described as 'raids, ambushes, enormous marches ... whole columns would disappear for weeks together, to burst out a thousand miles away. Patrols would stumble through jungles, and then suddenly find they were facing each other, not the enemy.' Yellow fever decimated the ranks, leaving few unaffected but Porch remained well.

Whenever Jennie saw Winston in those months, an attack on Turkey was his continuing obsession. Unfortunately, his intelligence service, the famous Room 40, was sadly inadequate: it should have informed him that the Germans, under the brilliant General Liman von Sanders, had vastly increased the defences at Gallipoli, but no such reports were obtained.

He clearly wanted to emulate the expedition of February 1807, when Admiral Sir John Duckworth, in the fever of a Russian-Turkish war, had forged a passage through the Dardanelles and gone on to the very gates of

Constantinople. As recently as 1912, during the Tripolitan War between Italy and Turkey, when Italian warships bombed the installations, a clear picture of their military strength had been obtained. But now Room 40 failed to update that information.

Jennie's worst anguish at the time was that Jack, who in many ways she loved more than Winston (though they had far less in common), was with the army's 29th Division and sailed for Gallipoli under the command of General Sir Ian Hamilton; he had already served in the Oxfordshires, with Sunny Marlborough, in several skirmishes in France.

She received letters from him at the front: he arrived in the midst of a slaughter for which Winston would always be blamed. He urged Winston to add aeroplanes to the attack, but Winston was unable to make the arrangements. Jack wrote to Jennie that, as he watched from the deck of his HMS *Queen Elizabeth*, men were killed by the thousand; the stench of death lay heavily in the air as flies swarmed over the corpses.

Jennie could take comfort in Jack's display of gallantry when he at last went ashore to join the battle he longed for. He cut a fine figure, wearing very short shorts and acting with deliberate effeminacy to cheer the men up; they dubbed him Lady Constance. Though surrounded by shellfire, he led, like Montagu Porch, a charmed life; by July, after four months of service, he was still uninjured.

In May 1915, Winston was assailed again; the *Lusitania* was torpedoed off the Irish coast, and he was blamed for the sinking. For Jennie, the disaster was especially painful because she had heard from her friend Nancy Leeds, that wealthy American whom by now George Cornwallis-West had also abandoned, that she would be on board; fortunately, Mrs Leeds changed her reservation, but Jennie didn't find out until later.

On 4 February 1915, the German government had issued a warning, laid firmly on Winston's desk, that after two more weeks U-boats would attack any Allied vessel that falsely flew a neutral flag. Winston failed to respond or supply all such ships with armed escorts.

Room 40 must surely have advised Winston that the *Lusitania*, the most luxurious of British passenger ships, was in outright defiance of German warnings when she sailed from New York at the outset of May, absurdly flying the Stars and Stripes, although her true origin and registration were well known. With recklessness that amounted to the criminal, she had been allowed to carry 4,200 chests of Springfield cartridges and 11 tons of black gunpowder to Liverpool – a fact determined by the Austro-Hungarian emissary in Washington, Kinsky's old boss Constantin Dumba, and by his colleague in Berlin, Kurt Hahn, who in 1915 was head of the German Foreign Ministry's American Information Bureau.

Winston should never have allowed such a sailing; if he had to allow it, because of the need for American supplies, he should have provided a full-scale armed escort, and been ready in London for the slightest indication of trouble. He was accused of the same irresponsibility he had shown at the Battle of Coronel; he flew to Paris the week the *Lusitania* was crossing the Atlantic on the excuse that he needed to help secure support at high-level meetings with Italian and French officials to secure neutral Italy's co-operation in the war.

But the truth was that several days before the *Lusitania* sank, on 26 April, in a secret treaty on Winston's and every other desk in Whitehall, Italy had already joined France and Russia in a mutual guarantee of co-operation against Germany and Austria. Italy had been promised Libya, Eritrea and Somaliland as prizes of conquest, and the Pope in Rome was forbidden to sustain peace arrangements with the Kaiser. The Naval Convention that followed, and called for Winston's presence, did not start its meetings until after the *Lusitania* was sunk off the Irish coast on 7 May, with a loss of 1,198 lives.

Already in trouble over Gallipoli, Winston ran into a firestorm. Many accused him of letting the *Lusitania* sink because Americans were on board, in a bid to lure the United States into war. In the House of Commons, Lord Charles Beresford fired a broadside: he wanted to know why, if merchant vessels carrying horses to Liverpool were protected by torpedo boats, the *Lusitania* was not; why had reports of U-boats sighted off the coast of Ireland been consistently ignored? To boos from the opposition, and murmurings from his own backbenchers, Winston lamely stated that an official inquiry had been ordered, to be run by Lord Mersey; he overlooked the fact that in the same waters the HMS *Candidate* and *Centurion* had just been lost to enemy action, and he even lied: 'The entire seaport trade has been carried off without loss . . . merchant traffic must take care of itself.'

The cover-up that followed was shocking. To conceal the fact that the *Lusitania* had been carrying her clandestine cargo it was claimed that U-boats had fired two torpedoes instead of one. The official report then added that the extra torpedo had struck at a point far removed from the location of the black powder and cartridges, whose existence was consistently denied. At the farce of an official inquiry, Lord Mersey placed the blame for the sinking on the Germans and the Germans alone. Many took a different view: when a coalition government was formed on 26 May, Winston was sacked from the Admiralty and made Chancellor of the Duchy of Lancaster, a practically meaningless post, which in fact was in line with his position as debtor to Sir Ernest Cassel, since it involved keeping an eye on King George V's Casselian investments.

Winston did everything to avoid the job. He begged Asquith for the job of First Air Lord so he could rain bombs on the Turks; the application was refused. Each day Jennie had to read at her breakfast table the litany of anti-Churchill charges: that he had wantonly removed the popular and ageing Sir George Callaghan as Commander in Chief of the First Fleet; that he had pressed too hard on a cautious naval staff for an attack on German ships before war was declared; that he had been responsible for the sinking of the British cruisers *Aboukir*, *Cressy* and *Hogue*; and that he, who never rose above the rank of lieutenant in the Hussars, had, as a mere stripling of forty, been put in charge of the greatest navy in the world.

Jennie and Clementine knew they must do something to save Winston's reason in that summer of agonised discontent. Money was tight – Natty Rothschild had died – so a new home must be found. The Ivor Guests lent Jennie a rather cramped house in Arlington Street, and soon after that the family moved to Jack's house at Cromwell Road, with many dissents and conflicts inevitable in so confined a space. They also rented Hoe Farm, near Godalming in Surrey, as a much-needed summer retreat.

Winston may have been on the verge of suicide over Gallipoli (and perhaps, although he would have denied it, the *Lusitania*). He sent a letter to Clementine from London on 17 July, telling her the terms of his will should he die soon. ('Don't grieve for me too much. Death is only an incident.') He revealed he had about three thousand pounds in assets, more than a third of it through Cassel investments in railways, plus his life insurance policy.

At Hoe Farm, the family gathered around its most prominent member in full force. Jack Jr and Randolph with the other children were as noisily healthy as ever. Recently at Blenheim, they had driven everyone mad by ceaselessly pulling the tail of a stuffed lion in the entrance hall; through an internal mechanism, the mangy beast had roared. At Godalming they ran around constantly; Winston, working off his tension and misery, dressed up in his shabbiest clothes, humped over, swung his arms and bared his teeth, scratched himself and hopped up a tree, a gorilla to the life, making the boys scream with laughter.

Melancholy again, he was talked into painting the farm gardens and trees; this acted as therapy, which as a perennial Sunday painter, he would enjoy all his life. Less happily, he managed, with an emphasis on red, his cousin Nellie Hozier's portrait. As paint splashed on him, he looked down in agony and cried out, 'There is more blood than paint on these hands. All those thousands of men killed. We thought it would be a little job. And so it might have been if it had begun the right way.'

Jack wrote and offered a solution to his despair: why not become a soldier again and serve at Gallipoli itself? Jennie and Clementine were horrified; Kitchener gave his approval but the Cabinet ruled against it.

Jennie had no cheering news from Jack. A disastrous British defeat at Suvla Bay was followed by a notorious episode when the troops, weary of flies, disease and slaughter after so many months of action, when ordered to charge the Turkish guns, stripped naked and swam in the straits, surrounded by a hail of bullets.

Porch was transferred from the front line in Nigeria to British Resident in Zaria and, in October 1915, he was given a long leave in England, dividing his time between Jennie in London (he stayed at the United Empire Club) and his family at Weston-super-Mare. It was a happy, though limited, reunion of husband and wife.

Winston swallowed his pride and asked Asquith for Command of British East Africa; he was again refused. He announced in desperation that he would leave for the trenches as a soldier. Jennie and Clementine again protested, but there was nothing they could do; Jack, on a short leave, was very proud of him.

The atmosphere at Cromwell Road was charged as Winston packed to leave for front-line service: Jennie could hardly speak from anxiety; Clementine was distraught; Winston's devoted secretary Edward Marsh was in tears; the boys were excited. Winston arrived at the front with a travelling bathtub and boiler and soon sent for sardines, chocolates, potted meats, Stilton cheese, cream, dried fruit and a beefsteak pie.

He served with gallantry and his men came to adore him; like Jack, he enjoyed a charmed life, and he was far happier in the line of fire, shells and bullets around him, than in the genteel jungle of Whitehall. He became a legend in the annals of his regiment, the 6th Royal Scots Fusiliers.

He returned to London in May 1916; he could talk to Jennie of nothing except his experiences and of bringing down the hated government. His continuing association with a demented Lord Fisher was a mistake, though, and soon in the wake of action, his gloom returned. On 2 June, he attended a dinner party at Lady Cynthia Asquith's; she was the daughter-in-law of the prime minister, and fiercely catty. She described him in her diary as melodramatic, purple in rhetoric, brooding, scowling and miserable; she quoted him as saying that watching the Gallipoli disaster from afar was 'like being bound hand and foot and seeing your girlfriend raped'. Later, in conversation with George Moore, Cynthia would describe Jennie as black, commenting that she must like the idea of being the only white woman in Nigeria as opposed to being the only black one in London.

In 1917, Jennie finally had cause for rejoicing: America came into the war, following Room 40's interception of the telegram signed by the German Foreign Minister Alfred (not, as almost every historian has given it, Arthur[2]) Zimmermann, indicating that Germany would continue to attack and sink American ships and that Germany would support a Mexican invasion of Texas.

Winston's continuing unpopularity, and Porch's inevitable return to the hell of Nigeria, depressed Jennie; the attacks of the German Zeppelins, vast cigar shapes roaring through the sky over London, bombs dropping and killing, grated on her nerves. In February 1916, her left toe became infected after she stubbed it and it had to be amputated. On 15 April, thieves broke into her house at 72 Brook Street and stole money as well as gifts from Edward VII, Queen Alexandra and Consuelo Yznaga, and a valued locket with miniatures of Winston and Jack as children.

---

[2] All contemporary records of World War I show the correct name, and so do newspapers. Even Barbara Tuchman, author of the famous *The Zimmermann* telegram, made this serious mistake.

CHAPTER TWELVE

On 9 March 1917, the report on the Gallipoli fiasco was published in London. To Jennie's relief, it was quite fair to Winston. It had been hastily completed under severe pressure by the dying commission chief, Lord Cromer, who had signed the conclusion on his deathbed. A further handicap for the commission was the death of Kitchener at sea when HMS *Hampshire* was sunk; unable to speak now, he was dealt with harshly as the chief instrument of the folly. Asquith issued a spirited defence, but the newspapers, fearless of libel, attacked the dead man like vultures. After a brief pause, with no living target, the press began eating Winston's bones. He didn't help matters by attacking the dead Cromer. Instead of re-emphasising Cromer's findings that he was only part of the tragic clumsiness of the War Council, he denounced the commission as guilty of using 'chippings and slippings' or 'single sentences only from witnesses and documents', and that the result was 'an instalment of fair play by apportioning the blame among several prominent figures'. He charged the commission with being 'pernicious to the last degree'.

In view of the report's fairness to him, and its largely favourable treatment, his attack was considered unwarranted and a public disgrace. He was more unpopular than ever.

Despite difficulty in walking because of her amputated toe, Jennie never ceased her work for the troops at Paignton, at Lancaster Gate and at Lady Limerick's canteen at Tower Bridge station. She was still the most severe of matrons: a force nobody dared contradict. When one orderly nodded off, she slapped him awake so hard his teeth rattled. She refused all applications from society women as volunteers, and stuck with hardened professionals.

On 17 July 1917, Lloyd George, by now prime minister, appointed Winston minister of munitions through the extraordinary step of not consulting his Cabinet, which was furious. Forty MPs signed a joint letter of complaint; but Winston did win a Liberal campaign as MP for Dundee, with a 5,266 majority; and now as minister he was able to introduce the caterpillar tanks he had so long wanted to see in action in France. He also raised a hundred-million-pound loan from the banker Bernard Baruch in New York, pressed for increased gas warfare, and quashed a munitions factory strike by threatening that unless it were called off, every man on the assembly line would be enlisted at once.

Late in 1917, Jennie moved from a house in Brook Street to another at Westbourne Street. She gave it extra touches: the light bulbs round the mirrors glowed softly, giving her the illusion of youth; she had her maids dressed daringly as half-men, with bowties, dinner jackets and Eton collars as well as skirts, a touch that Pearl Craigie would have approved.

In the midst of Zeppelin raids, Jennie lived it up with a new friend, the American Emerald Cunard. She attended concerts at the Aldwych Theatre conducted by Emerald's friend Sir Thomas Beecham. On 13 October, the actress and society beauty Lady Diana Manners wrote in her diary that she had seen Jennie and Emerald at Lady Wimborne's 'tipsy, dancing and talking wildly' while the Zeppelins rained bombs outside.

Winston had meanwhile turned his house at 33 Eccleston Square into an extra ministry of munitions. The Churchill children would invariably pick up the telephones to insult the switchboard operators.

When her grandsons, John Jr and Randolph, told Jennie they intended building a crane with a Meccano set in the dining room, Winston announced it would be better to have a bridge. To Clementine's despair, the dining room was turned into a miniature steel factory, with nuts and bolts all over the floor, girders scratching the mahogany dining table and sideboard, and Winston and the boys poring over vast diagrams, building a fifteen-foot-long, eight-foot-high structure, complete with a highway on wheels and cars and buses manipulated by clockwork. It took a heroic effort to have food served in the circumstances.

Jennie and Clementine had to put up with more mischief; the children's rebelliousness was not decreased by the insane diet to which both women subjected them through a succession of nannies: tapioca pudding mixed with beef blood, bread and dripping, and mustard put in chocolate creams. In the summer of 1917 at Lullenden, a family retreat in Sussex, the children again upset Jennie, Gwendeline (wife of Jack) and Clementine by emptying a chamber pot out of a window on the unsuspecting heads of Winston and Lloyd George. On another occasion, John Jr and Randolph put the younger children in a miniature covered wagon and pushed them so hard down a steep hill they were spilled out.

In April 1918, Montagu Porch ran into trouble in Nigeria. He had taken absence without leave to visit Jennie and marry her. In London he was ordered to report to the Colonial Office to explain his behaviour; he refused. He was told to go back to Nigeria on 9 May, charged with overstaying his leave when in fact he had deserted. He did not go back. He claimed he was in England to seek a transfer to Arabia, where he said he wanted to serve with Sharif Husayn, the self-styled Arabian king, against the Turks; but the Turks had long since left the area, and had made peace with Husayn. Caught in a lie, Porch was forbidden to wear his uniform, while his case was being considered.

He and Jennie set out to Ireland for a three-week stay with Clarita and her husband; they returned for their wedding on 1 June at Harrow Road Registry Office. Porch acted outrageously; refused permission to be in uniform, he had one made up at a London costumiers; he wore it at the ceremony, thus giving grounds for his dismissal from the army. Winston and Jack must have been aware of the action but they said nothing; when he saw the wedding pictures Porch's commander Lord Lugard was furious. He withdrew Porch and sent him for severe action at Zaria.

When the war ended in November, London was filled with rejoicing, but Jennie was acutely anxious over Porch's fate. White women were forbidden to join their husbands in Nigeria, but many accused Jennie of being disloyal in not going there. Then in June 1919, his case pending, Porch ran into even more serious trouble. He had fired an African cook and the embittered man charged him with attempted homosexual rape. A tribunal found Porch guiltless but it didn't help when his fellow officers caught the cook and beat him senseless; at a subsequent trial for assault, Porch was found guilty.

He was sent in disgrace to the garrison town of Kantagora while the possibility of court martial was considered; the Governor of Nigeria, Sir Hugh Clifford instead had him cashiered out of the colonial service. He sailed from Accra in low spirits and when he reached London was suddenly unable to deal with the social life he had once enjoyed. He left Jennie again, and returned to Africa; persona non grata in Nigeria, he settled in the Gold Coast.

He was convinced, he told Jennie, he had a future there; and women would be allowed to join their husbands now that war was over. He saw an opportunity to get in on the ground floor of the cocoa industry that would soon grow to the point where it supplied more than fifty per cent of the world's chocolate. Railways were needed to bring supplies from inland to Accra, and he managed to borrow money from Jennie, Jack and Winston to invest in the rolling stock and trains.

In her sixties, Jennie could take little satisfaction in what was arguably the bleakest period in Winston's career. Even worse than his disgrace over Gallipoli was his virtual invalidity as war secretary in Lloyd George's peacetime coalition, government following his recklessly ill-advised plan to launch counter-revolutionary actions in Russia after the revolution. Then there was the grotesque incident when, combining work at the air ministry with his normal duties, he was involved in an embarrassing crash-landing at Buc, near Paris, in June 1919, and in a plane he flew himself. Always in his own mind the belligerent successor to Marlborough and Wellington, alive with dreams of glory that his failure in Turkey had not suppressed, Winston believed that a war-weary England would rally to the colours yet again and crush the Bolshevists. The rash military misadventure, abortively launched in part in Russia itself, brought more ignominy to his name.

With a husband who was often in the Gold Coast, Jennie needed an emotional outlet, and she found an improbable one in the unstable sculptress Clare Sheridan, daughter of Moreton and Clarita Frewen. Tall, slim and blonde, Clare gave every appearance, unlike her father, of being reliable, and her marriage in 1910 to Wilfred Sheridan, a stock-broker colleague of Jack, had met with Jennie's approval. In 1915, her husband was killed in action; after that, and the birth of her son, who was pretentiously named Richard Brinsley Sheridan (after the eighteenth-century dramatist), she became wildly promiscuous, carrying on affairs with so many men that even free-thinking Jennie was given pause.

She advised Clare over lunch to be careful and discreet, advice from the oddest source that Clare ignored. Then Clare, defying Jennie's hatred of communism and Winston's counter-revolutionary campaign, took off to Moscow to cohabit with her Russian commissar lover, Lev Kamenev. Jennie was furious, writing to her sister Leonie warning her to have Clare reveal nothing of British matters, a futile request.

Clare's response to her family's annoyance, and Winston was among the most badly upset of all, was to inform them she was sculpting a bust of Lenin; Lenin told her that Winston was an odd sort of person for her to have as a cousin, as he was 'the most hated man in England'. She returned to London praising Trotsky and the butchers of Russia as 'perfect gentlemen', and wearing a sable coat stripped from an imprisoned Russian countess.

Christmas for Jennie was seldom a happy occasion, and 1920's was no exception, with Winston again embroiled in a legal challenge.

She had been very friendly with Sir John French, Lord Lieutenant of Ireland and formerly head of the British Expeditionary Force in France, a guest of her various homes in London and Winston's strong friend and supporter. It was known in intelligence circles that Sinn Fein, the Irish nationalist group, had him as well as Winston on a list for potential kidnapping and murder; Jennie can hardly have been unaware of this. And on 6 December 1915, French, in a near-repetition of the Phoenix Park killings of 1882, was ambushed and almost killed. He was on his way to the viceregal lodge through Phoenix Park when shots rang out, followed by exploding bombs; unlike Lord Cavendish and Thomas Henry Bourke, French was not walking at the time, but had commandeered an armoured car, and the assailant, the Sinn Feiner Martin Savage, who fired at him from a horse cart, was shot down. In the crossfire, an innocent bystander named Laurence Kennedy was also killed. On 1 January 1921, Kennedy's family brought suit against Winston as secretary for war, charging him with manslaughter for sending French into a danger zone, thus causing Kennedy's death and seeking heavy damages. The absurd case was quashed in the lower court, but it was severely unsettling for Jennie and the whole family.

It soon emerged that the attempted assassination was the work of Charles Diamond, proprietor of the London *Catholic Herald*, and an old enemy of Winston's; tried and found guilty, he was sentenced to hard labour for twenty years. Winston's call for punishment of Sinn Fein went unanswered; in May 1921, all but four of the elected candidates in Southern Ireland following the final introduction of Home Rule were Sinn Feiners.

In that same month, with Porch back in Africa after a brief reunion, Jennie was in Rome as the guest of her old friend the Duchess of Sermoneta, helping her to redecorate her palazzo on the Via Appia, and snapping up shoes to add to the collection that filled a glass cabinet in her drawing room in London. Soon after her return, she accepted an invitation to spend the weekend with her friend, the patroness of the arts Lady Frances Horner, at the Elizabethan Miles Manor in Somerset. She was changing for tea when the bell rang; always punctual to a fault, she threw on her high-heeled Italian shoes too rapidly, and when she began her run downstairs she tripped and fell to the bottom, breaking an ankle and bones in her left leg.

Rushed by ambulance to her home at Westbourne Street, she was attended by Winston, Jack and their wives, and by Clarita; Leonie was torn between attending Jennie and her own daughter, who was about to give birth. Bourke Cockran, ever faithful, was with Lady Warrender at her bedside. Two weeks later she was still unable to get up; then gangrene set in and she was forced to agree to an amputation of her left leg. Her typical request to the surgeon was that he 'cut high enough'. Matters weren't helped by Leonie's and Clarita's hysteria, though Jennie was brave and calm, saying she would put her 'best foot forward' in the future.

Told of Jennie's condition, Montagu Porch wrote to say that he was 'frantic with apprehension and fear' but disgracefully he made no attempt to come home. Instead, he informed her that he had a good business going in railway construction for a new route to Accra and didn't want to leave, and that once she was recovered she could come to his house at Coomassie and enjoy its benefits. He also took out a mortgage on Westbourne Street. There was no mention of Jennie benefiting from that arrangement.

On 29 June 1921, Jennie called out to her nurse that she was soaking wet; she thought her hot water bottle must have burst. The nurse drew back the bedclothes and saw that she had suffered a haemorrhage. Within an hour, she was dead. Winston and Jack were at her side when she passed away.

Even in death, Jennie was at the centre of a drama. As had happened with Blandford, her sons wanted to rule out foul play or suicide; they would lose the life assurance if these possibilities could be confirmed. They ordered an inquest; Montagu Porch, on his way at last, was not heard from. The coroner at Paddington, sitting without a jury, gave a verdict of accidental death, the insurance was paid to the sons.

The funeral was a simple affair; Jennie was buried next to Randolph at Bladon churchyard near Blenheim. It is sad that Jennie didn't live another twenty years. At 87 she would have seen Winston, her fractious and difficult boy, become the greatest statesman of the twentieth century. But she lived on in him: he reflected her strength, her single-minded optimism, her passion for living in the face of adversity, her patriotism, and her superb authority. In the last analysis, she would have been proud of him – as a lasting extension of herself.

POSTSCRIPT

Apart from her audacity in having affairs with, or marrying, men young enough to be her sons, still taboo in many ways today, it is possible to see the heroine of this book as a political figure in her own right – the first American woman to influence British history both in and out of parliament. In all the vast mass of Churchilliana, insufficient mention has been made of the influence Jennie Jerome of Brooklyn Heights had on her first husband and on her illustrious, elder son.

Lord Randolph, an unimpressive figure, in the unfortunate situation of being the second son of a duke, was of little importance when she met him but by helping him write his speeches, infusing him with a very American energy and drive, and forcing him to confront his Liberal enemies and his fuddy-duddy Conservative leaders, she helped him become the most exciting, dangerous and controversial political figure in England.

And the American elements of Winston Churchill's inherited character are undeniable, with his compulsive taking on of enemies, his crushing of obstacles, and his unconquerable optimism in the face of a disastrous early career. Taking into account his love of the underdog and his close relationship (rare in aristocratic circles) with the common man that later resulted in his overwhelming popularity one can scarcely estimate Jennie's influence on world politics in her shaping of the great war leader of World War II.

APPENDIX

THE MARLBOROUGH FAMILY (1874–1895)[3]

John Winston Spencer Churchill, 7th Duke of Marlborough. Married Lady Frances (Fanny) Anne Emily Vane.

Sons:
1. George Charles Spencer Churchill, Marquess of Blandford (later 8th Duke). Married (1) Lady Albertha Frances Hamilton, children: Charles Richard John (Sunny) 9th Duke (married Consuelo Vanderbilt), Frances Louisa, Lilian Maud, Norah Beatrice. Married (2) Lilian Hammersley (Lily). No issue.
2. Frederick John Winston Spencer Churchill. Died in infancy.
3. Lord Randolph Henry Spencer Churchill. Married Jeanette Jerome, sons: Winston Leonard Spencer Churchill, John Strange Spencer Churchill.
4. Charles Ashley Spencer Churchill. Died in infancy.
5. Augustus Robert Spencer Churchill. Died in infancy.

Daughters:
1. Cornelia Henrietta Maria. Married 1st Baron Wimborne. Issue.
2. Rosamond Jane Frances. Married 2nd Baron de Ramsey. Issue.
3. Fanny Octavia Louisa. Married 2nd Baron Tweedmouth. Issue.
4. Anne Emily. Married 7th Duke of Roxburghe. Issue.
5. Georgiana Elizabeth. Married 4th Earl Howe. Issue.
6. Sarah Elizabeth Augusta. Married Lieutenant Colonel Gordon Chesney Wilson. Issue.

---

[3] The period of Jennie and Randolph Churchill's marriage.

ACKNOWLEDGMENTS

I am deeply grateful to the following, without whose help this book would not have been possible:

The staff of the Glendale Public Library, Glendale, California.
Mark Adams, New York/Brooklyn genealogist.
Anthony Adolf, British genealogist.
Kirstie Addis, Virgin Books Ltd Editor.
Ian Allen, copy-editor.
Melanie Aspey, Rothschild Archives, London.
Chichi Barthelemy, French contact.
Emily Bergman, Occidental College, California.
Terry Coleman.
John Davis, Bodleian Library, Oxford.
Jane Eastwood, Virgin Books Ltd.
Clark Evans, Library of Congress.
The Earl of Fife.
Reginald Green, Grand National historian.
Don Greenwald, racing historian.
Dorris Halsey, Whitney Lee, fine agents.
Michael Haney, gifted advisor, fine theatre man.
Colin Harris, Bodleian Library, Oxford.
Luther H. Harris, New York Historical Society.
Joseph Jennings, racing historian.
Brian Jones, British genealogist.
Douglas Kemmener, racing historian.
Sally Keisel, National Archives, Washington.

Bruce Kirby, Library of Congress.
Edward Lowe, British genealogist.
Dr John H Mather, Churchill medical historian.
Hugo A Mauriera, Washington researcher.
Denis McCarthy, Dublin historian.
Patrick Melvin, Galway historian.
Maureen Moran, Galway librarian.
Richard D Nicoll, racing historian.
Bob O'Hara, British researcher.
Lawrence Overmire, New England genealogist.
Philip Parkinson, British researcher.
Jean Paule, Occidental College, California.
Robert Persauld, Royal College of Physicians, London.
Doyle Phillips, Big Spring, Texas historian.
Udana Power, genius transcriber of illegible manuscripts; sage
  advisor.
Jeremy Rex-Parkes, Christie's, London.
The Earl of Roden.
Marsha J Shapiro, New York book finder; researcher.
Sim Smiley, Washington, DC researcher.
John Taylor, National Archives, Washington.
Gerald Turbow, historian and friend.
Dorothy Turmail, Presbyterian Churches of Brooklyn, NY.
Lloyd Ultan, Bronx historian.
Mark Washburne, historian.
Kenneth C Wenzer, Washington historian/researcher.

ARCHIVES CONSULTED

Archives Nationales de France
Austrian Straatsarchiv, Vienna
Beinicke Library, Yale
Bibliothèque Nationale de France
Big Spring Library and Historical Society, Texas
Bodleian Library, Oxford
British Library, London
Brooklyn Historical Society
Bronx Historical Society
Christie's, London
Churchill College, Cambridge

Georgetown University, Washington, DC
Glastonbury Public Library, Somerset, England
Glendale Public Library, California
Library of Congress, Washington, DC
Los Angeles Public Library
Merseyside Museum Archives, Liverpool, England
National Archives, Washington
National Archives of Great Britain, Kew, England
New York City Historical Society
New York City Public Library
New York City Records Office
Princeton University, New Jersey, USA
Rochester Historical Society, NY
Rothschild Archives, London
Royal Archives, Windsor Castle
Royal College of Physicians Archives, London
Royal Naval Museum, Portsmouth
West Yorkshire Historical Society, Leeds

SELECTED BIBLIOGRAPHY

Adams, WS. *Edwardian Portraits*. London: Secker and Warburg, 1957.

Bain, David Howard. *Empire Express*. NY: Viking, 1999.

Balsan, Consuelo Vanderbilt. *The Glitter and the Gold*. NY: Harper and Co., 1956.

Barrie, JM. *Better Dead*. NY: Scribners, 1930.

Battenberry, Michael and Anne. *On the Town in New York*. NY: Scribner, 1973.

Beckert, Sven. *The Making of New York Bourgeoisie*. Columbia University, NY: Unpublished Dissertation, 1995.

Bellows, Henry. *Historical Sketch of the Union League Club*. NY; Privately Printed, 1879.

Bishop, Alan. *Gentleman Rider, A Biography of Joyce Carey*. London: Michael Joseph, 1988.

Blunden, Margaret. *The Countess of Warwick*. London: Cassell, 1967.

Brandon, Ruth. *The Dollar Princesses*. NY: Knopf, 1980.

Byrne, Thomas. *Rogues' Gallery: 247 Professional Criminals of 19th Century America*. NY: Chelsea House, 1886.

Caffyn, Gladys F. *Fragments in the Life of Ambrose Hall*. Palmyra, NY: Doris F Smith, 1956.

Cheshire, David T. *Portrait of Ellen Terry*. Oxford: Amber Lane Press, 1981.

Churchill, John Spencer. *Crowded Canvas*. London: Odhams Press, 1961.

Churchill, Lady Randolph. *Small Talks on Big Subjects*. London: Arthur Pearson, 1916.

Churchill, Peregrine and Mitchell, Julien. *Jennie*. NY: St Martins Press, 1974.

Churchill, Randolph and Gilbert, Martin. *Winston S Churchill*. And Companion Volumes. Boston: Houghton Mifflin, 1967, Passim.

Churchill, Winston. *My Early Life 1874–1904*. NY: Scribners, 1930.

Coates, Tim. *Patsy*. NY: Bloomsbury, 2003.

Cornwallis-West, George. *Edwardian Heydays*. NY: Putnam, 1930.

Cornwallis-West, Mrs George. *The Reminiscences of Lady Randolph Churchill*. London: Edward Arnold, 1908.

Corti, Count Egon. *Elizabeth, Empress of Austria*. New Haven: Yale University Press, 1936.

Costello, Peter. *Dublin Castle*. Dublin: Wolfhound Press, 1999.

Cowley, The Earl of. *Secrets of the Second Empire*. London: Harper, 1929.

Crozier, John Beattie. *Lord Randolph Churchill*. London: Swan Sonnenschein, Lowrey and Co., 1887.

Davis, Richard. *The English Rothschilds*. London: Collins, 1983.

Downes, Kerry. *Sir John Vanbrugh*. NY: St Martin's Press, 1987.

Ellis, Roger. *Victorian Britain*. NY: Stackpole Books, 1997.

Ferguson, Niall. *The House of Rothschild: the World's Banker*. Two Volumes. NY: Viking, 1999.

Foster, RF. *Lord Randolph Churchill*. Oxford: Clarendon Press, 1981.

Fowler, Marian. *Blenheim: Biography of a Palace*. NY: Viking, 1989.

Fowler, Marian. *In a Gilded Cage*. NY: St Martin's Press, 1993.

Gilbert, Martin. *The First World War*. New York: Henry Holt, 1994.

Goncourt, Edmond and Jules de. *The Goncourt Journals, 1851–1870*. NY: Doubleday, Doran, 1937.

Hamilton, Lord George. *Parliamentary Reminiscences*. NY: Dutton, 1916.

Hansard: British Parliamentary Debates. London: Government Printing Office, 1874–1921.

Harding, Mildred Davis. *Air-Bird in the Water: The Life and Works of Pearl Craigie (John Oliver Hobbes)*. Madison/Teaneck: Farleigh Dickinson University Press, 1996.

Harrison, Michael. *Painful Details: Twelve Victorian Scandals*. London: Max Parrish, 1962.

Heckstall-Smith, Anthony. *Sacred Cowes*. London: Alan Wingate, 1955.

Hegermann-Lindencrone, L. (Lillie Greenough). *In the Courts of Memory*. NY: Harper, 1912.

Hershkowitz, Leo. *Tweed's New York*. NY: Anchor Press/ Doubleday, 1977.

Hibbert, Christopher (Editor). *Queen Victoria: Her Letters and Journals*. NY: Viking-Penguin, 1985.

Hobbes, John Oliver (Pearl Craigie). *The Vineyard*. London: TF Unwin, 1904.

Hyde, H Montgomery. *The Cleveland Street Scandal*. NY: Coward, McCann and Geoghegan, 1976.

Jacobs, Arthur. *Arthur Sullivan: A Victorian Musician*. NY: Oxford University Press, 1984.

James, Robert Rhodes. *Lord Randolph Churchill*. NY: AS Barnes, 1960.

Jenkins, Roy. *Churchill*. NY: Plume, 2002.

Jenkins, Roy. *Gladstone*. NY: Random House, 1995.

Jenkins, Roy. *Victorian Scandal*. NY: Chilmark Press, 1965.

Kehoe, Elizabeth. *Fortune's Daughters*. London: Atlantic, 2004.

Koch, W John. *Daisy, Princess of Pless, 1873–1943*. Edmonton, Canada: Self-published, 2003.

Kraus, Rene. *Young Lady Randolph*. NY: GP Putnam's Sons, 1943.

Lamont-Brown, Raymond. *Edward VII's Last Loves*. London: Sutton, 1998.

Lang, Theo. *The Darling Daisy Affair*. NY: Atheneum, 1956.

Le Blond, Mrs Aubrey (Mrs Fred Burnaby). *Day In, Day Out*. London: John Lane, 1918.

Leslie, Anita. *The Fabulous Leonard Jerome*. London: Hutchinson, 1954.

Leslie, Anita. *Lady Randolph Churchill*. NY: Scribners, 1969.

Leslie, Shane. *Leonard Jerome* (unpublished) MS at Georgetown University, USA.

Longford, Elizabeth. *A Pilgrimage of Passion: The Life of Wilfrid Scawen Blunt*. NY: Knopf, 1980.

Loomis, Stanley. *A Crime of Passion*. London: Hodder and Stoughton, 1967.

MacColl, Gail and Wallace, Carol McD. *To Marry an English Lord*. New York: Workman, 1989.

Magnus, Philip. *King Edward VII*. NY: EP Dutton, 1964.

Matthews, Roy T and Mellini, Peter. *In Vanity Fair*. London: Scolar Press, 1982.

McCabe, James D. *Lights and Shadows of New York Life*. St Louis: National Publishing Company, 1872.

McCarthy, Justin. *Memoirs*, NY: Longmans, 1902.

Medbery, James K. *Men and Mysteries of Wall Street*. NY: R Worthington, 1878.

Montgomery, Maureen E. *Guilded Prostitution*. London and NY: Routledge, 1989.

Moore, George. *Celibates*. (Includes *Mildred Lawson*.) NY: Brentanos, 1915.

Nassau, F. *Conversations With Distinguished Persons During the Second Empire, 1860–1863*. London: Hurst and Blackwell, 1880.

Neill, Kenneth. *An Illustrated History of the Irish People*. Dublin: Gill and Macmillan, 1979.

Nevill, Lady Dorothy. *Reminiscences*. NY: Longmans, 1908.

Pakenham, Thomas. *The Scramble for Africa*. NY: Random House, 1991.

Palmer, Alan. *Bismarck*. NY: Scribner, 1976.

Pearsall, Ronald. *The Worm in the Bud: The World of Victorian Sexuality*. NY: Penguin, 1969.

Pearson, Hesketh. *Labby: The Life of Henry Labouchère*. NY: Harpers, 1937.

Peters, Margot. *Mrs Pat: The Life of Mrs Patrick Campbell*. NY: Knopf, 1984.

Pickle, Joe. *Gettin' Started: Howard County's First 25 Years*. Big Spring, Texas: Heritage Museum, 1980.

Pless, Daisy, Princess of. *Diaries*. London: John Murray, 1928.

Ponsonby, Sir Frederick. *Recollections of Three Reigns*. NY: FP Dutton, 1952.

Preston, Diana. *Lusitania: An Epic Tragedy*. NY: Walker, 2002.

Quench, Eileen. *Perfect Darling*. London: Cecil and Amelia Wolf, 1972.

Rayner, DA and Wykes, Alan. *The Great Yacht Race*. London: Peter Davies, 1966.

Robins, Joseph. *Champagne and Silver Buckets: The Viceregal Court at Dublin Castle 1700–1922*. Dublin: The Lilliput Press, 2001.

Rosebery, Lord. *Lord Randolph Churchill*. London: HA Humphrey, 1906.

Sandys, Celia. *Churchill, Wanted Dead or Alive*. NY: Carroll and Graf, 1994.

Sarnoff, Paul. *Russell Sage: The Money King*. NY: Ivan Obolensky, 1965.

Schama, Simon. *A History of Britain*. NY: Simon and Schuster, 2002.

Scobey, David. *Empire City*. New Haven: Yale University Dissertation, unpublished.

Seldes, George. *Witness to a Century*. NY: Ballantine, 1987.

Stancz, Clarice. *The Vanderbilt Women*. NY: St Martin's Press, 1991.

Simpson, Colin. *The Lusitania*. Boston: Little Brown, 1972.

Smith, Marrhew Hale. *Bulls and Bears of New York*. Freeport, NY: Books for Libraries Press, 1873/1972.

Soames, Mary, editor. *Winston and Clementine: Their Correspondence*. NY: Houghton Mifflin, 2001.

St Aubyn, Giles. *Edward VII Prince and King*. NY: Atheneum, 1979.

Taine, Hippolyte. *En Angleterre*. Gallimard: Paris, 1925.

Terry, Ellen. *Ellen Terry's Memoirs*. NY: Putnam, 1932.

Valentine's Manual, 1917–1918. NY: The Old Colony Press, 1917.

Voigt, Charles Adolph. *Famous Gentlemen Riders at Home and Abroad*. London: Hutchison, n.d. (c. 1924).

Vosbrugh, WS. *Racing in America: 1866–1921*. NY: The Jockey Club, n.d.

Weintraub, Stanley. *Edward the Caresser*. NY: The Free Press, 2001.

Weintraub, Stanley. *London Yankees*. NY: Harcourt Brace Jovanovich, 1979.

Whittle, Tyler. *The Last Kaiser*. NY: Times Books, 1977.

"X" *Myself Not Least*. NY: Henry Holt, 1923.

NOTES ON SOURCES

With over 200 books and over 15,000 pages of documents read, a full list of sources would fill a separate volume. The following is intended as a shorthand guide to those who wish to investigate the subject further. All documents will be found at Occidental College, Eagle Rock, California. I have preferred to go to primary sources, including letters, diaries, current newspaper accounts, contemporary eyewitnesses, works published close to the events, censuses and certificates of birth, deaths and marriages rather than recent volumes; in the case of the medical histories, Dr John H Mather has been of indispensable assistance, and the genealogists listed in the Acknowledgments have been of incalculable help.

ONE

BIRTHPLACE: Brooklyn/New York City Directories; censuses; JEROME FAMILY: Larry Overmire, genealogist; HALL FAMILY: Caffyn; PRINCETON: Princeton Archives; ROCHESTER: Rochester Historical Society; FILLMORE: National Archives, Washington, DC; Library of Congress; NON-BAPTISM: All New York/Brooklyn dioceses searched; LIND: *Grove Dictionary of Music and Musicians*; JEROME BUSINESS: *Men and Mysteries of Wall Street*; *Bulls and Bears*; SOCIAL LIFE: *Lights and Shadows of New York Life*; WALES VISIT: All New York newspapers; SHOPPING: *Sights and Sounds*; PACIFIC MAIL: All New York newspapers; New York City Records Office; LINCOLN: Higham: *Murdering Mr Lincoln*; MISS GREEN'S SCHOOL: Research by Luther H Harris, New York Historical Society; Also: *Valentine's Manual: 1917/1918*; PATTI: *Grove*; JEROME PARK: RACING: Vosbrugh; NEWPORT: Research by Bert Lippincott, Newport Historical Society; SANITARY COMMISSION FAIR: New York Historical Society; BOND THEFT: *Rogues Gallery*.

TWO

RAILROADS: *Men and Mysteries*; RACETRACK: Bronx Historical Society; Jockey Club Records; 30 books; YACHT VOYAGE: *The Great Yacht Race*; SPEECH BY WRONG JEROME: London *Times*; CITY OF BALTIMORE: Merseyside Museum Archives, Liverpool; PARIS: Archives Nationales; Moulton; PETIT VAL: Grenough memoirs; (Hegermann-Lindencrone); PERSIGNY: Archives Nationales; BREAKIN: New York *Herald*.

THREE

PARIS: Archives Nationales; WASHBURNE: Washburne papers; LONDON: *The Times*; JEROME TROUBLES: *New York Herald*; COWES: *Sacred Cowes*; *New York Times*.

FOUR

RANDOLPH: Churchill papers, Churchill College, Cambridge (hereafter CCC); *Lives* by RF Foster, Robert Rhodes James; RELATIONSHIP ISSUES: Correspondence in companion volumes to Churchill/Gilbert (hereafter CCV); MARLBOROUGH DEBTS AND SALES: CCC; Christie's; BLACK THURSDAY: All New York newspapers; FINANCIAL DEAL ON MARRIAGE: CCV; BAZAINE: Archives Nationales; PRASLIN: *A Crime Of Passion*; WOODSTOCK: All London/Oxford newspapers; HONEYMOON LOCATION: Greenough memoirs; CCV; BLENHEIM: Fowler, *Blenheim*; VANBRUGH: biographies, various; Taine; DRAWING ROOM: London *Times*; CHARLES STREET: Nevill reminiscences; GLADSTONE: Roy Jenkins; ADDISON'S: Dr

John H Mather; BIRTH: Dr John H Mather; MARRIAGE(S): Burke's Peerage 1953–2003; EVEREST: Brian Jones, British genealogist; censuses; birth records; FANNY RONALDS: Sullivan papers, Beinecke Library, Yale; Jacobs: *Sullivan*; GORDON-CUMMING: Giles St Aubyn; RING EPISODE: CCC.

FIVE

AYLESFORD: Divorce court records, British National Archives; FRACAS OVER DIVORCE: St. Aubyn; YZNAGA: *New York Times*; Fowler, *In a Gilded Cage*; TRIP TO NEW YORK: *New York Times*; IRELAND: Irish National Library and Archives; Denis McCarthy, Dublin Castle historian; Robins: *Champagne*; *New York Times*; Dublin newspapers; various; BLANDFORD: CCV; MARLBOROUGHS/QUEEN: CCV; BEEF SCANDAL: *New York Times*; SIR BERNARD BURKE: Denis McCarthy; ROBINS: *Champagne*; IRVING/HAMLET: Ellen Terry memoirs; ST. PATRICK ORDER: *New York Times*; LETTER TO HICKS-BEACH; CCV; DILKE/AYLESFORD: Big Spring, Texas, historical archives; CARMEN: London *Times*; Grove; ATTACKS ON GLADSTONE: *Hansard*; FAMINE RELIEF: London *Times*; JACK CHURCHILL: Earl of Roden interviews; letters; Edward Lowe, genealogist; all records of births searched with no results in UK and Ireland; ATTACK ON COACH: *New York Times*; 'STAR' RAPE: letter courtesy Earl of Roden; WOODSTOCK CAMPAIGN: *New York Times*; CCV; FOURTH PARTY: Justine McCarthy memoirs; NORTHCOTE: Northcote biographies, various; BRADLAUGH: McCarthy memoirs; Hansard; RANDOLPH AS DANDY: *New York Times*; FOURTH PARTY MEETINGS: Nevill memoirs; THEIR CHARACTERS: McCarthy memoirs.

SIX

KINSKY: Vienna State Archives; VOIGT: *Gentlemen Riders*; FREWEN: *New York Times*; NEW YORK VISIT: *New York Times*; MURDER IN PHOENIX PARK: *New York Times*; RONALDS CRISIS: Beinike, Yale; WINSTON WITH DUCHESS: CCV; EGYPT: *New York Times*; GLADSTONE INVESTMENTS: Ferguson: *Rothschild*; MALTMAN BERRY: Holroyd:

Shaw correspondence; FLOWER: Ferguson: *Rothschild*; WINS-
TON AT SCHOOL: CCV; RANDOLPH IN COMMONS: Han-
sard; RAYNAUD'S DISEASE: Mather; JENNIE ILL: CCV;
JAMES DINNER: *Vanity Fair*; ZOEDONE: *Famous Gentlemen
Riders*; NORTHCOTE/BEACONSFIELD: British Library;
KILMAINHAM: Jennie reminiscences; MARLBOROUGH
DEATH: Fowler; Blenheim; AUCTION: Christie's; BAD GAS-
TEIN: *New York Times*; NATIONAL UNION: Foster; Rhodes
James; SCHOOL REPORTS: CCV; BAY MIDDLETON: *Gentle-
men Riders*; BLANCHE'S FATHER: *Burke's Peerage*; LEONIE
MARRIAGE: *New York Times*; BURNABY: *Day in, Day Out*;
National Archives; Pakenham: *Africa*; MISS THOMSON'S: CCV;
INDIA: London *Times*; DELACOUR: National Archives military
records, family history; Dublin Archives; National Library of
Ireland; West Yorkshire Archives; censuses; Brian Jones, geneal-
ogist; Bob O'Hara; ORLEANS CLUB: CCV; De Grey; Harcourt
diaries; Bodleian Library, Oxford; RANDOLPH IN COMMONS:
Hansard; CASSEL: National Dictionary of Biography; NATTY:
Ferguson; BURMA: India Office secret files, London; Burmese
nationals' accounts, various; JENNIE AT WINDSOR: CCV.

SEVEN

DIVORCE: Harcourt diary: Bodleian; CRAWFORD CASE: Brit-
ish National Archives; RIOT: *New York Times*; WINSTON ILL:
CCV; PARIS STAY: Paris newspapers; DINNER PARTY: St
Aubyn; others; NATTY: Ferguson; AUCTION: Christie's cata-
logues; SCANDAL OF EXPENDITURE: Randolph Churchill
speech, Commons; DARTFORD SPEECH: London *Times*; RUS-
SIAN TRIP: *Truth*; RESIGNATION CRISIS: Edward Hamilton
diaries; CCV; Ferguson: *Rothschilds*; George Hamilton memoirs;
Jennie memoirs; etc.; *New York Times*; London *Times*; SALIS-
BURY pieces: London *Morning Post*; GOSCHEN: CCV; BLAND-
FORD/CAMPBELL CASE: British National Archives; *New York
Times*; LETTERS FROM RANDOLPH: CCV; RANDOLPH
COMMITTEE: Hansard; OVENDON: Biographies of Rosa
Lewis, various; MAYNARD: Blunden: *Warwick*; FRENCH AP-
POINTMENTS: London *Times*: French National Archives;

CRAIGIE: *Air Bird in the Water*; KINSKY IN LONDON: Vienna Archives; Lives of Crown Prince Rudolph, various; RUSSIA: London *Times/New York Times*; Hansard; EVEREST/MARLBOROUGH: CCV; LILY: *In a Gilded Cage*; Blenheim; WINSTON/HARROW: CCV; BEEFSTEAK CLUB: Ellen Terry's memoirs; lives of Henry Irving, various.

EIGHT

CLEVELAND STREET: H Montgomery Hyde; British National Archives; FAILURE AT BIRMINGHAM: Foster/Rhodes James; JENNIE/WINSTON: CCV; TRANBY CROFT: Biographies of Edward VII, various; DAISY AFFAIR: *Life of Countess of Warwick*; SOUTH AFRICA: Ferguson; Foster; Rhodes James; KINSKY VISIT: CCV; BANSTEAD: CCV; WINSTON ACTIONS: CCF; OVENDON/COMB: biographies of Rosa Lewis, various; RAYNAUD'S DISEASE: Mather; WOLVERTON: CCC; also Churchill/Mitchell *Jennie*; MANDEVILLE: British National Archives; JENNIE ILL: CCV; Churchill/Mitchell; DEATH OF BLANDFORD: *New York Times/London Times*; LADY CAMPBELL AS REVENANT: Fowler, *In a Gilded Cage*; JEROME PARK DEMISE: *New York Times*; CENTRAL AVENUE/ JEROME: Bronx Historical Society; WINSTON'S FALL: CCV; Dr Mather; EVEREST DISMISSAL: CCV; SWITZERLAND: CCV; SANDHURST: CCV; RAYNAUD'S: Mather; LETTERS: CCV; Churchill-Mitchell; ASQUITH/BICYCLES: Hansard; BRAIN TUMOUR: Mather; NEW COURT/TRIP: Mather; CCC; KINSKY/BOYS: CCV; TRIP HOME/LETTERS: Churchill/ Mitchell; WILL: Obtained by Brian Jones; FANNY MARLBOROUGH LETTER: CCV; ESTATE MATTERS: Ferguson: *Rothschild*; MEETING AT NEWMARKET: CCV; WILDE STORY: Jennie memoirs; COCKRAN: *New York Times*; CRAIGIE DIVORCE: Court records; EVEREST DEATH: CCV; VANDERBILT MARRIAGE: *The Glitter and the Gold*.

NINE

WINSTON SCANDAL: CCV; *Issues of Truth*: Hansard; CONSUELO RETURN: *The Glitter and the Gold*; ASTOR: *New York*

Times; Vanderbilt family biographies, various; CRUIKSHANK: CCV; OVERDRAFT: CCV; DIAMOND JUBILEE: Ponsonby: *Reigns*; DEVONSHIRE BALL: Pless memoirs; CHRISTMAS RAG: CCV; RAMSDEN: Churchill/Mitchell; EFFORTS FOR WINSTON IN EGYPT: CCV; SUDAN: CCV; CORNWALLIS-WEST: his memoirs; TOWN TALK: British National Archives.

TEN

MAGAZINE LAUNCHING: *Air Bird in the Water*; issues of magazine at British Library; WINSTON AS PARSON: CCV; FUND RAISING FOR REVIEW: *Air Bird in the Water*; Jennie memoirs; *MAINE* VOYAGE AND SOUTH AFRICA: Jennie memoirs; London *Times*; War Office Records; National Archives; LETTERS/WEST: CCV; Churchill/Mitchell; OPPOSITION TO MARRIAGE: CCC; MARRIAGE TO GEORGE: *New York Times*; London *Times*; others; SULLIVAN: *Life of Arthur Sullivan*; CURZON NOTE: CCC; LETTER FROM WINSTON: CCC; PLESS: her memoirs; QUEENS DEATH: all London newspapers; GEORGE PROBLEMS: his memoirs; LOOSE BOX: Weintraub works, various; *New York Times*; DE GREY CONCERTS: Professor Gerald Turbow; PEARL CRAIGIE: *Air Bird in the Water*; WINSTON CHANGE OF PARTY: London *Times*; SEANCES: Pless memoirs; TWEEDMOUTH: *New York Times*; GOONIE: *Crowded Canvas*; BAY MIDDLETON: *Burke's Peerage*; MARRIAGES: *New York Times*; FIRE: *New York Times*; HIS BORROWED PLUMES: Peters: *Mrs Patrick Campbell*; GALSWORTHY/JUSTICE: Life of John Galsworthy, various; CRIPPEN: *New York Times*; MORRISON: *New York Times*; SIDNEY STREET: *New York Times*; SHAKESPEARE BALL: *New York Times*; SHAKESPEARE'S ENGLAND: *New York Times*; DIVORCE: National Archives.

ELEVEN

PORCH: Army files, family records; British National Archives; Bob O'Hara, Researcher; census reports; Victoria State Library, Geelong; Melbourne Public Library; Glastonbury Public Library; Magdalen College Archives, Oxford; NIGERIA: Niger Archives;

Army service/diplomatic files, British National Archives; letters in Peregrine Churchill/Mitchell *Jennie*; LAWSUIT: *New York Times*; DAISY PLESS: Koch biography; IRELAND/WAR: Churchill: *Small Talks on Big Subjects*; JENNIE/WAR EFFORT: *Small Talks*; WINSTON CONTROVERSY: Jenkins: *Churchill*, many others; TURKEY/CONFLICTS IN LONDON: CCV; CCC; Jenkins, Churchill/Gilbert; LUSITANIA: London *Times*; *New York Times*; Maritime Enquiry, British National Archives; HOE FARM: Longford: *Passion*; CYNTHIA ASQUITH: Asquith diaries; ALFRED ZIMMERMAN: All current records; *New York Times*; London *Times*; THEFT: *New York Times*.

TWELVE

WINSTON/MUNITIONS: Churchill/Gilbert; CHILDREN'S AN-TICS: John Churchill memoirs; UNIFORM AT WEDDING: Army reports, British National Archives; also COURTMARTIAL THREAT; HOMOSEXUAL CHARGES; CLARE SHERIDAN: Shane Leslie papers, Georgetown; FRENCH AFFIAR: *New York Times*; DIAMOND: *New York Times*; ROME VISIT: Leslie; PORCH ATTITUDE: Peregrine Churchill/Mitchell; DEATH AND INQUEST: London *Times*, *New York Times*.

INDEX

Bazaine trial, attends 40
birth 1–2, 7–8
Blenheim Palace, first sees 43–6
Burma, encourages RC's annexation of 111, 112, 113
childhood 9, 10, 11, 12, 16, 17, 19, 20, 21, 24, 26, 31, 32
Cleveland Street Affair, involvement in 141, 142
Crippen case, interest in 206–7
death 2, 236–7
divorce 212, 217–18
Dublin 62–5
father, relationship with 8, 20, 22, 23, 27, 144–5
finances 83, 86, 93, 94, 107, 158, 159–60, 169, 170–1, 173, 189, 191, 205, 217
first social event 11
fundraising 68, 181–2, 209–12, 220–1
funeral 237
gambling 144, 148
health 85–8, 150, 151, 153, 236
Jack (son), relationship with 69, 173, 181, 184, 202, 216–17, 224, 228
literary references to 136, 159, 184–5
lovers and admirers 54–5, 60, 68–9, 77, 78–80, 86–7, 89–90, 97, 98, 114–15, 117–18, 121, 131, 133, 138, 144, 147, 148–9, 156–7, 161, 168, 169–70, 173–7, 184–5, 194, 214–16, 219, 223, 228
Macbeth, donates gown to production of 140
marries for second time 186, 195
marries for third time 232–3, 236
memoirs 167, 195–6 *see also under individual title*
mother, death of 161–2
music, love of 14, 21–2, 47, 67, 133, 192
name 7
Order of the Crown of India 113
Oscar Wilde, writes to 160
Phoenix Park assassins, interest in 91
playwright 191–3 *see also under individual title*

Praslin case, interest in 40–1
Queen Victoria's Diamond Jubilee, attends 171
Queen Victoria's funeral, attends 188
Queen, first presented to 46
RC, aids political career of 71–2, 75–6, 84–5, 86, 90, 96, 100, 105, 108–9, 111, 112, 113, 119, 121–2, 132, 134, 143
RC, first meets 34, 35–40
RC, marries 39–43
RC, nurses 110, 148, 154, 157
RC, talk of divorce from 114, 120–1, 127
RC's affair with Gladys de Grey, reaction to 105, 114, 117–18, 122, 160
RC's family, relationship with 50, 53, 55
RC's resignation, reaction to 124, 127
raped 70
Russia, visits 134–5
schooling 13, 20, 24, 29, 30
'Shakespeare's England' exhibition 209, 202
war effort 220–1
Winston (son), relationship with 51–2, 81–2, 84, 97, 116, 136, 146, 147, 152, 159, 163, 165, 169, 170, 171–2, 180–1, 186, 187, 188, 191–2, 194, 197–200, 204–5, 208, 216–17, 221, 223, 224, 227
Jerome, Julia 7
Jerome, Kate 151
Jerome, Lawrence 4, 6, 7, 9, 151
Jerome, Leonard W 35, 39, 168
 ancestry 3
 Blandford, attempts to find wife for 130, 131, 137
 business interests 8, 9, 11, 18–20, 23, 25–7, 33, 107, 109, 112, 146
 Civil War, involvement in 11–12, 172
 Consuelo Yznaga, arranges marriage of 60
 death 145
 early life 4–5